The New Black Politics

The New

The New Black Politics

Black Politics

THE SEARCH FOR POLITICAL POWER

Edited by
Michael B. Preston
Lenneal J. Henderson, Jr.
Paul Puryear

Longman
New York & London

The New Black Politics
The Search for Political Power

Longman Inc., 95 Church Street, White Plains, N.Y. 10601
Associated companies, branches, and representatives
throughout the world.

Developmental Editor: Irving E. Rockwood
Editorial and Design Supervisor: Diane Perlmuth
Manufacturing and Production Supervisor: Anne Musso
Composition: Book Composition Services, Inc.
Printing and Binding: Fairfield Graphics

Library of Congress Cataloging in Publication Data
Main entry under title:

The new black politics.

    Bibliography: p.
    1. Afro-Americans—Politics and suffrage—
Addresses, essays, lectures.   I. Preston,
Michael B.   II. Henderson, Lenneal J.   III. Puryear,
Paul Lionel, 1930–
E185.615.N38   323.1′196073   81-13734
ISBN 0-582-28351-5   AACR2
ISBN 0-582-28212-8 (pbk.)

Manufactured in the United States of America

9 8 7 6 5 4 3 2

Several persons were of great help in preparing this book. At the University of Illinois–Urbana, Anna Merritt performed a wide variety of tasks with uncommon skill. Florence Edmison and Lorena McClain typed the bulk of the manuscript. Velma Sykes, Jean Baker, and Darlene Ricchiuto provided indispensable support services. I would also like to thank Professor Samuel K. Gove for his supportive assistance. Finally, I am indebted to a very competent and patient editor at Longman, Irving E. Rockwood.

MBP

Contents

List of Figures and Tables

About the Authors

Lucius J. Barker, Ph.D., Illinois, is Edna Fischel Gellhorn Professor of Political Science and former chairperson, Department of Political Science, Washington University. He is the author of *Black Americans and the Political System* (with Jesse J. McCorry, Jr.), and coauthor of several books in the judicial politics area, including *Civil Liberties and the Constitution* (with Twiley Barker).

Twiley W. Barker, Jr., Ph.D., Illinois, is a professor in the Department of Political Science, University of Illinois, Chicago Circle. He is the author of *Civil Liberties and the Constitution* (with Lucius Barker), and numerous other articles on judicial politics.

Marguerite Ross Barnett, Ph.D., Chicago, is a professor of political science and in the Program in Politics and Education. She is also director, Institute for Urban and Minority Education, Columbia University. She is the author of *The Politics of Cultural Nationalism in South India* and *Public Policy and the Black Community* (with J. A. Hefner) and numerous other articles on black politics and the Congressional Black Caucus.

Mary Coleman, Ph.D., candidate at University of Wisconsin–Madison, is currently an assistant professor of political science, Jackson State University. Her major teaching areas are public law, senior research and law-related courses, and women and politics. She has written "Teaching Black Politics in Political Science" (with Leslie Burl McLemore) and is currently writing a book on Mississippi politics (with Professor McLemore).

Charles V. Hamilton, Ph.D., Chicago, is Wallace S. Sayre Professor of Government, Columbia University. He is the author of *Black Power* (with Stokley Carmichael), *The Bench and the Ballot,* and numerous other books and articles on American politics, black politics, and public administration.

Lenneal J. Henderson, Jr., Ph.D., Berkeley, is currently an associate professor in the School of Business and Public Administration at Howard University. He formerly served as associate director of research at the Joint Center for Political Studies, director of Ethnic Studies at the University of San Francisco, NASPAA fellow in the U.S. Department of Energy, and a fellow of the Moton Center for Independent Studies. He has edited *Black Political Life in the U.S.* (1972); coedited *Public Administration and Public Policy: A Minority Perspective* (1977), and authored *Administrative Advocacy: Black Administrators in Urban Bureaucracies* (1979). His articles have appeared in the *Public Administration Review*, the *Black Scholar*, the *Annals*, the *Review of Black Political Economy*, and other publications.

John O'Loughlin, Ph.D., Penn State University, is associate professor of Geography, University of Illinois–Urbana. He is the author of several articles on the election of black mayors and reapportionment, both in the United States and Europe. He currently has a Rockefeller Grant to study the reapportionment process in several European countries.

Leslie Burl McLemore, Ph.D., University of Massachusetts–Amherst; Post Doctorate, Johns Hopkins. He is chairperson, Department of Political Science, Jackson State University. He has published "A Theory of Black Politics" in the *Journal of Black Studies,* "The Closed Society in Transition," and many other articles on black politics in Mississippi. He is currently writing a book on Mississippi politics (with Mary Coleman). Professor McLemore was also recently a congressional candidate in the Fourth Congressional District in Mississippi.

William E. Nelson, Jr., Ph.D., Illinois, is head of the Department of Black Studies and a professor in political science, Ohio State University. He is the author of *Electing Black Mayors* (with Philip J. Meranto), "Black Elected Administrators" in *Public Administration Review* (with Winston Van Horne), and numerous other articles on black and urban politics.

Michael B. Preston, Ph.D., Berkeley, is an associate professor, Political Science and Institute of Government and Public Affairs, University of Illinois–Urbana. He is the author of *Race, Sex, and Policy Problems* (with Marian Lief Palley), "Black Machine Politics in Chicago in the Post-Daley Era," "Black Elected Officials and Public Policy," "Minority Employment and Collective Bargaining in the Public Sector," and "The Limitation of Black Urban Power: The Case of Black Mayors."

Paul Puryear, Ph.D., Chicago, is professor, Afro American Studies, University of Massachusetts, Amherst. He is the author of numerous articles on black and American politics (especially southern politics).

Wilbur, C. Rich, Ph.D., Illinois, is director, MAPA Program, Wayne State University, Detroit. He is the author of *The History of the New York*

Civil Service System (forthcoming), "Political Power and the Role of Housing Authority," "Civil Servants, Unionism, and the State of Cities," and "Municipal Civil Service Under Fire," *Public Administration Review.*

Alvin J. Schexnider, Ph.D., Northwestern, is associate dean, School of Community Services, Virginia Commonwealth University, Richmond, Virginia. He is the author of numerous articles on black and urban politics.

Douglas St. Angelo, Ph.D., Chicago, is professor of government and research associate, Institute for Social Science, Florida. He is the author of numerous articles including "Black Candidates: Can They Be Aided by a New Populism?" (with E. Lester Levine) in *Journal of Black Studies* and is coauthor of several books.

Eddie N. Williams is president of the Joint Center for Political Studies, Washington, D.C. He received his B.S. degree in journalism from the University of Illinois–Urbana and studied political science in the graduate schools of Atlanta and Howard Universities. Mr. Williams is the author of numerous articles on black politics (*Focus*) and has recently completed a book on *The Black Vote: Election '76.*

Foreword

If a book on black politics had been written twenty years ago, it very likely would have emphasized the role of the federal courts and the rise of a new wave of mass protest demonstrations. That book probably would have discussed the decline and virtual demise of the white primaries, but it would have noted the continuing difficulty southern blacks encountered to register and vote. The activist role of the Warren Court, especially in school desegregation, as well as in aiding the Montgomery bus boycott, would probably have led the authors of that book to be more than mildly optimistic about the Supreme Court. But Congress, with its entrenched southern-based chairmanships, would have posed question marks. A handful of black congressmen would have been seen mostly as spokesmen (not yet spokespersons!) but with the possible exception of Adam Clayton Powell, Jr., who was becoming chairman of the influential House Education and Labor Committee, probably not as political bargainers who needed to be taken seriously. There would perhaps have been some hopes that a Democratic President would help matters by being a more outspoken advocate for "civil rights" than his predecessor. But that would likely have been more predilection than prediction. (Kennedy's southern judicial appointments would soon balance his otherwise progressive rhetoric.) A book twenty years ago *might* have forewarned of the spread of mass demonstrations to the urban northern communities, but that would have been stated cautiously, one suspects. Indeed, any emphasis in that book on northern black politics would probably have concentrated on a few places where there were reasonable prospects of blacks getting into and controlling local political machines.

So much for such a book twenty years ago.

Today the subject matter has expanded, as this volume demonstrates. The focus today is not so much on the *right* of black Americans to participate, but rather on the search for *reasons* to participate and on the *means* of that participation. The courts are still important, as the chapter by Twiley and Lucius Barker indicates, but the courts' role is more one of protecting against sophisticated manipulation of electoral arrangements under Section 5 of the Voting Rights Act of 1965.

We have seen two decades of mass protest actions creating a crisis that forced decision makers to take notice. Barnett and Nelson suggest that such actions should not be abandoned.

Several chapters in this book (e.g., those by Rich, Preston, Schexnider) stress the need for black politics to make a more conscious effort to link politics to economics. This is certainly a proper emphasis, and if it had been overlooked—or at least not stressed—in a book twenty years earlier, that omission would have been understandable. When a group has to spend so much time and energy simply defining legal and constitutional rights, it should not necessarily be faulted for making some excessive assumptions about the utility of those rights once obtained.

"Give us the ballot," Dr. Martin Luther King, Jr., implored in a speech in May 1957, "and we will no longer have to worry the federal government about our basic rights. . . . Give us the ballot and we will fill our legislative halls with men of good will. . . . Give us the ballot and we will help bring this nation to a new society based on justice and dedicated to peace."

Quite an agenda for just one instrument called the vote. Naive perhaps, even for the time, but not necessarily unexpected. White Americans had spent so much effort denying the vote to blacks that there was good reason to believe that they must be protecting some tool of vast importance. Perhaps it was reasonable to put so much emphasis on the one fundamental process that clearly distinguished first-class from second-class citizens.

But that naiveté is no more. This volume dispels any notion of a simple correlation between process and product. Gaining the right to vote does not, ipso facto, lead to the public goods and services needed or sought. More frequently than not, gaining the *right* to vote is only the beginning of an arduous task of transforming that tool into some meaningful substantive results. A number of authors in this volume, for instance, discuss the necessity for and the problems inherent in organizing and organizations (Barnett, Williams, St. Angelo and Puryear, Coleman and McLemore, Preston, Nelson). Some (Henderson, Williams, Rich) discuss the leeway and limits of black electoral strategies. Others (the Barkers, O'Loughlin) remind us of the concrete institutional and socioeconomic impediments to a useful exercise of the vote.

No student of black politics and American politics generally is or should be unaware of the highly fragmented nature of the American political system. It is a system with several layers and many access points. It was deliberately designed by its framers to slow up political action, to provide checks and balances, to guard against hasty (read, irrational) actions. Change at best has been incremental. Black Americans would have to conclude that those goals have been substantially achieved. If the black political experience has been anything, it has been a testament to the incremental nature of American politics.

While this can be understood and perhaps even appreciated, it can nonetheless be a source of frustration. This is the risk such a system runs. If the system is too unresponsive over too long a period of time, it may foster alienation and cynicism. When these reactions occur, people tend to withdraw or seek nonsystemic means of pursuing their demands.

As one reads the essays in this volume, it is rather easy to see how this can be a serious problem for many black Americans. In a precise sense, these essays all discuss political legitimacy. The black political experience is one that tests the viability of the society. As Barnett clearly points out, it is not an adequate response to tell blacks that they should pursue a traditional ethnic political model. Their situation is too fundamentally different. In fact, since blacks predate the European immigrant groups by centuries, if one wished to be sarcastic, one might suggest that the more recently arrived ethnics should be emulating the political mobility of *their* predecessors—many of whom were black. The sarcasm of that observation is precisely relevant to understanding why blacks cannot now equate their status with those who arrived long after they did. But it is not necessary to overkill the ethnic politics analogy to demonstrate its invalidity.

This brings us to a consideration of what I characterize as the *P* paradigm: Process, Product, Participation. The essays in this book in their various ways speak to a central proposition: Where the *process* (e.g., voting, marching, caucusing, lobbying) is perceived to be related to the *products* sought (e.g., full employment, decent housing, good schools), *participation* will likely increase. If there is no such perception, participation will likely decline. Thus, people participate where, when, and how they think it matters. To be sure, this is a very instrumental formulation of the causes of political activity, and some might argue that it overlooks less tangible things, such as civic duty. It does not overlook this; it simply recognizes that some things are of more immediate concern to some people than other things. Certainly, as discussed by St. Angelo, Puryear, and Coleman and McLemore, we know that those citizens lower on the socioeconomic scale tend to participate less than their higher-SES counterparts. These citizens, who need more from the political system, usually receive less. They have a more difficult time connecting process with product, thus they fail to participate, especially in the process of voting. Would they receive more if they participated? Perhaps so; but the critical question is, more of what? Is the political process capable of delivering the vast indivisible benefits needed by many people—decent housing, good medical care, good schools, decent jobs? This is the question the new black politics is posing, and the American political system must answer.

The constituents of the new black ethos need far more from the political system than the immigrant groups that came to this country in the late nineteenth and early twentieth centuries. Then, there was a growing private sector economy that was reasonably available to absorb the masses of uneducated who simply had strong backs and a willingness to work. The political system could work for these people precisely because that system was not asked to do too much. It was asked to bridge the brief gap between entry and movement into and up the private-sector ladder. (It was able to help people get naturalization papers and a pushcart license and possibly a patronage job for a newly arrived uncle. Little else beyond these divisible benefits were needed.) But that manifestly is not the case today. There is no private-sector expanding economy. There is talk of retrenchment, not expansion. There is talk of the public sector "getting off the backs" of people. This is a far cry from the days when the public sector, through the GI Bill, paid the tuition of millions to go to college. A far cry from the days when VA and FHA loans were available to help working-class people make a down payment on a modest home and begin to build equity in property that they could pass on to their children—who, ironically, would perhaps complain about some people taking handouts from government.

Without question, the new black politics operates in a fundamentally different milieu, and few would envy its task. It must ply its trade in a fundamentally different economic environment. It must raise substantially new and more piercing questions about the capacity of the system to deliver. It is not permitted the luxury, if that is the word, of assuming that process inevitably leads to product. This is why it is important to focus not only on the *right* to participate but also on the *reason* to participate. Perhaps—but only perhaps—this question was premature for a book written twenty years ago. But it is certainly relevant for a volume appearing today.

Charles V. Hamilton

For Mary, Sherry, Sonja, Adrienne, and Rymicha

PART ONE

Blacks and National Politics

ONE

Black Politics and American Presidential Elections

Lenneal J. Henderson, Jr.

In contrast to the 1976 presidential election, black voters contributed little to the 1980 presidential election outcome. Black voters in 1976 were integral to Jimmy Carter's primary as well as general election victories. Blacks gave Carter 90 percent of their vote in 1976. Assertions and hypotheses about "the pivotal role" of the black vote were frequently heard.[1] Conversely, Ronald Reagan could have triumphed in both the Republican primaries and the general election without the black vote. His overwhelming margin of victory over incumbent Jimmy Carter rendered the black vote all but insignificant. Clearly, when either Democratic or Republican presidential candidates win by a landslide, the black vote pales in national significance.

Nevertheless, the significance of black presidential voting to the *political self-image* and *confidence* of blacks is equally important. The symbolic and substantive association of black voters with the Democratic party encourages blacks when Democrats win and discourages blacks when Democrats lose. Except for those few black Republicans who may benefit by Ronald Reagan's election, most blacks interpret Reagan's victory as damaging to their political interests. The 1980 presidential election is therefore illustrative of the agony and ecstasy of black voting in presidential elections in both *the black political context* and in America as a whole.

Clearly, black voting in presidential elections is tied to many variables: international and national events, economic conditions, mass media influences, political organization, and past patterns of American political behavior in elections. Collectively, these variables comprise *the external factors* related to the black vote in presidential elections. Economic conditions, political values, political organization, voter awareness and behavior, and political leadership are *internal* variables among blacks that influence black presidential preferences. Together these internal and external variables constitute *the political environment* in which the black presidential vote takes place.

This chapter therefore examines selected aspects of black voting behavior in American presidential elections. What has been the pattern of black voting in quadrennial presidential elections? Are there significant differences in black and national voting patterns in these elections? What difference do these differences make? Have recent legislative and judicial policies facilitated black voter participation in presidential elections? How relevant are shifts and changes in national and regional voting trends to black voting behavior in presidential elections? What contributions to black voting in presidential elections has increased black voter mobilization and organization made? What is the conceptual and theoretical significance of the black vote in presidential elections? Finally, what are the strategic implications of black voter participation in presidential elections for prospective presidential candidates and black political development? These questions underscore the importance of black participation and voting for the highest elective office in American politics and government.

The black presidential vote assumes a fourfold significance. First, many political leaders and analysts consider it *a barometer of political participation and influence*, particularly in national politics. Second, as a largely cohesive bloc vote, *it may be pivotal in close presidential elections*. Third, it represents *a symbolic and substantive expression of black values and preferences* through interest-group articulation and mobilization. And fourth, it is *an instrument of political brokering and bargaining by black leaders* seeking to advance black economic, political, and policy goals through the Presidency.[2]

Black Presidential Voting and Concepts of Political Participation

Historically, the key issue in the participation of blacks in presidential elections was the acquisition and maintenance of the right to vote. The concept of political participation thus revolved around the vote. The black vote must be examined in conjunction with other concepts of political participation, however. Analysts of electoral trends in presidential elections employ a variety of political participation concepts to explain voting behavior. Milbrath identifies and arranges in hierarchical order fourteen types of participatory acts ranging from mere exposure of oneself to political stimuli at the bottom to holding public and party office at the top.[3] Others conceptualize political participation as varied efforts to influence public policy outcomes. Verba and Nie seem sensitive to cultural variances in modes of participation.[4] However, their analyses exclude subcultural variances in political participation within a single political system such as the United States. Milton Morris is more aware of these intrasystem subcultural differences. He categorizes black political participation into "electoral and nonelectoral modes." [5] Electoral modes include voting, party participation, and the holding of elective office. Nonelectoral modes include interest-group activity and leadership. Thus the historical evolution of black participation in presidential elections must include electoral and nonelectoral participatory concepts to embrace those years in which blacks were totally denied the right to vote.[6]

For example, Larry Nelson points out that blacks participated in the presidential election of 1864 even without the widespread use of the vote:

> Although generally denied the vote, black leaders hoped to promote their cause by presenting their views to the electorate. During the winter and spring of 1864, they took advantage of the opportunities presented by abolitionist meetings, informal gatherings, speaking tours, and the press to voice their opinions and anxieties publicly. They seldom spoke without commenting on the fate of slavery.[7]

The activities Nelson describes are examples of nonelectoral political behavior aimed at the candidates in the 1864 presidential election. These activities presaged black voting during the Reconstruction period. Black political conventions, newspapers, race advancement organizations and other types of political participation were also used in conjunction with the black vote during and after the Reconstruction period to widen the spectrum of black political participation.

Once blacks secured the right to vote through the Fifteenth Amendment, electoral as well as nonelectoral modes of participation in presidential elections became important. These modes included party registration and participation, participation as delegates to party conventions, party officeholding, and election or appointment to public office. Each of these kinds of participation became particularly critical during presidential election campaigns.

For instance, black party affiliation has switched from predominantly Republican from 1866 to 1934 to predominantly Democratic from 1934 to the present. This switch in party affiliation is particularly manifest in presidential elections. Levy and Kramer argue:

Until 1934 the black vote in the U.S. was decidedly Republican. Those blacks who voted did so for the G.O.P. with the same singlemindedness as Southern whites went for the Democrats, and for precisely the same reason—the Civil War. The G.O.P. was the party of Lincoln and with the exception of his successor, Andrew Johnson, who vetoed a bill providing for black suffrage in the District of Columbia (Congress overrode the veto), the Republicans, perhaps by design, perhaps not, aided the black advance with popular executive orders and selective federal appointments during the succeeding 20 years.[8]

Paradoxically, the budding black influence in presidential campaigns was all but destroyed by a Republican presidential candidate. Rutherford B. Hayes promised to return control of the politics of race to the southern states in the presidential campaign of 1876 if the South promised him their vote. Both Hayes and the white South were victorious.

Until this pernicious compromise, the number of black delegates to Republican national conventions increased. Nowlin points out that there were only four black delegates at the Republican convention in 1868, the year black participation began in Republican convention politics.[9] By 1872, as Reconstruction politics permeated the southern states and registered more black voters for the Republican party, the total number of black delegates to the Republican national convention reached twenty-seven. From 1868 to 1896, the politics of these black delegates differed little from their white counterparts. Nowlin suggests that they gave "unstinted support to candidates whose records they believed to favor the welfare of their race and other oppressed people's and in turn for their support, focused the attention of the Convention upon the problem of securing civil rights and protection for their groups." [10]

But, following the compromise of 1876, the black-white Republican coalition in the southern states began to disintegrate. White Democratic party leaders viciously attacked the coalition with words, ostracism, and violence. White Republicans began an exodus from the regular party organization and established what came to be known as "lily-white Republican clubs." Following a riot between black and white Republicans at the state Republican convention in Texas in 1888, the white flight from the Republican party increased. Blacks remaining in the regular party organization became known as the Black and Tan Republicans. Hanes Walton and C. Vernon Gray indicate that:

the lily-white movement gained support and was officially recognized in several states by President Benjamin Harrison in 1889 as the only Republican organization . . . although the era of disfranchisement stripped away most black support of Black and Tan Republicans, both groups became important in the struggle for presidential nomination.[11]

The number of black delegates to Republican national conventions continued to decline between 1880 and 1912 (see Figure 1.1).

By 1934 the economic devastation of the Great Depression, black urbanization, and President Franklin Roosevelt's New Deal combined to turn the majority of the black vote to the Democratic party. This dramatic transition to the Democratic party underscored the increasing importance of the black presidential vote. When the 1942 off-year elections suggested that some black voters were returning to the GOP, some white and black Republican leaders predicted that Republicans would substantially reclaim many black votes in the 1944 presidential election. Two prominent black organizations, the Chicago Citizen's Committee of 1,000 and the National Negro Council, joined with the Republicans in opposing Roosevelt for a fourth term. But the 1944 general election only demonstrated the strength and resiliency of black support for Roosevelt. Blacks provided a key margin of victory for Roosevelt in Pennsylvania, Maryland, Michigan, Missouri, New York, Illinois, and New Jersey. These seven states contributed 168 electoral votes to Roosevelt's victory.[12]

Nevertheless, it is important to note that southern states and southern black voters were not pivotal in presidential elections prior to 1944. Seven months prior to the 1944 presidential election, the U.S. Supreme Court, in the case of *Smith* v. *Allwright* (321 U.S. 649 [1943]) declared the white primary unconstitutional, stimulating black voter registration. But not until the massive civil rights and voter registration efforts of the 1950s

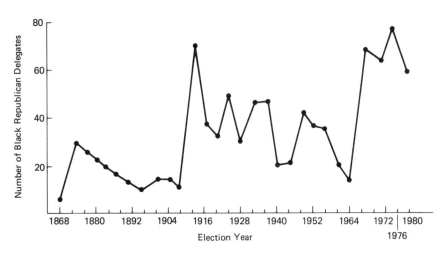

FIGURE 1.1   Number of black delegates to Republican National Conventions, 1868–1972. (Adapted from Hanes Walton, Jr., Black Republicans: The Politics of the Black and Tans (Metuchen, NJ: Scarecrow Press, 1975, p. 179.)

would the southern black vote become a factor in presidential elections. The focus was primarily on the black voter in large cities in the Midwest and North. Voting registration figures generated by the U.S. Commission on Civil Rights indicate that in the last years of the 1950s, black voter registration in the South began to rise significantly (see Table 1.1).

In 1948, black support for President Harry Truman contributed to his victories in the three key states of Ohio, Illinois, and California, accounting for 68 percent of his 115 electoral vote margin. Truman's Executive Orders 9980 and 9981 establishing a Fair Employment Board within the Civil Service Commission and outlawing segregation in the nation's armed forces proved enormously popular with black voters.[13] There can be no doubt that black voters participated in the presidential contest with a keen rational self-interest and some political acumen.

Nevertheless, in the 1952 and 1956 presidential elections, some blacks defected to the Republican party candidate, Dwight Eisenhower. Also, a number of blacks perceived Democratic party candidate Adlai Stevenson's pursuit of an illusory black-southern Democratic coalition as a political setback. According to a Gallup poll in January 1957, black voting for Republican candidates rose 18 percentage points from 1952 when only 20 percent of the black vote went to Eisenhower. The poll also indicated that "of all the major groups of the nation's population, the one that shifted most to the Eisenhower-Nixon ticket last November was the Negro voter." [14] The southern black vote seemed particularly important to this

TABLE 1.1   BLACK VOTING REGISTRATION IN SOUTHERN STATES, 1959 AND 1964

State	Percentage of Voting Age Blacks Registered 1959	1964	Estimated Number of Blacks Registered 1964
Alabama	13.7	21.6	104,000
Arkansas	37.7	43.5	80,000
Florida	39.0	51.1	240,616
Georgia	25.8	39.1	240,000
Louisiana	30.9	31.6	162,866
Mississippi	6.2	6.7	28,500
North Carolina	38.2	45.0	248,000
South Carolina	14.8	34.2	127,000
Tessessee	na	67.2	211,000
Texas	38.8	57.7	375,000
Virginia	23.0	27.7	121,000
TOTAL	—	38.6	1,937,982

SOURCES: For 1959: 1959 Report, *Civil Rights Commission, pp. 559–86; and 1961* Report, *U.S. Civil Rights Commission, pp. 251–311.* For 1964: Second Annual Report, *Voter Education Project of the Southern Regional Council, Inc., April 1, 1964.*

trend. An NAACP survey of election returns from predominantly black areas of 63 cities throughout the nation pointed out that the Republicans gained 19.9 percentage points in black communities in 1956. But black voters in 23 southern cities increased their vote for Eisenhower by 36.8 percentage points while blacks in 40 nonsouthern cities increased their support for Eisenhower by only 9.9 percentage points. This dip in black support for Democratic presidential candidates is illustrated in Figure 1.2.

What is also important to underscore about the slowly emerging influence of the black southern vote is its underlying nonelectoral participatory base. The Montgomery bus boycott of 1955, the desegregation crisis at Little Rock in 1957, the North Carolina Agricultural and Technical sit-ins of 1960, and other civil rights actions began to infiltrate themselves into the major issues that characterized the 1960 presidential election. Black voters in the North and South began to use events in the South as a method of evaluating prospective Democratic and Republican presidential candidates. Thus, although most civil rights actions in the South were aimed at influencing racial norms and mores, laws and customs, they also influenced politicians and political systems. But, as will be discussed later in this chapter, black southern voters would be critical to presidential hopefuls in 1960, 1968, and 1976.

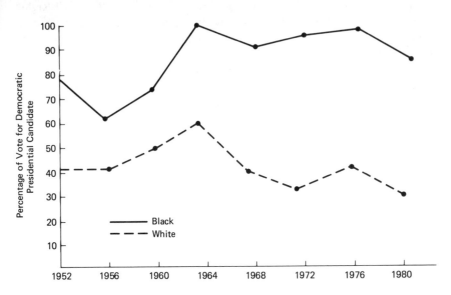

FIGURE 1.2 Electoral support for the Democratic party candidates in presidential elections, 1952–1980. (Based on Gallup poll survey data in the Gallup Opinion Index, 1974, 1977; data from the Joint Center for Political Studies and the New York Times, November, 1980.)

Testing the Pivotal Black Vote Thesis

The focus on voting as the key political resource in the acquisition and maintenance of black civil rights was dramatically illustrated in the 1960 presidential election. John F. Kennedy symbolized a youthful political genesis more sensitive to black goals and aspirations. Black votes substantially contributed to his 110,000-vote margin over Republican Richard M. Nixon. This pivotal role of the black vote in the 1960 presidential election elated civil rights leaders and notified political strategists that black votes were no longer of minor significance.

The 1964 and 1968 presidential elections seemed to argue *against* the pivotal black vote thesis. Although more than 90 percent of the black vote went to Democrat Lyndon Johnson, how critical were these votes to Johnson's victory margin of 434 electoral votes and 61.1 percent of the popular vote? In Louisiana, Mississippi, Alabama, Georgia, and South Carolina, electoral votes went to Republican Barry Goldwater in spite of civil rights activity and the emerging black southern vote. Although it is possible that the visibility of black politics in these states triggered the Goldwater vote, it is clear that the national and southern black vote were minor factors submerged in the Johnson landslide in 1964.[15]

The 1968 presidential election was another and more distinctive and complex test for the pivotal black vote thesis. Both the 1964 Civil Rights Act and the 1965 Voting Rights Act were expected to combine with continued black voter registration to increase the strategic significance of the black vote in both the presidential primaries and the general election. Ghetto unrest, the emerging black power movement,[16] and the Poor People's Campaign and other civil rights actions maintained race as a controversial national issue. Moreover, several prominent hopefuls in the Democratic party primary intensified interest in the campaign. Edmund Muskie, Hubert Humphrey, and Robert Kennedy all seemed viable presidential nominees at the Democratic convention. All seemed sensitive to civil rights and black needs.

But key circumstances deprived black voters of the opportunity to become electoral arbiters in the 1968 presidential election. First, George Wallace's defection from the Democratic party and his show of political strength as the nominee of the American Independent party seriously weakened the regular Democratic party coalition, which included blacks. Wallace's candidacy was an antidote to emerging black voter strength. He symbolized reaction to increasing black political power. His 46 electoral votes and 9 million popular votes were captured in Arkansas, Louisiana, Mississippi, Alabama, and Georgia—states targeted by civil rights advocates.

Also, the assassination of Robert F. Kennedy during the Democratic primary eliminated the most popular black presidential choice and pitted civil rights against the Vietnam war as the principal issues in the general election. Black voters supported Robert Kennedy more than any other Democratic or Republican presidential hopeful (see Table 1.2). His association with his brother John F. Kennedy, with civil rights advocacy, and with the liberal wing of the Democratic party made him attractive to many black leaders. His opposition to the Vietnam war distinguished him from Vice-President Hubert Humphrey. Had he become the Democratic party nominee, the Vietnam war would have been less a stigma than it became for Humphrey. Given the saliency of the war and the divisiveness of the Wallace campaign, blacks and civil rights could hardly have elected a President in 1968.

The 1972 presidential election was the antithesis of the 1964 election for the black vote. In spite of the visible role of black party leaders in McGovern's nomination and the fact that almost 90 percent of the black vote went to McGovern, black voters could not reverse his landslide loss by 503 electoral votes and Nixon's capture of 60.7 percent of the popular vote. Black voters were as submerged in McGovern's loss in 1972 as they were in Johnson's victory in 1964.[17]

The role of the black vote in the 1976 presidential election revived and reinforced the pivotal black vote thesis. According to the Joint Center for Political Studies, the black vote proved to be the margin of Carter's narrow victory in 13 states: Alabama, Florida, Louisiana, Maryland, Mississippi, Missouri, New York, North Carolina, Ohio, Pennsylvania, South Carolina, Texas and Wisconsin (see Table 1.3).[18] The Joint Center monitored election results from 1,165 predominantly black sample areas in 23 states. Their analysis is based upon careful manipulation of data from these sample areas.

TABLE 1.2 BLACK PERCEPTIONS OF PRESIDENTIAL HOPEFULS, 1968[a]

Wallace (AIP)	Humphrey (D)	Nixon (R)	McCarthy (D)	Reagan (R)
12.1	85.0	55.1	56.5	40.6

Johnson (D)	Romney (R)	R. Kennedy (D)	Muskie (D)
81.5	49.0	90.0	69.3

SOURCE: Survey Research Center, University of Michigan.
[a] Each respondent rated every candidate on a scale of 0 to 100 with 0 indicating great dislike and 100 indicating a very positive evaluation. The scores in the table are mean ratings for each candidate.

TABLE 1.3 1976 PRESIDENTIAL ELECTION; BLACK VOTER TURNOUT IN
STATES WHERE BLACK VOTES WERE CARTER'S VICTORY MARGIN

State	Black Voter Turnout [a] (%)	Estimated Total Black Vote	Percentage for Carter	Estimated Number of Black Votes for Carter	Winning Margin	Electoral Votes
Alabama	68.1	211,246	86.4	182,517	148,631	9
Arkansas	60.8	74,412	84.3	62,729	229,196	6
Florida	67.3	275,866	94.9	261,797	186,087	17
Georgia	60.3	272,074	96.3	262,007	482,507	12
Kentucky	54.5	49,181	80.0	39,345	85,239	9
Louisiana	67.2	282,708	93.6	264,615	77,308	10
Maryland	55.5	163,709	91.5	149,794	86,638	10
Mississippi	52.9	140,526	87.4	122,819	11,537	7
Missouri	72.6	137,504	91.4	125,678	67,510	12
New York	69.0	681,581	89.5	610,015	275,970	41
North Carolina	55.6	220,670	92.8	204,782	184,508	13
Ohio	75.2	304,091	80.0	243,273	7,586	25
Pennsylvania	70.3	294,551	87.2	256,849	128,456	27
South Carolina	64.8	184,632	90.4	166,907	101,492	8
Tennessee	65.5	150,723	92.2	138,967	188,863	10
Texas	48.2	267,770	96.8	259,202	155,246	26
Wisconsin	84.5	43,741	93.4	40,854	34,017	11

SOURCE: Adapted from The Black Vote: Election '76 (Washington, DC: Joint Center for Political Studies, 1977).
[a] Percentage of black registrants who voted.

Three elements seemed critical in the 1976 black presidential vote. First, the full impact of the 1965 Voting Rights Act, renewed in 1970 and 1975, seemed to be felt (see Table 1.4 and Figure 1.3). What is most critical to underscore is the substantial increase in black voter registration in Georgia, President Carter's home state. Black support for Carter in Georgia and Carter's Georgiacentric black politics can be largely attributed to this substantial increase in black voter registration in Georgia, as well as the visible and sophisticated black political infrastructure in the state.

Second, in contrast to the 1960, 1964, 1968, and 1972 elections, black southern voters were indispensable to a winning presidential candidate. Cromwell points out that "with heavy support from black voters, Carter carried every southern state of the old confederacy except Virginia where President Ford won with a 23,906 vote margin. Without this massive black support, many political observers have noted, Carter would have lost his native South. A majority of whites voted for President Ford." [19]

Third, what is somewhat paradoxical about the pivotal role black voters played in Carter's election is that they did so without as much influence in the Democratic party convention as they enjoyed in 1972 and with less overt support for Carter than either McGovern enjoyed in 1972 or Humphrey had in 1968. Once Carter captured the Democratic nomination, black politicians found themselves selling an unknown to black voters. This was particularly difficult because Carter often seemed ambiguous and elusive on major election issues, particularly those of concern to blacks.[20] This may suggest that party participation is less positively correlated with election outcomes than is commonly believed. Campaign issues, the characteristics of presidential contestants, televised debates between presidential candidates, and other variables may be more causal in presidential elections than are party participation variables.[21]

Thus, *external political events* and *internal black political organization* combined to make the 1976 black presidential vote pivotal. The lingering

TABLE 1.4   VOTER REGISTRATION IN THE SOUTH BEFORE
AND AFTER THE VOTING RIGHTS ACT OF 1965

| | *Percentage of Voting-Age Population Registered* | | |
	1964	*1972*	*1975*
Black	43.3	56.6	54.8
White	73.2	67.8	78.3

SOURCES: *Southern Regional Council Data in the 1968* Congressional Quarterly Almanac, *pp. 772, 1055; and in Congressional Quarterly,* Revolution in Civil Rights, *p. 70,* The Voting Rights Act: Ten Years After, *Report of the U.S. Commission on Civil Rights; (Washington, DC: Government Printing Office, 1975), p. 43; and Voter Education Project, Atlanta.*

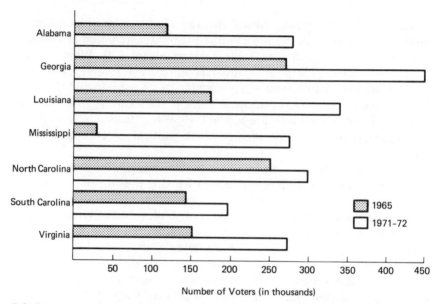

Number of Voters (in thousands)

FIGURE 1.3   Increase in black voter registration in the seven southern states covered by the 1965 Voting Rights Act. (The Voting Rights Act: Ten Years After, Report of the U.S. Commission on Civil Rights [Washington, DC: Government Printing Office, 1975] p. 53).

shadow of Watergate certainly favored Jimmy Carter. Ford's association with Richard Nixon reinforced Carter's anti-Washington-establishment image. Black voter mobilization, particularly through Operation Big Vote, stressed not only the necessity of a high black voter turnout but also the need to vote for more ethical and accountable elected officials.

The cumulative impact of internal black political organization began to be felt. The Civil Rights Acts of 1960 and 1964, the Voting Rights Act of 1965, party reforms—particularly those preceding the 1972 Democratic National Convention—and coalitions of black political organizations bolstered the surge of black voters. Moreover, the sharp increase in the number, distribution, and visibility of black elected officials stationed elective leadership in many black communities during the 1976 presidential election. This increase in black elected officials, from little more than 600 in 1962 to 4,503 in 1978, symbolized both the need for and the result of more conscientious black voting behavior.

Despite this temporary rise in the influence of black presidential voting, blacks had yet to realize their full political potential in presidential elections. Of the 15.6 million blacks eligible to vote in 1976, only 9.2 million registered to vote, and only 5.7 million (64.1 percent) actually voted. Thus, just over one-third of the eligible black voting population actually voted in 1976. Although black voting has increased sharply over past trends, many black adults remain to be registered, and many have yet to vote.[22]

Thus, although the black vote has been numerically pivotal in the 1960 and 1976 presidential elections, whether it will continue to be pivotal is related to the following factors: (1) whether it is the margin of victory in a precinct, county, city, or state needed by a candidate to capture the popular and electoral vote; (2) whether the election is close enough to require a decisive bloc vote; (3) whether blacks contributed to the issues that were decisive in the election; (4) whether black primary votes in individual states and the aggregate primary vote secured the nomination for a candidate; and (5) whether blacks coalesced with other interest groups to contribute to the margin of victory for a candidate.

Ronald Reagan's election severely tests the pivotal black vote thesis. Reagan's victory margin was the second largest (behind that of Richard Nixon in 1972) attained by any Republican presidential candidate in the twentieth century. Reagan acquired 43,267,462 popular votes, 489 electoral votes, and 51 percent of the popular vote, despite the 7 percent of the popular vote captured by Independent party candidate John Anderson.[23] Carter obtained 34,968,548 popular votes, only 49 electoral votes, and 41 percent of the popular vote. Approximately 16,967,000 blacks were eligible to vote in the 1980 presidential election, or 10.8 percent of the total voting-age population in America. According to the Joint Center for Political Studies, 61.3 percent of the eligible black voters actually voted, *2 percent more than turned out in the 1976 race.* Only 7.0 million, or 40 percent of the total black voting-age population, actually voted. The key element in the Joint Center's analysis is the relationship of Reagan's strongest regional support to the strongest regional black voting turnout (see Table 1.5). Reagan's strongest electoral and ideological support came from the West and the South. Turnout by black registered voters,

TABLE 1.5   TURNOUT RATE OF REGISTERED BLACK VOTERS BY REGION,[a]
1980 PRESIDENTIAL ELECTION

Region	Number of Precincts	Percent of all Sample Precincts	Total Registered	Votes Cast	Turnout (%)
Northeast	116	21.2	64,857	43,782	67.5
North Central	108	19.7	63,414	39,014	61.5
South	284	51.8	362,884	217,813	60.0
West	40	7.3	21,455	13,763	64.1
TOTAL	548	100.0	512,610	314,371	61.3

SOURCE: *Joint Center for Political Studies 1980 election study of sample precincts.*
[a] *All data weighted by region.*

however, was highest in the Northeast (67 percent) and lowest in the South (60 percent). And although black voter turnout was relatively high in the West (64.1 percent), a much smaller percentage of black voters exists in the West than in the South or Northeast.[24]

What is particularly interesting is the comparison between black support for Carter and Hispanic support for Carter. More than 80 percent of the black vote went to President Carter. But according to the *New York Times,* only 54 percent of the Hispanic vote went to Carter. More than 36 percent of the Hispanic vote went to Reagan. What this suggests is the weakening of the black-Hispanic coalition support for Democratic presidential candidates coupled with relatively weak black support for Reagan in strong Reagan regions. It is also evident that the southwestern and western configuration of the Hispanic population appeared to be influenced by strong Reagan support in those regions.

In brief, a number of preconditions for pivotal status eluded the black vote in 1980. There were few precincts, counties, cities or states in which the black vote could have been the margin of victory for Reagan or Carter. National election results were not nearly close enough to make any racial or ethnic bloc vote decisive. Blacks were an unspoken but significant issue in national support for Reagan. Since only 2.7 percent of the Republican party delegates were black, black support in the Republican primaries was insignificant. And black coalitions with Hispanics, labor unions, Jews, and others were considerably weaker than in previous presidential elections.

Components of a Conceptual Framework for Assessing Black Politics and American Presidential Elections

Black Political Values and Interest-Group Aggregation

Whether pivotal or not, "the black vote" exhibits distinctiveness, cohesiveness, and predictability. A general commonality of group values and preferences explains these characteristics. Civil rights, equal educational and employment opportunities, improved social services, and greater political access are among consistent black interest-group values and preferences. Blacks regard presidential elections as opportunities to advance their group interests and goals. As Kirkpatrick argues:

> Elections are, after all, the process through which popular participation and political accountability are secured, the nexus of a system of interlocking institutions through which political leaders are recruited, governments criticized, alternatives presented and examined, and decisions finally made by masses of people about who should rule and to what broad ends.[25]

But two points should be made. First, blacks are historically a submissive group seeking to reduce their dependency on other, more dominant groups through politics. As Mack Jones argues, "the concepts of dominant and submissive groups distill the essence of the black political experience and give us an analytical tool which will allow us to isolate, categorize and interpret the important variables in the black political experience." [26] Participation in presidential elections is a key part of the black political experience through which dominant-submissive group struggle occurs. Second, black voters are less a single, monolithic national interest group than a consistent coalition of local and specialized interest groups that display remarkable voting cohesiveness. Nationally, "the black vote" is the collective expression of values emanating from the black vote in specific cities, states, regions, parties, unions, and other interest groups and institutions. Black political values and aims are expressed through civic, community, union, church, educational, fraternal, and other organizations, as well as through exclusively black political organizations. Black interest-group behavior in presidential elections must therefore be considered at every level and through every institution in which it is manifest. [27]

Black political caucuses are particularly important in presidential elections. Aggregated within or independent of larger organizations, black political caucuses mobilize their members and constituents around strategies that pursue specific political objectives. These caucuses challenge legal or social constraints on their members and constituents. They broker and bargain with larger political entities for concessions. And they may join coalitions with other groups and caucuses to pursue mutual interests.

Political analysts have seldom appreciated the role of black political caucuses and organizations in advancing civil rights aims. They attribute increased black voter registration and political action to the removal of legal or institutional barriers. For example, Herbert Asher writes:

> Since 1952, a number of developments have occurred that have increased the potential electorate dramatically. One important set of events is the breakdown of the legal barriers, particularly in the South, that had prevented blacks and other minorities from voting. The 24th amendment to the Constitution abolished the poll tax, while congressional passage in 1965 of the Voting Rights Act enabled federal examiners to register cities in countries (mostly southern) where literacy tests were used and fewer than 50 percent of the people were registered. [28]

Asher fails to discuss how these legal developments were translated by black organizations into effective political advocacy, particularly during presidential campaigns.

Two kinds of black political caucuses are critical in presidential elections: voter registration/education organizations and intraparty caucuses. Historically and recently, the NAACP, Southern Christian Leadership Conference, Student Non-Violent Coordinating Committee, Voter Education Project, National Urban League, Congress of Racial Equality, Joint Center for Political Studies, and many other organizations have diligently educated and registered black voters. They have translated opportunities provided by voting rights and civil rights law into concrete voter mobilization.

For example, massive voter registration campaigns conducted by Operation Big Vote, the Voter Education Project, labor unions, the Democratic National Committee, and a plethora of local organizations contributed to the substantial black voter turnout that proved so crucial to Jimmy Carter's victory. Big Vote represented a coalition of more than fifty civil rights, labor, business, and community organizations that targeted thirty-six cities for intensive voter registration activity during the 1976 presidential election year. These efforts provide black voters with the instruments to exercise group power to achieve group goals. They also bolster the political infrastructure of the black national and local communities while mobilizing black voters.

Although essentially external to party decision making, this mobilization of black voters facilitates black intraparty participation. For example, the reforms initiated by the Democratic party in the 1972 convention resulted from the work of a special party task force headed by Senator George McGovern. McGovern revealed that various devices had been used to discourage minorities and other groups from participating in party decision making, particularly at the state level. McGovern's findings were the result of testimony provided by the same civil rights organizations involved in black voter registration and education. The task force findings resulted in structural changes within the party that provided blacks and other groups with greater access to party decision making.

As a result, blacks, women, Hispanics, and youth formed caucuses at the 1972 and 1976 Democratic conventions. Pressman points out:

> The Black and Women's caucuses showed marked organizational development during this period. In 1972 they existed largely as forums to hear speeches by their own members and by presidential candidates. But by 1976 these two caucuses had established stable leadership structures and sophisticated communications networks. They held large meetings for caucus members, whose votes ultimately sanction caucus actions. But their leaders also engaged in a series of concrete, specific negotiations with the presidential nominee.[29]

Perhaps the zenith of black participation in the Democratic party was the 1972 Democratic National Convention in which black state delegations and caucuses successfully challenged entrenched party regulars; held critical positions during the convention such as Credentials Committee Chairman, party Vice-Chairman, and Convention Co-Chairman; and spurred a liberal thrust that helped George McGovern capture the Democratic presidential nomination. Key black leaders became conduits for black demands channeled to party leaders and linkages between black delegates and Democratic party leadership.

Black caucus action was particularly crucial to McGovern in California. Gray and Walton write:

> The occasion for the display of black delegate influence was the California challenge. If McGovern won the California challenge, his nomination was assured; if he lost, his nomination would be more difficult to achieve. In a crucial vote on the California challenge, black delegates overwhelmingly voted with the McGovern forces for the seating of the duly elected slate of delegates. Of the 452 black delegates, more than 350 voted to seat the full McGovern delegation.[30]

California Assemblyman Willie Brown, leader of the California delegation, played a key leadership role in the challenge. His brokering and strategy were particularly important to McGovern's nomination.

Although less influential in the 1976 Democratic National Convention, the black caucus enjoyed vestigial authority. Because Carter's early start for the nomination and his surprising control of convention processes left little room for brokering and bargaining among and between groups supporting different candidates, black and other caucuses had less to trade than they did in 1972. This suggests that black caucuses are likely to attain more influence in heavily contested primaries and conventions than those in which a single candidate is dominant.

Conversely, the black caucus at the 1976 Republican National Convention was important because Ford and Reagan ran neck and neck through most of the primaries. Although there were only seventy-six black delegates at the convention, they held several meetings and receptions with Ford and Reagan during the convention week. The National Black Republican Council, a group closely affiliated with the Republican National Committee, continuously discussed platform planks, candidates, and convention procedures with their members and with prospective nominees. Black Republican delegates and alternates were concerned about the appointment of blacks to top-level administrative posts, soaring unemployment among black youth, the platform's antibusing plank, and other issues. But because several leading black Republican delegates were fearful that too aggressive a strategy would endanger President Ford's nomination, they were neither vociferous nor diligent in pursuing their demands.

At the 1980 Republican convention, the number of black delegates declined significantly, from 76 in 1976 to 56 in 1980. Conversely, an unprecedented number of black delegates attended the Democratic party convention. Of the 3,331 delegates and 2,053 alternates, 481 and 297 respectively were black. Sixty-eight percent of the black delegates supported President Carter, and 32 percent supported challenger Senator Edward Kennedy.[31]

In addition to brokering and lobbying as caucuses within the Democratic or Republican parties, blacks have occasionally pursued more independent action during presidential campaigns. At the 1964 Democratic National Convention, the Mississippi Freedom Democratic Party (MFDP) mobilized a 68-member delegation to unseat the regular white Democratic party delegation from Mississippi. Although they failed in 1964, they continued political activity in Mississippi. In 1968, former MFDP leaders returned as the Mississippi Loyalist party (MLP) to again challenge the regular state Democratic delegation. The MLP was seated with Aaron Henry as a delegate.

Also in 1968, the District of Columbia nominated Channing Phillips as a black favorite son for the Presidency. He received 67.5 votes. Black Georgia state legislator Julian Bond was nominated for the Vice-Presidency, but declined. Also in 1972, without the endorsement of the Congressional Black Caucus or the National Black Political Convention, Congresswoman Shirley Chisholm announced her candidacy for the Democratic party nomination for President. Chisholm entered the 1972 Democratic National Convention with only 26 delegate votes. However, the Congressional Black Caucus failed to agree on the endorsement of a presidential candidate in 1972 and 1976.

What is important to underscore about black political caucuses in presidential elections is the two-dimensional nature of their function. They simultaneously mobilize their membership and constituents to consolidate themselves internally while seeking to affect productive exchange relations with other groups and institutions external to themselves. The emergence of the National Conference of Black Elected Officials, the National Caucus of Black State Legislators, the National Caucus of Local Elected Officials, the National Conference of Black Mayors, and other black caucuses will seek greater influence in upcoming presidential elections both as voter mobilization institutions and as effective sources of black demands and policy preferences. More than 85 percent of the 4,912 black elected officials in 1981 served local government. Caucuses representing black local elected officials as well as black congresspersons are particularly important stimulants to black voter mobilization.

The extent to which present or future black political caucuses influence presidential outcomes depends upon a host of variables beyond the con-

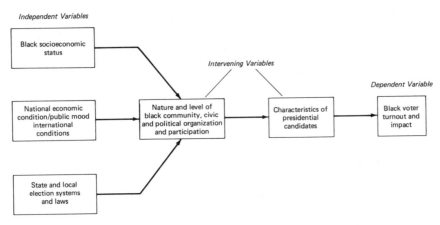

FIGURE 1.4   Independent and intervening variables affecting black voter turnout.

trol of the caucuses, however. The socioeconomic status of the black voter, state and local election systems and laws,[32] the level of black civic and community participation, the characteristics of particular presidential aspirants, international events, and the national mood and condition during a presidential year are variables that black political caucuses must address. These variables are causally related to black voter participation in presidential elections (see Figure 1.4). Some, like the socioeconomic status of black voters and state and local election systems, are independent variables. Others, like the level of black civic and community activity and the characteristics of presidential aspirants, are intervening variables.[33] Whether independent or intervening, these variables comprise the strategic environment in which black political caucuses strive.

International and National Conditions and Events

In addition to black interest-group aggregation, international and national conditions and events are critical in presidential elections. Although black interest-group aggregation is an example of an *internal black political variable*, international and national conditions and events are *key external variables* related to the black presidential vote. Public satisfaction or dissatisfaction with the way in which incumbent presidents handle international and national conditions influence voter propensity to support or oppose incumbents. Combined with the charisma, conviction, and image of the challenging presidential aspirant, the public mood can swing from incumbent to challenger or from challenger to incumbent.

For example, McGovern's unsuccessful effort to generate voter support by exploiting Nixon's method of "winding down" the Vietnam war contributed to his electoral demise. Ford's failure to dissociate himself from the Nixon administration and respond adequately to the energy crisis helped Jimmy Carter in the 1976 general election. Carter's inability to stimulate the economy and win freedom for Americans held hostage by the Iranian government contributed substantially to Reagan's electoral margin.

It will be important to follow President Reagan's handling of the federal budget, the civil conflict in El Salvador, the economy, and other issues, as well as public opinion of his performance. His proposals to reduce social security benefits, for example, may stimulate a reexamination of his entire national economic recovery program by voters and could gradually erode his margin of popular support as the 1984 presidential primaries draw closer.

Continued Mobilization of Black Voters

In addition to black interest-group aggregation, continued direct mobilization of black voters will be necessary to maintain and expand the level of black influence in presidential elections. The continued efficacy of Operation Big Vote, a nonpartisan coalition of some eighty local, regional, and national organizations will be essential. As Hillman indicates, "through voter registration and get-out-the-vote campaigns, Operation Big Vote coalitions in 50 target cities not only raised the level of participation in those cities, but helped to raise political consciousness and participation in other areas as well."[34]

Specifically, black voter mobilization must consider the following:

1. Targeting key precincts, cities, counties, and states where presidential sweepstakes in the primaries may be close.
2. Increasing the *number and distribution* of black elected officials, particularly in Congress and statewide offices. This will contribute visible black leadership able to influence party decisions and electoral strategies in a presidential election year.
3. Increasing the proportion of eligible black voters.
4. Strengthening black voter coalitions with other key interest groups.
5. Continued internal review of values, policy preferences, and political strategies between and among political caucuses and organizations within the black community.

Blacks, Presidential Elections, and Public Policy

Black political caucuses articulate black public policy concerns during presidential campaigns. The success of these caucuses in persuading presidential candidates and party leaders to incorporate black public policy concerns into party platforms determines whether blacks can hold an elected President accountable for implementing them once in office. The saliency, clarity, and consistency of black public policy positions coupled with the role of the black vote during the primary and general presidential elections can increase or decrease the ability of black political leaders to bargain with successful presidential candidates for political or public policy concessions.[35] For example, in 1960 black leaders were vocal and clear about their civil rights demands during the presidential election, particularly within the Democratic party. The saliency of the civil rights issue and the key role of black votes in the general election put black leaders in a favorable position to bargain with John F. Kennedy for civil rights and antipoverty legislation.

In contrast, in the 1972, 1976, and 1980 presidential elections, the linkage between black public policy demands and the role of the black vote was less firm. In 1972 blacks articulated a strong and clear set of public policy issues for George McGovern. But the black vote failed to elect McGovern. In 1976 blacks were less unified and clear about their public policy expectations of Jimmy Carter. But the black vote was decisive in Carter's election. As a result, both in 1972 and in 1976, the ability of blacks to successfully bargain with the President-elect was more limited than in 1960. Once Carter was nominated in 1976, many black politicians who in 1968 and 1972 were almost ideological purists on such issues as affirmative action, aid to the cities, black participation in Democratic party decision making, and other concerns now exchanged a belated and bewildered commitment to Jimmy Carter in the hope that he would be responsive to black concerns.[36]

It is important to note that public policy issues are not the sole concerns of black leaders in presidential campaigns. Frequently, the price of black voter support is the appointment of blacks to key leadership and administrative positions in the party or the new administration. The assumption is that a black presidential appointee will be sensitive enough to blacks to pursue their public policy concerns while in office. But the failure of black leaders to clearly identify those blacks best able to implement specific black policy concerns leaves the President-elect with the discretion to appoint a black who may or may not inspire the confidence of the national black community. For example, when President Carter appointed Housing Secretary Patricia Roberts Harris, many black leaders complained that she was not the ideal choice for the post. *After,* rather than *before,* the appointment, black leaders identified other, "more acceptable," choices for the post of Secretary of Housing and Urban Development.

Nevertheless, the public policy issues identified as critical by black leaders during presidential campaigns reflect both national and black economic, social, and political conditions. These policy issues must therefore be considered in relation to larger national public policies and policy issues to determine whether they are politically feasible. Often, black leaders will demand that a presidential aspirant declare himself on a policy issue that is politically unfeasible. They may do so as a political ploy rather than a genuine attempt to evaluate the suitability of the presidential prospect. In either case, larger policy issues must be considered by black leaders in presidential elections not only to know who the significant others of the various presidential prospects are but also because those larger issues may have overt or covert implications for the black community. For example, the fiscal and monetary policies of presidential aspirants are seldom explicitly racial but have underlying implications for the economic opportunities of nonwhite communities.

Summary

Ultimately, blacks participate in presidential elections to affect public policy outputs and outcomes. Their social, economic, and political development and quality of life depend heavily on government action and intervention. The policies that influence the nature and extent of that government action and intervention are therefore of principal concern to black voters. Given the importance of multidimensional participation in presidential elections, factors that encourage or restrain black voters, black party officials, black elected officials, and other black leaders must be isolated in order to identify strategies for maximizing black participation in the selection of the President. Historically, blacks have struggled from virtually negligible participation in presidential elections to an occasionally pivotal role. As black voters increased, black delegates to the Democratic and Republican conventions increased. As black delegates increased, more conscious and collective black group strategies resulted. Black group strategies not only occasionally affected the nomination of presidential candidates but also resulted in the periodic development of black presidential and vice-presidential aspirants.

It is important to reiterate that black southern voters are growing in political influence in presidential elections. Unable to overcome racist third-party mobilization or the incursion of conservative Republicans into the South for decades, black southern voters gave Jimmy Carter decisive support in southern states in 1976. Still, Reagan victories in these states in 1980 reminded black voters of the mobilization yet to be done and the limits of even maximum black voter mobilization.

Although the role of the black vote in 1976 illustrates how pivotal black presidential voting can become, the Reagan election illustrates that the black vote is only pivotal when elections are close, when black votes help presidential candidates to win key states, and when blacks forge effective coalitions with other groups whose support is indispensable to the presidential candidate.

Whether pivotal or not, black votes result in and are the result of effective black political caucuses and organizations. These entities exist at the local, state, and regional levels as well as at the national level. Often, they emerge in a union, church, or other large organizations. But their leadership, advocacy, and strategies during presidential campaigns determine whether black interest-group values are effectively articulated and accommodated by political parties and party leaders.

It is also important that these black political organizations and caucuses articulate clear and consistent public policy goals for presidential aspirants and their parties. If they fail to do so, their ability to bargain with successful presidential candidates, even when the black vote is pivotal in the election, may be significantly reduced. Blacks must therefore articulate their public policy expectations effectively, formulate workable participatory strategies for black voters, design efficacious group strategies within and outside party structures, and bargain effectively with successful presidential candidates if they are to maximize their role in presidential elections.

NOTES

1. See Lucius Barker and Jesse McCrorry, *Blacks in the American Political System* (New York: Winthrop, 1980).
2. Scholarly literature on blacks and presidential elections is surprisingly scarce. Among the key works are Henry Lee Moon, "The Negro Vote in the Presidential Election of 1956," *Journal of Negro Education* 26, no. 3 (Summer 1957): 219; Hanes Walton, Jr., *Black Republicans: The Politics of the Black and Tans* (Metuchen, NJ: Scarecrow Press, 1975); Milton Morris, *The Politics of Black America* (New York: Harper and Row, 1975), chaps. 8 and 9; Hanes Walton, Jr., *Black Politics: A Theoretical and Structural Analysis* (Philadelphia: Lippincott, 1972), chap. 5; Eddie Williams and Milton D. Morris, *The Black Vote in a Presidential Election Year* (Washington, DC: Joint Center for Political Studies, February 1981); see also Ronald W. Walters, "Black Presidential Politics in 1980: Bargaining or Begging?" *Black Scholar* 11, no. 4 (March/April 1980): 22–31.
3. Lester Milbrath, *Political Participation* (Skokie, IL: Rand McNally, 1965).
4. Sidney Verba and Norman Nie, *Participation in America: Political Democracy and Social Equality* (New York: Harper and Row, 1972).
5. Morris, *Politics of Black America*, p. 147.
6. Lenneal J. Henderson, "The Historical Evolution of Black Political Participation" (unpublished paper, Howard University, Department of Political Science, 1978).

7. Larry Nelson, "Black Leaders and the Presidential Election of 1864," *Journal of Negro History* 6, no. 1 (Jan. 1978): 43.
8. Mark R. Levy and Michael S. Kramer, *The Ethnic Factor: How America's Minorities Decide Elections* (New York: Simon and Schuster, 1972), p. 38.
9. William Nowlin, *The Negro in American National Politics* (New York: Russell & Russell, 1970; originally published in 1931).
10. Ibid., p. 65.
11. Hanes Walton, Jr., and C. Vernon Gray, "Black Politics at the National Republican and Democratic Conventions, 1868–1972," *Phylon* 36, no. 3 (1975): 272.
12. Henry Lee Moon, *Balance of Power: The Negro Vote* (Garden City, NY, Doubleday, 1948).
13. See Ruth Morgan, *The President and Civil Rights* (New York, St. Martin's Press, 1970).
14. Quoted in Moon, "The Negro Vote in the Presidential Election of 1956," p. 219.
15. See *Presidential Elections Since 1789* (Washington, DC: Congressional Quarterly Service, 1975).
16. See Stokely Carmichael and Charles V. Hamilton, *Black Power: The Politics of Liberation in America* (New York: Vintage Books, 1967).
17. See James A. Michener, *The Presidential Lottery* (New York: Random House, 1969).
18. See *The Black Vote: Election '76* (Washington, DC: Joint Center for Political Studies, 1977); and Oliver Cromwell, "Black Impact on the 1976 Elections," *Focus,* November 1976, p. 4.
19. Cromwell, "Black Impact on the 1976 Elections," p. 5.
20. Lenneal J. Henderson, "Black Politics and the Carter Administration: The Politics of Backlash Pragmatism," *Journal of Afro-American Issues* 5, no. 3 (Summer 1977): 245.
21. A good discussion of sex and race differences in political participation may be found in Susan Welch and Philip Secret, "Sex, Race and Political Participation," *Western Political Quarterly* 34, no. 1 (March 1981): 3.
22. *The Black Vote: Election '76,* p. 31.
23. Anderson, a Republican, captured 5,588,014 votes as an independent candidate. He received only 1.49 percent of the black vote.
24. Williams and Morris, *Black Vote,* p. 229.
25. Jeane J. Kirkpatrick, "Changing Patterns of Electoral Competition," in *The New American Political System,* ed. Anthony King (Washington, DC: American Enterprise Institute, April 1980), p. 249.
26. Mack Jones, "A Frame of Reference for Black Politics," in *Black Political Life in the U.S.,* ed. Lenneal J. Henderson (San Francisco: Chandler, 1972), p. 10.
27. See Harold F. Gosnell and Richard G. Smolka, *American Parties and Elections* (Columbus, OH: Charles E. Merrill, 1976).
28. Herbert Asher, *Presidential Elections and American Politics: Voters, Candidates, and Campaigns Since 1952* (Homewood, IL: Dorsey Press, 1976) p. 44.

29. Jeffrey L. Pressman, "Groups and Group Caucuses," *Political Science Quarterly* 92, no. 4 (Winter 1977–78): 673; see also Jeffrey L. Pressman, Denis G. Sullivan, and F. Christopher Arterton, "Cleavages, Decisions, and Legitimation: The Democrats' Mid-Term Conference," *Political Science Quarterly* 91, no. 1 (Spring 1976).
30. Walton and Gray, "Black Politics," p. 270.
31. Williams and Morris, *Black Vote*, p. 219.
32. See Steven J. Rosenstone and Raymond E. Wolfinger, "The Effect of Registration Laws on Voter Turnout," *American Political Science Review* 72, no. 1 (March 1978): 22.
33. See Christopher Arterton and Harlan Hahn, *Political Participation* (Washington, DC: American Political Science Association, 1975).
34. Gracia Hillman, "Black Voter Participation Rose by 2 Percent in 1980." *Focus* 8, no. 12 (December 1980): 5.
35. On blacks and public policy, see Marguerite Ross Barnett and James A. Hefner, eds., *Public Policy for the Black Community* (New York: Alfred Publishing, 1976); Michael B. Preston, "Blacks and Public Policy," *Policy Studies Journal* 6, no. 2 (Winter 1977): 245; and Lawrence Howard, Lenneal J. Henderson, and Deryl G. Hunt, eds., *Public Administration and Public Policy: A Minority Perspective* (Pittsburgh: Public Policy Press, 1977).
36. Henderson, "Black Politics and the Carter Administration," p. 246.

TWO

The Congressional Black Caucus: Illusions and Realities of Power

Marguerite Ross Barnett

In the early 1970s, as black leaders shifted from an emphasis on movement-style protest politics to an emphasis on electoral politics, the Congressional Black Caucus (CBC) was viewed by many as a concrete manifestation of black political power. If, as many believe, the CBC is in fact the most powerful contemporary black political organization, analysis of the CBC will reveal many of the opportunities as well as the constraints associated with the use of electoral politics and the political process to achieve positive results for the black community.

Ironically, just at the time when a theoretical framework is most needed to elucidate the black political experience (including the role of organizations like the CBC), the level of theoretical engagement has declined. During the 1960s the "benign neglect" of pressing theoretical issues related to black participation in electoral politics led to the careless equation of black political presence with black political power. The mere existence of black elected officials was regarded as success. No one examined what these public officials did or, even more crucially, what they could or should accomplish. A theoretical vacuum continues to exist, causing confusion about the trappings of power[1] and the symbols associated with the presence of blacks in political roles where they have real power and enduring ability to make decisions and use political influence and authority to bring about social change. Therefore, an analysis of the CBC and other black political organizations and institutions must consider the circumstances in which black politicians can and do wield political power, the limits of that power, and the goals they seek through the political process.

This form of "middle-range" analysis and theorizing seems particularly appropriate to the pre-paradigmatic stage of political science in general and the study of American politics in particular. Much of the literature on black politics has neatly ignored the lack of a general, commonly accepted framework for an analysis of black political life. Without such a framework, a multitude of nagging methodological and policy questions remain unresolved, and even more serious, often unrecognized.

An example is the common practice of analyzing black politics using propositions, concepts, and ideas from pluralist theory. The unstated theoretical assumption is that Afro-Americans are simply another ethnic group with a structural relationship to the social and political system that is fundamentally the same as that of Irish-Americans, Italian-Americans, WASPS, and so on. One immediate problem with this theoretical posture is that it cannot explain the historical experience of blacks in America. That experience has been fundamentally different from the experience of nonblack groups. Second, even contemporary (twentieth century) black political activity differs dramatically from that of other ethnic groups, which might lead careful analysts to seek reasons for this divergence. Finally, many scholars fall into the policy trap of advocating special programs for blacks while still operating within the pluralist framework. It is often difficult for them to answer critics who argue that other groups (which their analyses show to be structurally similar to blacks) have "made it," why can't blacks? The same theoretical problem exists when blacks are referred to as an underclass, a colony, a nation, a nation within a nation, and so on. Frequently such an assertion is not accompanied by any systemic theoretical discussion, and therefore labeling replaces analysis.

This chapter does not attempt to develop a general theory of black politics. Rather, in the spirit of middle-range inquiry, it will point to a general framework while seeking to shed light on a specific phenomenon. It describes the CBC in the congressional setting but theoretically located within a hypothetical construct of black political life in the United States. Afro-American politics is viewed as reflecting fundamental, economic, social, and cultural realities. While Afro-American politics and governmental policy can influence the social, economic, and cultural patterns of black life, fundamental changes in that environment cannot be dealt with by political action alone.

The CBC must be viewed on two separate levels. At one level it is a caucus within Congress. Failure to see beyond that level trivializes the caucus, adds only incrementally to our knowledge of Congress, and provides misleading information about black political life. On another level the caucus is an authority structure within the black community. As such, it interacts with the small group of black leaders who seek to represent the community at the national level. They also help define a legislative agenda and posture for the black community. By focusing only on this level, however, one misses the real importance of individual ambitions, problems, and behaviors of those who make up the caucus. These behaviors are often explicable mainly within frameworks that have been established to help understand Congress. An analysis pitched at a level of abstraction that misses the importance of individual idiosyncrasies also misses immediate political outcomes.

In sum, then, the CBC may be seen, on the one hand, solely within the legislative framework and can best be depicted metaphorically as a "labor union for individual black representatives." The organization has improved the leverage of these individuals through joint action. It has also provided information, support, and a forum—all factors that improve the ability of the legislators to carry out their representative function. On the other hand, the CBC may be viewed solely as a *collective* political voice for the black community, in which case the best metaphors are a movement or an interest group. In that sense the CBC has represented black demands within Congress; it has been a vehicle for interest articulation and interest aggregation on the part of the black community. It has also participated in efforts to develop a mass movement base to influence politics within and outside of Congress.

The realities of the caucus weave among the metaphors of movement, interest group, and labor union. Analysis, therefore, must find patterns in and explanations for this intermittent fluctuating reality. Interpretation that is predictive and rich must rely heavily on understanding the caucus first as a part of Afro-American political life and only secondarily as a part of congressional politics.

The CBC in Congress

The CBC is one among a number of caucuses in Congress, and in outward appearance is similar to them: It is a "members only" group that meets to debate matters currently before the Congress. Like other caucuses, discussions in CBC meetings cover legislative strategy, the substance of issues, assessment of the import of activities of the judicial and executive branch on legislative matters, and so on. However, the Congressional Black Caucus focuses on issues of concern to the black community and consists solely of the black members of the House of Representatives. Therefore, from its formation, the CBC has reflected its dual locus both in the Congress and in the black community.

Formation

Although the Congressional Black Caucus was not formally organized until 1971, the idea of joint action by black members of the U.S. House of Representatives has a longer history. In 1954 Representative Charles Diggs (D-Michigan) was elected to the House. Diggs' election marked the beginning of an effort to promote communication among black congressional representatives. When he arrived in the House, there were only two black representatives, Adam Clayton Powell (D-New York) and William Dawson (D-Illinois). Diggs found there was little political communication between the two, but since Diggs was politically left of Dawson and right of Powell, he got along well with both men and formed a bridge between them.

As black congressional representation increased with the election of Representatives Robert Nix (D-Pennsylvania in 1957), Augustus Hawkins (D-California in 1962), and John Conyers (D-Michigan in 1964), informal discussions developed. Nevertheless, no efforts were made to institutionalize ties among black House members. The turning point came in 1968 when Representatives Louis Stokes (D-Ohio), William Clay (D-Missouri), and Shirley Chisholm (D-New York) were elected. Coming at the end of the tumultuous 1960s, their simultaneous elections seemed to encapsulate the rising black interest in electoral politics. Their impact, therefore, was psychological as well as numerical—with their arrival, the "critical number" for an organization seemed to have been reached.

In 1969 Diggs, by then the most senior active black representative (Dawson and Powell were often absent—both were ill, and Powell had been stripped of his seniority), called a meeting of the nine black members of the House and proposed the formation of what later became the Democratic Select Committee. Its purpose, according to Diggs, was to facilitate communication among black representatives and between those representatives and the House leadership. The Democratic Select Committee operated informally—no elections were held—and Diggs became "temporary" chairman simply by group consensus. Moreover, there was no separate staff, budget, or long-range planning, and many activities centered on social functions. Despite its informality, the Democratic Select Committee was an active organization. Members worked together to fight the Nixon administration on many issues, including Supreme Court appointments, social welfare problems, and civil rights. It was as the Democratic Select Committee that the black representatives sent a letter to President Nixon in February 1970 requesting a meeting to discuss public policy toward blacks and poor people in the United States.

Both internal and external factors contributed to the reorganization of the Democratic Select Committee. Externally, the climate of the Nixon administration and the development of a protracted confrontation between black members of the House and the President helped forge the group's sense of common purpose and identity. Internally, there was mounting concern, particularly among the more recently elected black members, about the informality of the Democratic Select Committee. Representative Clay was the most vocal. In 1970, in a terse memo to his black colleagues in the House, he warned that ". . . without adequate programming and planning, we might well degenerate into the Kongressional Koffee Klatch Club." [2] Clay's dissatisfaction led to the drafting of a proposal for a new organization. He suggested (1) that formal elections be held, (2) that an executive committee of three members be elected as the policy-making group within the organization with authorization to act in the absence of the total membership, and (3) that subcommittees be established in policy areas of particular concern to minorities. Finally, Clay recommended that the name Democratic Select Committee be changed because it politicized the group along party lines and might potentially exclude black members from a different party.

At the first meeting of the Democratic Select Committee during the Ninety-second Congress, Clay's suggestions were reviewed and agreement was reached on the reorganization of the Democratic Select Committee as the Congressional Black Caucus. The new name reflected a de facto policy decision about the nature and primary constituency of the new organization. Three other names were considered: Congressional Committee on Minority Interests, Congressional Committee on Minority Rights, and Congressional Committee for the Protection of Minority Rights. Some felt that if the group were to expand its areas of concern to include Chicanos, Puerto Ricans, Indians, and so on, then the word "black" would be constraining. Most members agreed, however, that for the foreseeable future at least, their focus would be on problems of the black community. In addition, there was a proposal for establishing an auxiliary organization, Friends of the CBC, that could include liberal whites (including members of Congress), nonblack minority-group politicians and leaders, and blacks from outside Congress. Another idea was to establish a network of black experts that would serve as a resource group to the CBC staff—much the way the current CBC "brain trust" works.

By 1971, when the CBC was officially launched, there were twelve black representatives: Ronald Dellums (D-California), Parren Mitchell (D-Maryland), and George Collins (D-Illinois) were the new members. Subsequently, Ralph Metcalfe (D-Illinois) replaced Dawson, and Charles Rangel (D-New York) defeated Powell. Walter Fauntroy (D-District of Columbia) joined the group as a nonvoting delegate on April 19, 1971, bringing the number to thirteen. Between 1971 and 1977 George Collins was replaced by his widow, Cardiss (after he was killed in an airplane accident), and the original group was joined by Yvonne Burke (D-California), Barbara Jordan (D-Texas), Harold Ford (D-Tennessee), and Andrew Young (D-Georgia), who subsequently resigned to become ambassador to the United Nations. This group constituted the CBC during the middle 1970s (Ninety-fourth Congress) when the CBC was undergoing institutionalization as a stable force in American politics.

During the Ninety-fifth Congress, Nix was defeated and replaced in the Ninety-sixth by William Gray (D-Pennsylvania); Metcalfe died in 1978 and was replaced by Bennett Stewart in the Ninety-sixth and by Harold Washington in the Ninety-seventh; Jordan resigned and was replaced by Michel Leland (D-Texas); and Burke resigned and returned to California, to be replaced by Julian Dixon (D-California). In the Ninety-sixth Congress Charles Diggs was forced from office by a prolonged scandal and finally a conviction for misappropriation of federal funds. Replacing him as representative from the Third District of Michigan in the Ninety-seventh Congress is Democrat George Crockett. In addition to their replacements, the CBC gained new ground in the Ninety-sixth Congress with the election of Melvin Evans (a nonvoting delegate from the Virgin Islands who was not returned in the Ninety-seventh Congress), Melvyn Dymally (D-California), and Gus Savage (D-Illinois). By 1981 (CBC's tenth anniversary) the organization had grown to eighteen members. All were from the House of Representatives. Edward Brooke, the black senator and a Republican, never chose to join the CBC while he was in Congress.

The CBC in the Policy System: A History of Contradictions, Dilemmas, and Opportunities

THE "COLLECTIVE" STAGE   In an earlier study, I noted three stages in the development of the CBC. The first was a collective stage in which the CBC depicted itself as a single unified group representing a political construct called the "national black community." It worked both inside and outside the congressional arena. In the second, ethnic stage, CBC members functioned more individually as "just" legislators inside Congress. The third, synthetic stage combined both ethnic and collective elements but was an inherently unstable transition period between an ethnic-collective oscillation.[3]

During the first year of its existence (from mid-1971 to mid-1972), the CBC saw itself as "representative-at-large for 20 million black people." In carrying through this mandate, the CBC staff attempted a variety of activities including the provision of casework services, gathering and disseminating information, administrative oversight, articulation of the interests of a specialized group within the black community, and development of legislative proposals.

Much CBC visibility that first year came from a series of hearings held around the country on health, education, black enterprises, the mass media, Africa, and racism in the military. Results of these hearings were to be incorporated in the CBC "Black Agenda." In turn, the "Black Agenda" was to be used both inside Congress as the basis for a caucus legislative agenda and outside Congress as a document to be presented to the Democratic and Republican presidential candidates. The idea, which later came to fruition in slightly altered form, was to use the "Black Agenda" as the criterion for determining which party and candidate blacks should support in 1972. Indeed, as 1972 approached, more and more energy of individual CBC members was consumed in efforts to fashion pragmatic personal or group strategies for the forthcoming party conventions and presidential elections. The Black Political Convention in March 1972 in Gary, Indiana, was conceived as part of that process.

Representative Charles Diggs, then chairman of the CBC, had issued the call for a national black political convention to be held in the spring of 1972 "for the purpose of developing a national Black Agenda and the crystallization of a national black strategy for the 1972 election and beyond."[4]

This call created conflict within the CBC. While Diggs had touched base with one of the CBC members on the convention idea, he had not cleared his announcement with the full caucus at a formal meeting. By the time the CBC met formally to discuss the matter, a majority voted to withdraw official CBC backing for the convention idea. Some caucus members were afraid the convention would leave the CBC with large debts; others feared it would get out of hand and cause bad publicity. A few individual CBC members remained active, however. Diggs was an official convenor of the National Black Political Convention (along with Mayor Richard Hatcher of Gary, Indiana, and former black nationalist Imamu Baraka), and Walter Fauntroy was chairman of the important platform committee. Almost all caucus members attended the convention; and Howard Robinson, caucus executive director, played an important role in organizing and orchestrating convention activities.

The Gary convention marked an important transition point in CBC history. Although the caucus was not the official sponsor of the convention, the CBC name was publicly associated with it as a result both of Diggs' call and the visible involvement of some CBC members. The CBC therefore was associated (much to its embarrassment) with the two most controversial resolutions passed at the convention—on busing and on Israel. Not satisfied with repeated informal personal disclaimers, the CBC issued press releases on these topics immediately after the Gary convention. The release on Israel reaffirmed "its friendship with the State of Israel" and stated:

> As the Black elected representatives to the U.S. Congress, we reaffirm our position that we fully respect the right of the Jewish people to have their own state in their historical National Homeland. We vigorously oppose the efforts of any group that would seek to weaken or undermine Israel's right to existence.[5]

While the National Black Political Convention was well attended and representative of a broad cross-section of black America, it had offended powerful black civil rights groups as well as influential white liberal, Jewish, and labor interests. These groups formed the backbone of financial support for many individual CBC members and lobbying support for key pieces of liberal legislation. There was substantial pressure on CBC members, therefore, to totally disassociate themselves from the Gary convention and from subsequent efforts to develop a new, more autonomous black politics. Whatever their individual feelings, many CBC members perceived the cost of maintaining identification with the Black political convention as high and the benefits as uncertain, distant, and possibly minimal.

The Gary convention also revealed the extent of internal CBC conflict. While Fauntroy, Diggs, and Dellums were active in the Gary convention, Shirley Chisholm viewed it as a personal rebuff. Indeed, the unenthusiastic and at times hostile response of some caucus members to her 1972 presidential candidacy created an enormous rift in the caucus and almost destroyed it. By mid-1972, the view that the CBC could be a "united voice for Black America" was discredited. Never actually a monolith, even the myths of unity were punctured by the events surrounding the Gary convention and the 1972 Democratic convention. The caucus's collective stage had come to an end.

While the collective stage was often confusing for outsiders and hectic for the representatives, some accomplishments mark that period. First, a staff was appointed, which performed a variety of tasks and laid the groundwork for later diversification and expansion of activities. Second, a method for financing the CBC through the annual $100-a-plate dinner was begun. Third, an internal structure was established consisting of a chairman, executive committee, and policy-oriented subcommittees. While some subcommittees were moribund from birth, others, such as the subcommittee on small business, chaired by Representative Parren Mitchell, were successful. Finally, the CBC gained visibility and backing from many blacks around the country who saw it as operating on their behalf.

Significant lessons can be learned from the collective stage. Despite stated collective intentions, atomizing and individualizing tendencies muted the effective realization of collective goals. Effective individual performance in Congress demands, among other things, access to organizations with power on Capitol Hill. Good interest-group contacts can be vital to a freshman or sophomore representative, and most members of the CBC were very low in seniority in 1971–72. Lobbying groups influence committee assignments and committee chairmanships in both houses of Congress; they provide legislative spokesmen and experts to testify at committee hearings; their staff members draft legislation, amend legislation already drafted, monitor legislation, and can often influence the votes of substantial numbers of congressmen. The most powerful lobbying groups keep records of congressional voting patterns and reward their friends at election time with campaign money, staff assistance, propaganda materials, and public support; similarly, they punish their enemies through staunch and vitriolic opposition.

Along with external lobbying groups that pressure congressional representatives, there are other sources of cross-cutting loyalty that fragment, divide, and separate legislators. State delegations hold meetings and try to deliver the vote of their members as a bloc on key issues; informal policy groups such as the Democratic Study Group (DSG) send out large quantities of material on legislation and hold meetings at which the "liberal line" on legislation is presented; the President and his staff attempt to win adherents to his legislative program; and so on. Black politicians, like all politicians, worry about being reelected and will be, at least partially, accountable to those groups and individuals most likely to help in achieving that goal. While the black Democrats that make up the CBC can cooperate with one another to increase the amount of political resources that are tacitly and informally allocated for the black community, they must also compete with one another for a share of these resources. For the CBC to have maintained and succeeded with a collective model, *they would have had to resolve the contradiction between individual political survival and group direction; they would have had to construct an innovative way of functioning within the congressional context.*

THE "ETHNIC" STAGE   From mid-1972 through the end of 1974 the CBC entered what is best termed an "ethnic" stage—ethnic because the model of politics was one supposedly provided by white ethnic groups. It is a model of joint effort that maximizes compatability, with an individualistic and incremental conception of political action, and assumes prior assimilation of the ethnic group on the economic and social levels. If social, economic, and cultural issues have been resolved, then political action can take place in a framework where black politicians operate in the same way as other ethnic politicians do. Members of the CBC turned away from the turbulence of visible national collective leadership to define themselves as "just legislators"—primarily representatives of individual constituencies. During this period, the CBC undertook two major unified efforts: extension of OEO programs under the Economic Opportunity Act of 1964 and countering fund impoundments by President Nixon. Although the CBC's efforts on OEO and impoundment were only partially successful, the process contributed to CBC institutionalization. It was able to initiate extensive relationships with key national black, liberal, and labor organizations; its support base was broadened; and the organization achieved greater visibility and stability.

Reflection on this period raises a serious question: Were a formally organized caucus and the staff and operating costs it entailed necessary? No doubt there were significant legislative achievements during the ethnic stage—most notably the District of Columbia Home Rule legislation—but they were primarily individual efforts. The CBC countered White House conservatism in many ways—for instance, by issuing its own state of the union message, "The True State of the Union"—but it could have united those purposes without a formally organized caucus. Similarly, the campaigns to save OEO and blunt Nixon's impoundment strategy could have been coordinated through the offices of individual members. The CBC staff attempted to develop a research capacity that reflected the black perspective through public policy briefs called "legislative alerts." Since neither the CBC members nor the CBC staff had defined what constitutes a black public policy perspective, the alerts were often ignored by black and liberal representatives in favor of liberal analyses from the Democratic Study Group (DSG), to which all CBC members belonged. In fact, it is difficult to think of many activities during the ethnic stage that necessitated an ongoing, formally organized CBC. The point is not that the CBC as an entity with staff capacity was useless. Rather, when black representatives define their role in the narrowest, most individualistic terms, they obscure the reasons for institutionalizing a racially based political caucus and thus undermine their own legitimacy.[6]

By the end of 1974, CBC members, the CBC staff, and outside supporters and observers of the caucus were becoming increasingly uneasy. There was an impression among many black elites that despite the individual capability of some caucus members, the caucus as a whole was ineffectual and foundering.[7] Accurate or not, this criticism and other internal problems led to a series of retreats and self-evaluation sessions during late 1974 and early 1975. These sessions were the basis for the CBC strategy and self-perception in the late 1970s.

Three major strategies emerged from this self-evaluation. The first involved renewed efforts to get more favorable committee assignments for CBC members. At the beginning of the Ninety-fifth Congress, all twenty-two of the standing committees of the House of Representatives had at least one CBC member. Ten CBC members chaired subcommittees. Of the six that did not, five had excellent committee assignments, including Harold Ford, the newest black member of Congress at that time. The "Big Three" committees of the House of Representatives all had black members—Rules (Chisholm), Ways and Means (Rangel and Ford), and Appropriations (Stokes and Burke). Charles Diggs and Robert N. C. Nix chaired full committees—District of Columbia and Post Office and Civil Service, respectively.

Better committee assignments resulted from CBC negotiations with the Democratic House leadership. In 1971, when the caucus sought a place on the Armed Services Committee, they recommended Ronald Dellums, an opponent of high levels of military spending. Dellums received the appointment over the opposition of the chairman of the Armed Services Committee. Similarly, when Stokes wanted a seat on the Appropriations Committee, it was approved over the vehement objections of fellow Ohioan and Ways and Means Committee member Charles Vanik. Another example of CBC impact on the committee system was the continuation of the House investigation into the assassinations of John F. Kennedy and Martin Luther King, Jr. Many Washington observers credit the CBC with preventing the Select Committee investigating the assassinations from being dismantled.

With the exception of Walter Fauntroy, whose work on the District of Columbia Committee was of direct relevance for his home constituency, committee assignments for CBC members reflected peer-group pressure, collective decisions of the CBC, and serendipity more than constituency characteristics. Most CBC members represented constituencies with high black unemployment, poor housing, high crime and drug addiction rates, large percentages of the population on welfare, and so on. Even when there were substantial numbers of middle- and upper-class residents in a CBC member's district, the district's most pressing problems tended to grow out of economic deterioriation. In the late 1960s most blacks in Congress wanted to be on the House Education and Labor Committee because it was and is most closely identified with social legislation. Black representatives soon realized, however, that not only is the committee structure the key to congressional power, but it must also be seen as a committee system, not as a conglomeration of individual committees. To have an effective say on social legislation, CBC members had to be on a variety of key committees—Rules, Appropriations, Ways and Means, and a host of others.

In addition, they had to become active in introducing and pushing major legislation and key amendments to legislation initiated by others. Of the 729 bills that became law in the Ninety-fourth Congress (588 bills became public law and 141 private law), only 16 (2 percent) were sponsored by members of the CBC. It should be remembered, however, that no legislation that winds its way through the complex congressional maze is ever the work of a single representative. There are co-sponsors, sub-committee chairmen, party leaders, interest-group leaders, agency spokesmen and White House negotiators, and many others who help shape an initial idea into law; only a minuscule 1.5 percent of all bills introduced in the Ninety-fourth Congress became law.

Various CBC members seek to influence this process at every step by testifying at subcommittee hearings, negotiating the content of legislation, and offering amendments. Indeed, the CBC emphasizes the introduction and acceptance of amendments as crucial to their behind-the-scenes impact on the direction and scope of legislation. One example: When the CBC found that a $4 billion public works bill did not contain strong provisions to ensure that minority firms share in contracts for construction of public works facilities, Representative Parren Mitchell introduced an amendment, passed by both houses, requiring that 10 percent of each contract under the bill must go to minority firms.

A second major strategy growing out of the 1974 retreat was the "Fauntroy strategy" employed to secure Home Rule for the District of Columbia. This strategy was based on a series of studies done by the Joint Center for Political Studies showing that blacks comprise 25 percent or more of the population of 58 congressional districts. In 51 of these districts, the black voting-age population was approximately two to three times the margin of victory for the winning candidate in the 1972 congressional elections, indicating that a heavy turnout of black voters in those districts could be decisive if other factors remained constant.

District of Columbia Representative Walter Fauntroy singled out southern constituencies with 25 percent or more black population. Letters were mailed to black elected officials and a few other prominent people in those districts requesting them to ask their congressman to vote for HR 9682, the District of Columbia Home Rule bill. Fauntroy then reached congressmen from those districts and asked support for the legislation. Thus the strategy involved a coordinated lobbying and peer-group approach to southern congressmen from targeted districts.

Subsequently, a modified version of the "Fauntroy strategy" was used in the 1973 mobilization for extension of OEO. In both the District of Columbia Home Rule and OEO examples, complicating factors prevent a precise assessment of the strategy's impact. Certainly, in both cases there were large differences between what black lobbyists and other organized interest groups wanted and the legislation finally passed. Nonetheless, it did point out the willingness of black elected officials and local black influentials to cooperate with the CBC. As a caucus strategy, the Fauntroy plan was supposed to be elaborated by the creation of nationwide congressional district caucuses in constituencies of high black voting-age population. These district caucuses were to consist of black elected officials and local black influentials and would form the basis of a "CBC whip system."

Although proposed at the beginning of the Ninety-fourth Congress, the "Fauntroy strategy" did not become fully effective. Indeed, a significant number of staff members from various CBC offices opposed the plan and advised their representatives not to use it. This hostility stems from a number of factors and reflects the reluctance of staffers to advise their bosses to employ strategies that violate existing congressional mores. Since the "Fauntroy strategy" assumes a good deal of CBC unity and staff effort to be effective, this was no small obstacle.

The third strategy, first utilized by Congressman Parren Mitchell, was an expansion of the network of professional and academic advisers. Beginning in 1973, Mitchell gathered three hundred advisers (called "brainstormers") to discuss public policy issues and congressional legislation. As adapted for the CBC as a whole, the "Mitchell model" has meant the creation of a much larger group with expertise relevant to the entire caucus. Each caucus member meets individually with his or her group on a regular basis. Although the network concept did not gain in momentum until the Ninety-fifth Congress, it rapidly became an important CBC technique for gaining the support and assistance of elements of the black middle class on legislative matters.

The Ninety-fourth Congress was also a turning point for the CBC in its self-perception about the potential influence of black congresspersons. Diggs chaired a House committee, the District of Columbia Committee, and a number of other CBC members moved into important slots as subcommittee chairpersons and/or members on key committees (see Table 2.1). With increasing longevity in Congress, many CBC members were also moving up in seniority (Table 2.2). The stage seemed to be set for the CBC to realize its goal of influencing public policy in directions beneficial to the black community. By the Ninety-fifth Congress it had a goal, a strategy, and experienced legislators in key positions in Congress.

The CBC in the 95th and 96th Congresses: A Synthesis of "Ethnic" and "Collective" Tendencies

The "Mitchell Model" and the "Fauntroy strategy" tell us a great deal about CBC activities in the late 1970s, perhaps best described as a synthesis of the "ethnic" and "collective" orientations. In the "collective" stage the CBC saw the black community in undifferentiated terms as a unified entity; the "ethnic" stage was distinguished by a limited, constituency-oriented focus. The new CBC focus was on the black middle- and upper-class professionals and political elites, a group that has the

TABLE 2.1 CBC CONGRESSIONAL COMMITTEE MEMBERSHIP, 94TH CONGRESS

Member	Committee and Subcommittee
Yvonne B. Burke 28th Congressional District California	*Appropriations* District of Columbia Foreign Operations State Justice Commerce and Judiciary *Select Committee on Assassinations*
Shirley A. Chisholm 12th Congressional District New York	*Rules*
William L. Clay 1st Congressional District Missouri	*Education and Labor* Employment Opportunities Labor-Management Relations Labor Standards *Post Office and Civil Service* Civil Service Investigations Postal Personnel and Modernization *Special Welfare Reform*
Cardiss Collins 7th Congressional District Illinois	*District of Columbia* Judiciary *Government Operations* Commerce Consumer and Monetary Affairs Manpower and Housing *International Relations* Africa Inter-American Affairs *Select Committee on Narcotics* *Abuse and Control*
John Conyers, Jr. 1st Congressional District Michigan	*Government Operations* Legislation and National Security Manpower and Housing *Judiciary* Crime
Charles C. Diggs, Jr. 13th Congressional District Michigan	*District of Columbia* [a] *International Relations* Africa [b] International Operations

TABLE 2.1 (CONTINUED)

Member	*Committee and Subcommittee*

Walter Fauntroy
District of Columbia
	Banking, Finance and Urban Affairs
	  Consumer Affairs
	  Economic Stabilization
	  Historic Preservation and Coinage
	  Housing and Community Development
	
	District of Columbia
	  Economic Development and Regional Affairs
	  Fiscal and Governmental Affairs
	Select Committee on Assassinations

Harold Ford
8th Congressional District
Tennessee
	Ways and Means
	  Health
	  Oversight
	Select Committee on Aging
	  Health and Long-Term Care
	Select Committee on Assassinations
	  King Assassination

Augustus F. Hawkins
29th Congressional District
Tennessee
	Education and Labor
	  Economic Opportunity
	  Employment Opportunities [c]
	  Select Education
	House Administration [b]
	  Accounts
	  Contracts
	  Printing
	Joint Committee on Printing

Barbara C. Jordan
18th Congressional District
Texas
	Government Operations
	  Environment, Energy and
	    Natural Resources
	  Government Information and
	    Individual Rights
	Judiciary
	  Administrative Law and
	    Government Relations
	  Monopolies and Commercial Law

Ralph H. Metcalfe
1st Congressional District
Illinois
	Interstate and Foreign Commerce
	  Consumer Protection and Finance
	  Transportation and Commerce
	Merchant Marine and Fisheries
	  Merchant Marine
	  Oceanography
	  Panama Canal [c]

TABLE 2.1   (CONTINUED)

Member	Committee and Subcommittee
Parren J. Mitchell 7th Congressional District Maryland	*Banking, Finance and Urban Affairs* Domestic Monetary Policy [c] General Oversight and Renegotiation Housing and Community Development *Budget*
Robert N. C. Nix 2nd Congressional District Pennsylvania	*International Relations* Africa International Development *Post Office and Civil Service* [a] Investigations
Charles B. Rangel 19th Congressional District New York	*House-Senate Conference Committee on Energy* *Select Committee on Narcotics Abuse and Control* *Ways and Means* Oversight Public Assistance and Unemployment Compensation *Special Welfare Reform*
Louis Stokes 21st Congressional District Ohio	*Appropriations* Foreign Operations HUD-Independent Agencies Labor-HEW *Budget* *Select Committee on Assassinations* [a] Special Welfare Reform

SOURCE: *Congressional Quarterly Research Service.*
[a] *Committee chairman and ex-officio member of all subcommittees.*
[b] *Committee vice chairman.*
[c] *Subcommittee chairman.*

potential to provide financial resources and technical assistance to CBC. This group can also legitimate CBC claims to be greater than the sum of its parts—to represent black America.

But these strategies were interwoven with a generalized CBC effort at revitalization. The most important decision was to emphasize joint efforts for passage of full-employment legislation, specifically the Humphrey-Hawkins Bill, HR 50. In one sense, the CBC had been overtaken by events at just the moment when it sought an effective vehicle for its own internal reorganization and new external posture. Black unemployment and the general economic crisis in the black community had received

TABLE 2.2   CBC SENIORITY RATINGS IN 94TH CONGRESS

Member	Seniority in House of Representatives
Charles C. Diggs, Jr.	14
Robert N. C. Nix	19
Augustus F. Hawkins	28
John Conyers	33
Shirley Chisholm	38
William Clay	38
Louis Stokes	38
Ronald V. Dellums	45
Ralph H. Metcalfe	45
Parren J. Mitchell	45
Charles B. Rangel	45
Yvonne B. Burke	50
Barbara C. Jordan	50
Cardiss Collins	52
Harold Ford	59
Walter E. Fauntroy	Nonvoting delegate

SOURCE: Congressional Quarterly Research Service.

increasing priority among black leaders since the late 1960s. During the stagflation of the Nixon-Ford Presidencies, black unemployment soared. The "official" unemployment rate for the black community was about 12.5 percent at the beginning of the Ninety-fifth Congress. Since 1954, the unemployment rate for blacks has never dropped below 6 percent. If people discouraged and no longer looking for jobs were counted, the joblessness of some inner-city black communities would reach the staggeringly high figures of 35 percent for most of the late 1970s; indeed, for males over age sixteen, it was 55 percent. Despite regional differences, personal ambitions, constituency makeup, and other alliances, employment issues presented the best opportunities for CBC consensus.

When originally drafted, HR 50, the Full Employment and Balanced Growth Act, had provisions for the government to become the employer of last resort. It was strongly worded legislation that would have mandated full employment within a specified period of time with government public works programs as the residual source of employment if private industry failed. At that point, most of the bill had been drafted by Augustus Hawkins' office with some input and support from the late Senator Humphrey.

The route from the introduction of a bill to final passage is usually long and difficult. When that legislation is progressive social legislation in a time of increasing inflation and economic crisis, the road is particularly rocky. In order to win congressional support, the CBC sought allies outside Congress—labor, liberals, civil rights organizations, and the Democratic party. At each stage the legislation was watered down to suit the preferences of a particular group. When it finally passed the House in the waning hours of the Ninety-fifth Congress, it had been significantly weakened. Senator Orrin C. Hatch (R-Utah) had so much influence over the final wording that some Washington wags called it the Humphrey-Hawkins-Hatch bill. Even the *Congressional Quarterly* was almost brutal in its assessment:

> As cleared, HR 50 was a far cry from the massive federal jobs and economic planning bill introduced by the late Senator Hubert H. Humphrey, D.-Minn. (1949–64, 1971–78) and Rep. Augustus Hawkins, D-Calif., during the depths of the mid-70s recession. The bill that finally reached President Carter's desk was stripped of its original provisions calling for government "last resort" jobs for the unemployed, although it still retained the central goal of reduction of the unemployment rate to 4 percent by 1983.
>
> In addition, the final version contained a new national goal calling for a reduction of the inflation rate by 3 percent by 1983 and 0 percent by 1988.
>
> Coretta Scott King, while conceding that "we did not get all of the provisions in the bill that we would have liked," called the bill ". . . an important first step in the struggle for full employment." Organized labor was less sanguine. "It does represent a small symbolic step forward," said Ken Young of the AFL-CIO, "but the Senate weakened it severely."[8]

The sad saga of HR 50 is indicative of the larger problems of the CBC. While CBC was successful in getting the legislation passed, using traditional lobbying and alliance techniques, the final law was utterly meaningless as a vehicle to aid the black unemployed. An optimist might say it shows how blacks can use the political system to achieve their legislative priorities, thereby arguing the electoral system's benefit to the black community. A more careful analysis, however, reveals the political weakness of black leadership, the black political community, and the CBC.

By the middle of the Ninety-fifth Congress, it became clear that not only was the CBC not revitalized, but (except for a year of vitality and activity under Parren Mitchell) the organization seemed to be slipping even deeper into political chaos. Scandal tainted the group when Representative Charles Diggs was convicted of payroll fraud and finally jailed. Diggs was the senior member of the group and had chaired the full District of Columbia Committee as well as the Africa subcommittee of the House International Relations Committee. Other members also left. Nix, a quiet somnambular but senior representative from Philadelphia, was defeated by William Gray; Yvonne Burke resigned, to be replaced by Julian Dixon; Metcalfe died and was replaced by Bennett Stewart, who in turn was replaced in 1980 by Harold Washington. Diggs was replaced by Judge

Crockett. And although he had never belonged to the CBC, Edward Brooke's defeat removed a sympathetic voice from the Senate.

All these changes plus the deepening crisis of the Carter administration and the almost two years of division within the Democratic party over the party's presidential nomination did little to unify the caucus. As in the past, some caucus members supported the President; others supported Senator Kennedy. The CBC, like the country, was split. After the dubious HR 50 victory, a number of issues galvanized the CBC momentarily, but none initiated a multiyear, all-out campaign the way HR 50 did.

As the CBC heads for the Ninety-seventh Congress with newly elected President Reagan, it continues to face a doubtful future. On the positive side, the CBC has eighteen members, including some very prestigious new members: Judge Crockett from Michigan and Representative Dymally, a seasoned California politician, are the best known. In addition, both Savage and Washington from Illinois have very good reputations in local politics.

A second advantage of the CBC in the Ninety-seventh Congress will be the greater levels of seniority for the group as a whole. This is, of course, relevant in determining committee assignments. Four CBC members will chair full House committees: Parren Mitchell, Small Business Committee; Louis Stokes, Ethics Committee; Augustus Hawkins, Administration Committee; and Ronald Dellums, District of Columbia Committee. Other members, such as Chisholm, Clay, Rangel, and Conyers, also have important committee and subcommittee assignments.

New leadership of the CBC will likely add energy and enthusiasm to its activities. Representative Walter Fauntroy is the new CBC chair and has already begun to make changes that he believes will put the group on the offensive. He is likely finally to implement his strategy for linking the CBC with groups across the country. He has already hired additional staff to monitor and draft legislation and has taken organizational measures to strengthen CBC functioning. More important, Fauntroy wants to strengthen the CBC as a political organization with a definite shared perspective on national problems.

On the negative side are a variety of fundamental problems. Most troublesome are the dubious long-range prospects for continued growth in CBC membership. Indeed, there may be the possibility that the CBC will lose seats with the legislative redistribution required by the last census. Of the 25 top population losers, blacks represent 9 districts. Table 2.3 shows the representative, district, location, and percentage population lost for districts represented by the CBC.

No black representatives are from the 25 top population gainers, all of which are in the sunbelt, Hawaii, and Colorado. When the district lines are redrawn and elections are held, blacks could lose as many as 9 seats, although in all likelihood only a few will be lost. On a base of 18, however,

TABLE 2.3   BLACK REPRESENTATIVES IN THE TOP 25 DISTRICTS SHOWING THE HIGHEST POPULATION DECREASES IN 1980 CENSUS

Representative	District	Location	Percentage of Population Lost
Crockett	13th Michigan	Downtown Detroit	−38.6
Chisholm	12th New York	Northeast Brooklyn	−32.1
Clay	1st Missouri	North St. Louis	−25.0
Stokes	21st Ohio	Cleveland East	−24.7
Rangel	19th New York	Manhattan	−21.8
Collins	7th Illinois	West Side	−21.5
Washington	1st Illinois	South Side	−21.1
Gray	2nd Pennsylvania	West Philadelphia	−17.2
Conyers	1st Michigan	North Central Detroit	−16.5

SOURCE: Data based on information from Congressional Quarterly, *January, 1981.*

2 or 3 seats are important. If black representatives with seniority and standing are lost, the problem will be exacerbated.

Another obvious problem in the Ninety-seventh Congress will stem from the association of the CBC with the Democratic party (all current members are Democrats) during a Republican administration. Even though the Democrats maintain a slim majority of seats in the House of Representatives, the number of liberals likely to support caucus causes has decreased. This at a time when conservatives are preparing to dismantle social programs, affirmative action, minority business programs, and other issues usually supported by the CBC.

The more important issue, however, is not the specifics of historical change from one Congress to another but the persistent pattern revealed by CBC's ten-year history. The pendulum metaphor is as apt now as when it was initially used in 1975.[9] Moving from ethnic to collective orientations, attempting accommodations of ethnic and collective organizational aspects, undergoing frequent revitalization programs (and thereby acknowledging the movement between periods of stagnation and vitality), the CBC has failed to assume a consistent, national leadership role in the black community. While struggling against the increasing conservatism of the country and the Congress, it has failed to deliver or initiate legislation that would benefit the total black community. Acceptance of that evaluation leaves us with a persistent question: Why? It also focuses us back on our initial theoretical concerns.

Theory and Practice

Black representatives are practically and symbolically linked through the CBC. Unfortunately, the symbolism of the CBC often overshadows the realities of individual member priorities and differences. Although all blacks in the House of Representatives belong to the CBC and thereby further the illusion of a unified black legislative voice, not all are equally interested in the CBC as a primary political vehicle.

I began this discussion with the cautionary view that analyses of the CBC or of any black configuration should contribute to black political theory. The CBC provides necessary lessons. Although CBC members can be viewed as individual representatives with separate ambitions, diverse constituency problems, and mixed performance records, the interesting possibilities for the black community flow from their joint efforts. As our discussion has shown, however, CBC members (and by extension, black politicians working through the electoral process) are caught in a double bind. They are caught between pressures to represent blacks collectively as a unit and constraints dictated by their individual political circumstances. Put another way, there is a conflict between individualizing and collectivizing templates for political action. Efforts to transcend this double bind by concentrating on a specific issue, such as HR 50, have fostered only temporary unity.

The CBC collective stage differentiates it from other caucuses in Congress and underscores the obvious need for explanations of the CBC that go beyond conventional discussion of the rise and behavior of legislative caucuses. Even the ethnic stage, in which the CBC attempted to become "just legislators" to closely emulate other congressional caucuses, had a curiously unstable quality that demands explanation. The ethnic stage produced intense dissatisfaction both within and outside the CBC. Fuller understanding of both the ethnic and the collective stages requires that the CBC be situated within a broader theoretical discussion of blacks and the American political system.

Blacks and the American Political System

Part of the difficulty in understanding black politics stems from flawed views of the larger economic and political systems in which black political actors operate. A common political analogy likens blacks to white ethnic groups and is followed by arguments that even if blacks are not precisely like white ethnic groups, their usages of group power can produce similar results. Blacks, therefore are encouraged to follow the white ethnic group example, including the supposed use of the political system to achieve status and economic power for the group. This model is troublesome because it distorts white ethnic group history (most significantly the way they really used politics) and the sociology of both the black experience and the white ethnic experience.

The black experience is too dissimilar from white ethnic groups for blacks to pursue derivative strategies. One obvious difference is that ethnic group political victories and economic assimilation occurred simultaneously. The ethnically balanced ticket, made famous in the era of machine politics, was not only a result of ethnic majorities in urban areas but also reflected growing white ethnic group economic clout. The vast immigrant influxes occurred when the United States was experiencing tremendous economic growth and could absorb large numbers of uneducated European peasants as unskilled laborers. White ethnic groups therefore did not have to use urban or national politics to improve their collective economic position—that was accomplished by the natural growth of a capitalist system expanding outward to foreign markets and regulated by the potential of the frontier. Politics provided status, symbolic recognition, individual rewards, and substitutes for nonexistent social welfare services. White ethnic groups were not attempting to use politics to transform the political-economic system or to produce any structural (i.e., radical) changes. They used politics to legitimize the economic and social assimilation that was already taking place.

The contrast with blacks is obvious. Blacks were involuntary immigrants, brought here as slaves, as another kind of property. Their arrival (in large numbers) in the central cities of the industrial North came fifty to seventy-five years after the large white ethnic group migrations and at a time when the economic system could absorb them only sporadically in war-related cycles. While white ethnics faced some prejudice, the intransigence against black social and political assimilation and economic mobility was not like anything this country, or any country, had previously faced. In the South, blacks were trapped in a decaying, oppressive sharecropper system until well into the twentieth century. In the North, they were grafted onto the labor force as a reserve labor supply—hired in times of labor scarcity, unemployed during periods of labor surplus. Blacks thus became a kind of cushion, absorbing and insulating whites from the worst effects of economic downturns. This distanced the political system from economic contradictions by narrowing much of the impact of economic swings to the relatively powerless black group.

Many contemporary economists use a dual labor market theory to sharpen the analysis of blacks in the contemporary economic system. According to this view, the labor market is divided into a primary and a secondary sector. In the primary sector, job mobility is possible, pay is higher, work is stable, and unions or professional codes protect workers against certain forms of economic hardship. In short, the primary sector is the stable, desirable, and institutionally sheltered sector of the labor market. In contrast, the secondary sector is not well unionized, unstable, and lacking in opportunities for vertical mobility. Historically as well as today, blacks have been disproportionately concentrated in that secondary labor market. Although some individual white members of ethnic groups may be trapped in dead-end secondary labor market jobs, no white ethnic group, *qua* group, faces collective channeling into a structurally differentiated and inferior position in the labor market.

Since the economic viability of a community is a means for political advancement, these structural barriers in the economic system are of enormous importance. And these barriers have been uniquely immune to legislation. Many studies of the antiblack features of the dual labor market were done after the passage of antidiscrimination and civil rights legislation. Employers who automatically place blacks in secondary labor market jobs or who redefine jobs into the secondary sector after they have become "Negro jobs" cannot be reached by most current legislation. The real point here is that the white/black hierarchy overtly manifested in Jim Crow laws can be continued even after the nullification of those laws. The structural reality of legal segregation was that blacks were treated as a racial collectivity, separate and inferior to whites. Dual labor markets are one crucial example of the maintenance of the two main structural features that have historically encapsulated the black presence in America: racial hierarchy and enforced, stereotypically based, collectivism.

The ethnic group myth not only distorts American political history but it obscures our perception of current politics. The American political system is designed for, thrives on, and encourages incremental politics—incremental, not in a real sense, but often in terms of a consumer "forced choice" dictated by marketing goals. With no significant left electoral presence, most issues in American politics do not involve fundamental questions about the nature of our society. Certainly white ethnic groups did not wrench substantial collective benefits from the national political system, but then they did not demand basic or far-reaching economic and/or political change. Even if the ethnic group analogy were relevant, the question would still remain: Does it make sense for blacks to aim for the same quality and quantity of collective benefits that white ethnic groups received through political participation almost a century ago?

Issues that involve redistribution, issues that involve racial or class collectivities, and issues that are fundamental and nonincremental have difficulty getting on the political agenda; and once on that agenda, they tend to engender symbolic rather than substantive response. There are exceptions—the most obvious being forms of crisis politics. Wars, rebellions, severe economic downturns and dislocations, and the like, all set the stage for crisis politics.

Crisis politics, along with class politics and racial politics, tend to be ideological and divisive. Under such circumstances, traditionally liberal and conservative labels lose their meaning. Efforts to handle issues symbolically with gestures and assertions that paper over ideological fissures are doomed to failure. When symbolic efforts fail, the public policy that does finally emerge can be repressive or ameliorative. Ameliorative policies, formulated in crisis situations, tend to be more redistributive, encompassing, and nonincremental than the policy output from the normal political processes. A crisis atmosphere cannot be sustained indefinitely, however. In the normal functioning of the political process, organizations and individuals that evolve long-range strategies and networks of power, and whose interests can be served through maintenance of the status quo, acquire vested institutional power. Incremental politics rewards early intervention in the policy process, often at the agenda-setting stage. It is typified by the array of special interest groups so lovingly depicted in political science literature.

Crisis politics, in contrast, is inherently unstable and most effective in the short run. You can mobilize a few hundred thousand people to march on Washington only once in a decade. Unless there is a climate of fundamental political change, and the normal rules of the game do not apply, you cannot routinely apply political pressure through mass demonstrations, mass mobilization tactics.

Black politics have historically been most successful in crisis situations. The greatest political gains won by the black community were on the heels of the demonstrations and rebellions of the late 1950s and during the 1960s. Furthermore, many blacks raised political issues defined as illegitimate in the American political system—questions of separation and black nationalism, attacks on capitalism and current patterns of economic distribution, constitutional questions relating to the nature and organization of the political system, and so on.

Some black theorists conclude that politically sophisticated blacks must eschew crisis politics and play the incremental political game more effectively than any other group. Using the ethnic group analogy, they cite that model as the one to be emulated. What is overlooked is the reality of black structural differentiation. It should be obvious that if blacks are structurally different from white ethnic groups, they cannot reasonably emulate ethnic political models. (Such emulation has a "fail-safe" fallback. If political goals are not reached, don't blame the model, try harder.)

For the sake of argument, let us pursue this one step further. Going back to our discussion of the economic system, it is useful to point up the contrast between the ideology of capitalism and its actual operation vis-à-vis blacks. The underlying assumption of traditional economic theory is that capitalism maximizes competition and so provides individual opportunities for profit and economic gain. Wages in this system are supposed to reflect, at least approximately, productivity, training, and demand. Monopolies have long since limited the applicability of the notion of unfettered economic competition, but less well known is the fact that the operation of the dual labor market keeps a substantial portion of the black population out of direct competition in the labor market. Put simply, the subordination of blacks has enhanced white economic opportunities.

There is an analogy in the political system. The ideology of American politics asserts individual ability to influence decisions. Nevertheless, large interest groups are similar to monopolies in their ability to significantly skew decision making, and individuals can influence policy only to get incremental, divisible benefits from the political system. It is just those groups whose demands are not inherently incremental that are most cruelly deceived by the process. Also, since blacks perform what may be referred to as a cushioning role in the political system by absorbing economic dislocations, we must ask: Is this function so crucial for the political system that black subordination must continue in some form in order to ensure that the remainder of the population does not also begin to demand redistributive, nonincremental, and fundamental changes?

The Congressional Black Caucus, in order to be effective within the electoral context, would have to understand and directly attack the structural conditions of black subordination. Otherwise, structural constraints will continually undermine seeming advances won through electoral politics and incremental strategies.

Summary

Examination of CBC operation and history has revealed a pattern of development that demanded explanation on two levels: the emergence of collective, ethnic, and synthetic stages and the shift from stage to stage. Emergence of collective and ethnic stages is a reflection of the more general structural contradiction of black political life. Black politicians are forced to operate in a system where they must either find a model to come to grips with the unique structural position of American blacks or act as if that structural position had already been mediated and, therefore, as if blacks were just another ethnic group.

The CBC "collective" stage was an innovative political invention. The ideological representation of the CBC as a voice for the black community (collectivity) articulated a form of organic solidarity as the basis for their joint action. Despite its congruence with fundamental aspects of Afro-American life and despite its creativity as a political invention, transformation of the collective stage resulted from the pressures of conventional, incremental, individualistically based politics. This point needs elaboration. The National Black Political Convention and even the caucus's brief collective self-perception represent at least a partial break with both the theory and practice of interest-group politics. In interest-group theory, each group is abstractly equivalent to every other group in a plurality of competing groups comprising the polity. Groups are consciously modeled on the image of the autonomous individual: They are putative starting points in politics the way individuals are considered natural starting points in American cultural ideology. Both the CBC "collective" stage and the National Black Political Assembly were inchoate projections of black structural differentiation. In contrast to the theoretical model of autonomous, equivalent abstract units, the theoretical model underlying these CBC forms was unconsciously collectivist. Opposing the autonomous unit was the organic collectivity; equivalence was contrasted with recognition of structural imbalance, asymmetry, and black domination; abstraction was replaced by a focus on politics as emerging out of and reflecting the authenticity of cultural configurations.

The "ethnic" stage also floundered, but for different reasons. Once the CBC retreated into this stage, it distorted and undermined its own legitimacy. If CBC members are to act simply as legislators, then white legislators are substitutable for black legislators. Voting records and activity within Congress would be the only relevant basis for assessment of the CBC. Rationalization for a racially based caucus and for special efforts on behalf of blacks must hinge on a clear understanding of the special needs of black constituents and the particular responsiveness of black representatives to those structurally created needs. The ethnic stage, therefore, failed to relate black representatives to critical realities of black existence.

The current synthetic stage results from the failure of the CBC (and other black political organizations as well) to resolve the fundamental contradictions of black political life. It is inherently unstable because basic decisions about the theory and operation of the CBC cannot be dealt with by focusing on specific issues or instrumental strategies.

In a broader sense, the false consciousness, contradictions, false starts, and oscillations associated with CBC history are part of the general black political dilemma in the United States. It is this dilemma that must be explored as part of an emerging black political theory.

NOTES

1. Mack Jones, "Black Politics: Symbolism and Reality" (unpublished paper prepared for delivery at the Second Annual Political Science Seminar, South Carolina State College, March 15, 1972).
2. Personal communication received from Michael MacPherson, former A.A. to William Clay.
3. Marguerite Ross Barnett, "The Congressional Black Caucus," *Proceedings of the Academy of Political Science* 32, no. 1 (1975): 34–50.
4. CBC press release, 1971.
5. CBC press release, March 21, 1972.

6. The CBC therefore leaves itself vulnerable to the charge that its presence makes little difference. See Bruce Robeck, "The Congressional Black Caucus" (paper presented to the American Political Science Association meeting in Chicago, 1974) for the germ of that argument. After a roll-call analysis, Robeck concluded that the voting performance of white northern Democrats would not be improved greatly by replacing them with blacks.
7. Many commentators agree with this point. For example, Alex Poinsett, "The Black Caucus: Five Years Later," *Ebony* 28, no. 8 (June 1973): 64, was careful to draw balanced conclusions about the CBC but pointed out many of the group's problems.
8. "Humphrey-Hawkins Bill: A Victory of Sorts for Labor," *Congressional Quarterly* 36, no. 42 (October 21, 1978): 3102.
9. Barnett, "Congressional Black Caucus."

THREE

The Courts, Section 5 of the Voting Rights Act, and the Future of Black Politics

Twiley W. Barker, Jr., and Lucius J. Barker

The Voting Rights Act of 1965 was hailed as a great victory in America's attempt to end racial discrimination. The chief purpose of the act was to remove the vices and vestiges of practices that prevented blacks (and other minorities) from voting. If there is one sacred feature of the American democracy, it is the right to vote. The sacredness of this right is grounded on what is perhaps an oversimplified belief that through political participation (mainly the right to vote), individuals and groups will be able to safeguard, protect, and promote their interests. Put another way, the intense competition for votes in our electoral system acts as a leverage on actions by government officials that might alienate large numbers of voters. In any event, regardless of theoretical or practical considerations, there is widespread popular support for guaranteeing and safeguarding the right to vote. To be sure, it took a long time for this widespread support to be converted into specific support to protect the voting rights of blacks. It began with the gradual elimination of the most blatant devices (e.g., literacy tests and white primaries) that disfranchised significant numbers of blacks and continued with the actions taken by Congress in the civil rights acts of 1957, 1960, and 1964. These acts, while indicative of a change in congressional mood, were not very effective in increasing the number of black voters. White officials, primarily in the South, continued to find ways to keep blacks off the registration rolls and from voting. Indeed, the major defects of these measures were that they left registration machinery in the hands of hostile state and local officials and that they relied too much on litigation.

The 1964 elections made clear that the right to vote was still not a reality for black Americans in the South. A year later, stirred by massive civil rights demonstrations and pressed by the strong initiative of President Johnson, Congress finally enacted comprehensive voting rights legislation. The major improvement of the Voting Rights Act of 1965 over earlier laws is that it provided federal machinery to secure voting registration. In addition, the 1965 law abolished literacy and understanding tests in states and voting districts where less than 50 percent of the voting-age population had been registered in 1964 or had voted in the 1964 presidential election. To be sure, white southern officials challenged the constitutionality of the Voting Rights Act, but the U.S. Supreme Court upheld its validity in 1966.[1]

The new legislation proved effective. There were significant increases in black registration and black voting.[2] These increases, coupled with well-established demographic factors, raised the possibility that blacks might gain control of local governments in some jurisdictions.[3] Southern reaction to such an eventuality had been indicated by a situation that resulted in the 1960 Supreme Court case *Gomillion* v. *Lightfoot*.[4] Here, the Alabama legislature had attempted in a rather bold (and somewhat crude) manner to prevent a black takeover of a municipal government by redefining the corporate boundaries of Tuskegee and thereby excluding nearly all black voters from the city electorate. The plan did not survive judicial scrutiny, and the Supreme Court found it an obviously racially discriminatory scheme violative of the Fifteenth Amendment.

The decision on *Gomillion* indicated that "racial gerrymandering" could not be used as a device to blunt the impact of an increasing number of black voters. Nonetheless, those who pushed for the passage of the Voting Rights Act knew that safeguards against the use of such discriminatory devices had to be included in the legislation. It was directed at state or locally imposed changes in voting practices that might thwart or blunt the increase in black voters and prevent black majorities in given jurisdictions. More specifically, the VRA forbids a "covered" jurisdiction* to institute voting qualifications, practices, and procedures different from those in effect on November 1, 1964, unless it first obtains from the district court of the District of Columbia a declaratory judgment that the

---

* The following states (or parts of them) meet the statutory definition: Alabama, Georgia, Louisiana, Mississippi, North Carolina, South Carolina, and Virginia.

changes do "not have the purpose and will not have the effect of denying or abridging the right to vote on account of race or color."[5] To expedite matters, the provision allows jurisdictions to change the voting and election laws if the U.S. attorney general does not interpose any objections to such changes within sixty days after their submission. The ultimate outcome of such changes are then subject to judicial determination. In terms of its potential impact on black voting, Section 5 therefore looms as one of the most important safeguards against the use of discriminatory voting devices. The effectiveness of that safeguard depends in great measure on the position of the judiciary, and ultimately on the U.S. Supreme Court.

The chief burden of this chapter is to discuss how the Supreme Court has dealt with actions brought under Section 5 of the Voting Rights Act.[6] This discussion, in turn, allows us to comment on the importance of court actions to the achievement of black policy objectives. It also permits us to view the influence of such court activity on the future course of black political participation and political representation.

Section 5: The First Decade

The initial impact of the Voting Rights Act came during the first decade of the so-called reapportionment revolution.[7] To be sure, the reshaping of electoral districts had long been used as a mechanism for manipulating the voting strength of particular groups, a fact specifically referred to in the *Gomillion* case. A key question about Section 5, therefore, was whether Congress had had such actions in mind when it created the measure.

This was the question before the U.S. Supreme Court in the 1969 case *Allen* v. *State Board of Elections.*[8] In its decision the Court rejected efforts to exclude reapportionment activity from the judicial and/or administrative scrutiny required in Section 5. Mississippi had argued that since some reapportionment plans are the result of judicial mandate and must have judicial approval before implementation, Congress could not have intended a judicial conflict in the area by having such plans subjected to judicial scrutiny. The Court did not accept this rather curious and strained argument.

Two years later, in *Perkins* v. *Matthews,* the Court explicated further its *Allen* decision when it held that several changes in the electoral procedures of a Mississippi municipality were subject to Section 5 clearance before they could be implemented.[9] In this case the city of Canton had sought (1) to change the location of polling places, (2) to provide for different municipal boundaries through annexation, and (3) to shift from single-member districts to at-large elections. Speaking for the Court, Justice William Brennan agreed with a district court judge, who had originally heard the case, and rejected the ruling of a three-judge district court that had later heard the case. Brennan argued that a proper reading of *Allen* made prior Section 5 clearance of such changes mandatory. Brennan also said that the three-judge court had examined the substantive aspects of the electoral changes but that such an examination was beyond its authority. Under the Voting Rights Act only the district court for the District of Columbia has jurisdiction to examine the substantive issues concerning changes in voting procedures that occur in "covered" jurisdictions.

In *Georgia* v. *United States,* the Court once again affirmed its *Allen* ruling that state reapportionment actions are subject to Section 5 scrutiny.[10] Georgia had made extensive changes in its state legislative districts, including the creation of several multimember districts to replace single-member districts. Noting that "Section 5 is not concerned with a simple inventory of voting procedures, but rather with a reality of changed practices as they affect Negro voters," Justice Potter Stewart made it clear that because such changes could dilute the votes of blacks, they were within the "standards, practices, or procedures" to which Section 5 is directed. Stewart observed further that, in considering the 1970 extension amendments to the Voting Rights Act, Congress had had an opportunity to make substantive changes regarding Section 5 coverage, but had declined to do so. Hence, the *Allen* ruling remained the proper interpretation of Section 5 with respect to reapportionment.

Despite these favorable procedural decisions, the Burger Court has adopted rather narrow standards of review in judging the substantive effect of reapportionment actions under Section 5. This has resulted in the dilution and/or blunting of black voting strength in several jurisdictions. In *Beer* v. *United States,* for example, when the New Orleans City Council reapportioned its wards and continued to combine an at-large election format with a single-member district (ward) plan, the Burger Court did not find the action in conflict with Section 5.[11] But the federal district court for the District of Columbia pointed out the "dilution" consequences of the plan. Looking at the seven-member New Orleans City Council and the black percentage of the population, the lower court noted that the "mathematical potential" of blacks was the control of three of the seven seats. The "predictive reality" under the plan, however, was control of only one of the five single-member districts.[12] Indeed, the history of racial bloc voting in New Orleans made it realistic to assume that blacks would be frozen out of the two at-large seats. The U.S. Supreme Court disagreed. It reasoned that since the at-large seats were established in the city charter a decade before the Voting Rights Act, they did not represent a change in established voting arrangements and procedures. Hence, they were not subject to Section 5 scrutiny. Accordingly, the Court reasoned that the at-large dimension of the election scheme and the consequent dilution of black voting power were "sealed in" the city charter and would have to remain unless or until the charter was amended.

More significantly, the Burger Court majority found the New Orleans plan valid since it did not diminish the electoral position of blacks. Indeed, as seen by the Court, black electoral representation would in fact be enhanced since, prior to the reapportionment, there were *no black councilmen,* and under the new plan blacks would constitute a population majority in two of the five districts and a registered voting majority in one of them. Thus, to the Court majority, the reality of the reapportionment plan was that prior to the institution of the plan there were no blacks on the council, and now under the plan there would almost certainly be *one* black (the district having a registered black voting majority). On this basis the Court concluded that black representation would be increased by *100 percent,* and this certainly would not offend Section 5.

Justice Thurgood Marshall sharply criticized the Court majority for what he termed a simplistic application of its "non-retrogression" standard. A plan might be ameliorative and produce some gains for blacks but nonetheless be discriminatory in its overall effect. The inescapable fact, said Marshall, is that while blacks constituted 45 percent of the New Orleans population at the time of the 1970 reapportionment, under the plan accepted by the Court they could realistically expect to elect (and did in the next election) only one black person to the seven-member city council. To be sure, as Justice Marshall noted, proportional representation of blacks is not constitutionally required. But he did think that the burden of proof should be shifted to those officials who allegedly caused the dilution of black voting strength, compelling them to show that the revised election structures and processes are equally open to participation by the complaining blacks.

Marshall's view did not prevail, and the *Beer* decision was a definite blow to black political aspirations in New Orleans. When the history of racial bloc voting in the city is coupled with the entrenched at-large plan for the election of two-sevenths of the council, it seems clear that blacks are effectively frozen out of the at-large seats and can hope to elect black candidates only from the remaining single-member districts. It would seem that the at-large scheme should be viewed as part of a total plan for the election of the New Orleans City Council and not separate from the changes in election procedures subject to Section 5 scrutiny. Whatever the motives of those who adopted it in 1954, the overall plan *at the time it was instituted* serves today to discriminate against black voters. One wonders how long such a bifurcated election scheme will last if and when blacks become a voting majority. More than this, one wonders how long the at-large seats under the New Orleans plan will continue to be immune from Section 5 scrutiny.[13]

A more blatant method of dilution of black voting strength resorted to by some jurisdictions is territorial annexation. Illustrative of this strategy is the action taken by the city of Richmond, Virginia, in 1969. Up to that time, there had been a steady flight of whites to suburbia, resulting in an increasing black proportion of the Richmond population. Annexation proceedings had commenced in the early 1960s but had languished in controversy over an extended period of time. In fact, Richmond dropped its effort to annex one parcel as not being in its "best economic interest." But continued negotiations led to the annexation of some 23 square miles in the Chesterfield County area in 1969. Just prior to the annexation, the black proportion of Richmond's population had increased to 52 percent, and given the at-large election procedures for the city council, coupled with the historic practice of racial bloc voting, a black takeover of the city in the not too distant future was a realistic assumption. The new territory added slightly more than 47,000 inhabitants, of whom 45,700 were white or nonblack.[14] Hence the postannexation black proportion of Richmond's population was 43 percent, a substantial 10 percent decrease.

Upon the initial request under Section 5, the attorney general refused to approve the annexation because it portended the dilution of black voting strength. The attorney general did suggest that the "impermissible adverse racial impact" of the annexation on black voting strength might be avoided by the use of single-member districts for ward elections. Thereupon, Richmond devised a single-member district plan with the population apportioned so that four of the districts had substantial black majorities, and four were substantially white. For all practical purposes the Ninth District was white-dominated with a 59 percent white, 41 percent black population. Following the 1971 Supreme Court ruling in *Whitcomb* v. *Chavis,* Richmond officials sought a modification of the single-member district proposal.[15] The effort failed.

While the city was attempting to get approval of the annexation from the attorney general, litigation was commenced alleging that it constituted a violation of the voting rights of blacks as protected by the Fifteenth Amendment.[16] The district court for the eastern district of Virginia accepted the plaintiff's racial-purpose argument and ordered elections under a bifurcated scheme for the original city area and the annexed territory to avoid dilution of black voting strength. But the court of appeals did not accept such an application of the Fifteenth Amendment to the annexation action, and the Supreme Court sustained this position when it denied the plaintiff's petition for *certiorari*.

The district court for the District of Columbia (as provided for in Section 5 of the VRA) entered the controversy when Richmond sought a declaratory judgment to validate the annexation. Upon a special master's findings, the district court held that the annexation had a dilutive effect on black voting contrary to the proscription of Section 5.[17] Citing the Supreme Court decision in a 1971 case on the applicability of Section 5 to annexation actions, the district court noted that the obvious was implicit: If blacks constitute a lesser proportion of the population in the new jurisdiction with the annexed territory than they constituted in the old territory (prior to annexation), and when this fact is coupled with the well-established pattern of racial bloc voting, the voting strength of blacks as a class is diluted.[18] The lower court made it clear that the annexation had a discriminatory purpose and effect and that the city of Richmond had not met the burden of proof that there were "objective, verifiable legitimate economic and administrative reasons" supporting annexation.

The Burger Court rejected the district court's holding.[19] Justice Byron White, who spoke for the Court, discounted any racial motive in the 1969 annexation. The district court, as Justice William J. Brennan noted in dissent, had explicitly pointed to such a motivation:

> Richmond's focus in the negotiation was upon the number of new white voters it could obtain by annexation; it expressed no interest in economic or geographic considerations such as tax revenues, vacant land, utilities or schools. The mayor required assurances from Chesterfield County officials that at least 44,000 additional white citizens would be obtained by the city before he would agree upon settlement of the annexation suit. And the mayor and one of the city councilmen conditioned final acceptance of the settlement agreement on the annexation going into effect in sufficient time to make citizens in the annexed area eligible to vote in the city council elections of 1970.[20]

The Court majority was not satisfied with the evidentiary considerations of the district court, particularly the current justifications for annexation, and remanded the case for a further consideration of the justification issue.

The crucial part of the Court's decision in *Richmond* was its holding that Section 5 does not proscribe a city from annexing territory (and adding new voters) and thereby diminishing black voting strength so long as *there is no finding of a discriminatory purpose*. The discussion at any stage of the annexation for any "legitimate" and "justifiable" reasons, such as administrative and economic benefits, seems to be the Court's standard for meeting Section 5 scrutiny in such cases. To the majority, the fact that the proportion of the black population—and hence voting strength—diminishes when compared with the preannexation proportion does not in and of itself make the action defective. Of crucial importance is whether or not the enlarged jurisdiction gives fair and equitable recognition to blacks.

In 1980 in *City of Rome, Georgia* v. *United States* (100 S.Ct. 1548), the Court, speaking through Justice Thurgood Marshall, affirmed a federal district court's ruling rejecting several annexation actions because of their vote dilution effect. The territory proposed for annexation would have added almost 2,600 whites and about 50 blacks to the city's population, including 823 white and only 9 black registered voters. Under *City of Richmond* these facts alone do not condemn the annexation. But Rome did not meet its burden of proof that the new electoral jurisdiction "fairly reflects the strength of the black community after annexation."

More significantly, *City of Rome* emphasizes the Court's refusal to allow a local governmental unit in a "covered" state to initiate independently a "bail out" action under Section 4(a) of the VRA. Under that section, a "covered" jurisdiction may escape the preclearance requirement of Section 5 if it satisfies a three-judge panel of the district court for the District of Columbia that it has not employed for voter registration, at any time during the preceding seventeen years, any of the "tests" or "devices" (e.g., literacy and understanding tests) outlawed in VRA. Justice Marshall made it clear that Section 5 applies to the city of Rome because it is part of a "covered" state, and any exemption action under the "bail out" provision must be initiated by the "covered" state.

Justice Marshall noted further that two years earlier, in *United States v. Board of Commissioners of Sheffield, Alabama* (435 U.S. 110), the Court had made it clear that any political unit within a "covered" state must preclear new voting procedures. But he emphasized that the Court there made a distinction between a political unit as described in *Sheffield* and "political subdivisions" referred to in the "bail out" provision of Section 4.

Both *Sheffield* and *City of Rome* portend increasing and vigorous efforts on the part of local political establishments, particularly in "covered" states of the South, to free their electoral arrangements from initial scrutiny by the attorney general. They also underscore the nature of the changes being effected. In *City of Rome,* much as in Richmond, Virginia, and Houston, Texas, earlier, the annexation of new territory infused into the electorate a new group of white voters to "dilute" and blunt black electoral objectives. And in *Sheffield* a change to the at-large election for the city council was the device used to shut blacks out of the city council.

This latter device was reaffirmed as a constitutionally valid electoral arrangement in a Fifteenth Amendment action in *City of Mobile* v. *Bolden* (100 S.Ct. 1490, 1980), decided on the same day as *City of Rome.* While arguing that the amendment does not embrace the "right to have black candidates elected," Justice Stewart's plurality opinion emphasized that proof of purposeful and intentional discrimination is essential to a successful Fifteenth Amendment challenge of an at-large election scheme. What this does, in effect, is to validate electoral arrangements that have a discriminatory impact where the more stringent requirement of intentional or purposeful discrimination cannot be established. The Mobile case suggests that despite the finding of the lower courts that the factual situation strongly supported an inference of discriminatory purpose, convincing this Supreme Court of that fact will not be easy. It appears that the Court will be satisfied as long as the scheme does not abridge or deny blacks the right to vote. This disturbing development led Justice Thurgood Marshall to argue in a sharp dissent that the motivational analysis of the discriminatory intent cases was misapplied in cases like *Mobile* where the fundamental right to vote is at issue. For him, the discriminatory impact test, developed in *Fortson* v. *Dorsey* (379 U.S. 433, 1965) and applied to protect blacks and Mexican-Americans against dilution of their votes under a Texas multimember legislative districting plan in *White* v. *Register*, is the proper method to protect voters from actions that result in the "inequitable distribution of political influence."

A rather interesting and controversial question concerning the dilution of the voting strength was presented in 1977 to the Supreme Court in *United Jewish Organizations of Williamsburg* v. *Carey*.[21] The plaintiffs here were Hasidic Jews, not blacks. New York's legislative reapportionment statute of 1972 was questioned by the attorney general under a Section 5 submission because in some proposed districts the state had not demonstrated that its action "had neither the purpose nor the effect of abridging the right to vote by reason of race nor color." Subsequently, New York attempted to remedy these objections by focusing on the size of nonwhite majorities in certain districts, rather than the total number of districts. The emphasis was on a nonwhite population large enough in certain districts to effect the election of nonwhite representation. To accomplish this, population shifts were made in racial terms. The result was that a Hasidic Jewish community in New York City was divided between two districts.

In a subsequent constitutional challenge, the Hasidic Jews contended that their voting strength was being diluted for the purpose of effecting a "racial quota." Three members of the Court supported Justice Byron White in rejecting this position. They held that New York's use of racial criteria in fashioning its legislative districts was in effect an attempt to comply with Section 5 and obtain the attorney general's approval. As such, the challenged plan was not intentionally racially discriminatory. In fact, the Court held that the New York plan, while enhancing the possibility for nonwhite representation in several districts, did not "minimize or unfairly cancel out white voting strength." The Court concluded that as long as whites as a group were provided with fair representation in the overall reapportionment plan, increasing the nonwhite majorities in some of the districts did not constitute discrimination against whites.

The crucial lesson of *UJO* v. *Carey* was the Court's approval of the use of a racially based remedy to meet the mandate of Section 5. It may be argued that in doing this the Court opened the door to racial gerrymandering. However, the effect of shifting the percentages of nonwhite voters in several districts was not an invidious manipulation. Rather, the result reflected a possible fairer share of legislative representation to their population in the areas involved. It does not disturb the "nonretrogression" principle. And, as noted in *Beer,* rigid application of that principle can result in a severe dilution of black voting strength.

Chief Justice Burger's dissent in *UJO* poses an interesting dilemma for the future of black voting strength. Questioning the proposition that racial interests can be represented properly only by persons of that race and that this would result in a move away from a "truly homogeneous society," the chief justice sounded a note of caution for the future:

> This retreat from the ideal of the American "melting pot" is curiously out of step with recent political history—and indeed with what the Court has said and done for more than a decade. The notion that Americans vote in firm blocs has been repudiated in the election of minority members as mayors and legislators in numerous American cities and districts overwhelmingly white. . . .[22]

Burger's cautionary note does not seem to represent a realistic view of political behavior in the United States. Certainly it is possible to applaud the election of Mayor Bradley by a predominantly white electorate in Los Angeles. Nevertheless, this single instance does not reflect racial voting behavior in most American jurisdictions. The simple fact is that in the overwhelming majority of governmental units in the United States, black candidates do not get elected to any office unless they can count on a large black vote, usually a majority of the electorate. For this reason, the "proportionate" principle is crucial to such political events as reapportionment.

Black Political Participation and the Voting Rights Act

That the Voting Rights Act has had a monumental impact on the expanded participation of blacks at all levels of the political process is unquestioned. For the first time since Reconstruction, blacks have registered and voted in very sizable numbers in the one and one-half decades since the act's passage. According to a comprehensive study of the U.S. Commission on Civil Rights, more than one million new blacks registered in the "covered" southern states during the first seven years that the act was in effect.[23] Vigorous registration drives continued to add blacks throughout the 1970s and helped swing the electoral vote to President Carter in a number of states in the 1976 election. Furthermore, this newly acquired political power was instrumental in the election of 18 blacks to Congress in 1980 and almost 5,000 blacks to a wide variety of offices at the state and local levels.

Unlike the response of whites to Title II of the 1964 Civil Rights Act, where black use of all kinds of public accommodations has caused hardly a raised eyebrow, many whites, particularly those in the political establishment, have given ground to the political aspirations of blacks only grudgingly. To be sure, the likelihood that a century of blatant discriminatory voting policies and practices would be eradicated in five years or ten years or even more was overly optimistic, given the deeply rooted nature of racism in the political systems of the "covered" southern states. But Congress did respond to such reality with successive extensions of the VRA in 1970 and 1975. Had it not allowed the continuation of the range of protections and scrutiny of governmental officials that the act provides and requires, the political gains of blacks in some jurisdictions might have been all but obliterated by now, since state legislatures would probably have instituted more stringent voter registration requirements and general election system changes. This is well illustrated by the number and nature of electoral changes that "covered" jurisdictions are required to submit to the attorney general for preclearance under Section 5. As late as 1979 there were over 1,900 submissions of such changes, and in 23 of them objections were filed because the changes were alleged to have the effect of diminishing the voting strength of blacks. The nature of many of the changes to which objections were lodged—annexation, multi-member districts, at-large elections, full-slate voting, numbered posts, and so on—indicates how intense many advocates of the old political order are to discover ways to circumvent and ultimately subvert the VRA and the voting rights of blacks.

The controversy over another extension of the VRA has begun to accelerate as the 1982 expiration date of the act approaches. With significant changes in the congressional power structure resulting from the 1980 general elections—for instance, South Carolina Senator J. Strom Thurmond, a Republican and a veteran civil rights antagonist, will chair the Senate Judiciary Committee, which must initially clear such legislation—and a new national administration committed to the enhancement of states' rights, supporters of extension are probably in for a tough legislative battle. And Section 5, as the core of the act, will be under particular fire.

The Future of Black Politics

The discussion of how the Supreme Court has interpreted Section 5 points up several important factors with respect to the future of black politics.

First, the enactment of Section 5 and the Voting Rights Act itself suggests the incremental nature of the development of public policies. The Civil Rights Act of 1957, the first such civil rights legislation enacted since Reconstruction, represented an initial congressional response to the civil rights movement designed to safeguard the right to vote. But the effectiveness of the 1957 law, as well as the voting rights provisions of the 1960 and 1964 acts, depended primarily on the use of lawsuits and litigation to protect voting rights. Moreover, such court orders as might be forthcoming depended for their enforcement on state and local officials. Thus the protracted and limited coverage of such legal action, plus dependence on generally hostile white southern officials for enforcement, made it obvious that the voting provisions of such legislation would prove ineffective. The futility of these earlier laws was vividly pointed up by massive civil rights demonstrations that eventually led to the passage of the much stronger Voting Rights Act of 1965. This act allowed federal officials to register black voters and see that such persons could vote and have their votes counted honestly. Overall, then, starting with the very weak 1957 legislation, it took some eight years before an effective congressional policy evolved with respect to black voting rights.

Second, this discussion points up the enormous resources needed to win a major public policy enactment. The 1965 Voting Rights Act, for example, required a broad coalition of racial, religious, ethnic, and labor groups; persistent and massive street demonstrations; bipartisan support from congressional leaders; and vigorous support and arm-twisting from President Lyndon B. Johnson. This means that the enactment of major public policies, especially controversial ones (as civil rights laws tend to be), requires efforts and resources that are very difficult to harness.

But the enactment of policy is only one stage, albeit a very important one, in the overall policy process. Policies, once enacted, must be implemented. And this implementation depends in large measure on how various institutions and individuals interpret the policy. As this chapter illustrates, both the U.S. attorney general and the federal courts can be important in determining whether or not Section 5 will be effective in deterring racial discrimination in voting. The attorney general, for example, may be called upon to determine initially if a particular change in voting qualifications, practices, or procedures in "covered" states has the effect of "denying or abridging the right to vote on account of race or color." A decision at this stage can prove crucial, for it signals that the nation's highest legal officer has reviewed the matter and rendered an opinion. The fact that officials have such authority clearly demonstrates that blacks must be ever vigilant about who holds administrative positions, such as the post of attorney general.

The major focus of this chapter has been the role of courts, specifically the U.S. Supreme Court, in the formulation of public policy. The application of a law or public policy (e.g., Section 5) to specific cases allows courts to determine, in large measure, their meaning and effectiveness. Taking our example of black political participation and representation, a Court decision opting for "at-large" or "single-member district" elections might well determine the electoral opportunities open to blacks. The nature of electoral politics today and in the future would seem to indicate that *race* will be an important—perhaps the determining—factor in voting behavior in areas having sizable black populations. With few exceptions, black officials are elected from constituencies in which blacks compose a majority or nearly a majority of the population. Consider, for example, the fact that 13 of the 18 black members of Congress come from districts in which blacks constitute more than 50 percent of the population, and all but 2 are from districts with over 40 percent black populations (Dellums, D-California, 7, and Dymally, D.-California, 31). Undoubtedly the same phenomenon operates in other election units (e.g., state legislative districts and city wards). Because of losses in big city populations and reapportionment subsequent to the 1980 census, however, some black officeholders may have a difficult time retaining the kind of constituency from which they were elected. Nonetheless, in terms of Section 5-type voting policies, who the judges are and what they do remains important to black political participation and representation.

Given the above context, it becomes altogether understandable why comparisons are made between how actions of particular courts and judges affect the hopes and aspirations of blacks and other minorities. Thus, we continue to see comparisons of the role between the Warren Court and the Burger Court in terms of support given to civil rights interests. In general, the Warren Court had been viewed as both a strong supporter—and sometimes a stimulator—of policies favorable to blacks. By contrast, policies of the Burger Court with respect to blacks and civil rights have been viewed as mixed, uncertain, and negative. For example, the Burger Court's interpretation of Section 5 has not been generally supportive of black interests. On the other hand, certain 1978 and 1979 Court decisions in other areas, such as affirmative action and school busing, have provided marginal to strong support for policies favorable to blacks.[24]

In any event, studies of the role of the Court in the policy process indicate that (1) the position of the Court can prove important in the struggle for policy objectives; and (2) Court decisions, though important, are not necessarily determinative and are subject to change by the Court itself and by the "pushes and pulls" of the political process.[25] Given the nature of American politics—and the relatively meager representation, resources, and influence that blacks have in the nation's political councils—black citizens may well continue to need strong and persistent judicial support if they and other minorities are to reach threshold enjoyment of the responsibilities and benefits of the American political-social system.

Notes

1. *South Carolina* v. *Katzenbach*, 383 U.S. 301 (1966).
2. With respect to increases in black registration and voting, see Lenneal J. Henderson, Jr., "Black Politics and American Presidential Elections," Chapter 1 in this volume.
3. Most significant was the increasing proportion of urban black voters left behind by whites fleeing to suburbia.
4. 364 U.S. 399 (1960).
5. 42 U.S. Code 1973c. The statute requires the constitution of a three-judge court to make such determinations.
6. A fairly extensive literature exists on this general topic. See generally: "Voting Rights Act of 1965—Municipal Annexation," 10 *Georgia Law Review* 261 (Fall 1975); "Section 5 of the Voting Rights Act of 1965 and Reapportionment," 7 *Indiana Law Review* 579 (1974); "Multi-Member Districts and Minority Rights," 87 *Harvard Law Review* 1851 (June 1974); Robert L. Bell, "The At-Large Election System," *Howard Law Journal* 19:177 (Spring 1976); James W. Ozog, "Judicial Review of Municipal Annexation Under Section 5 of the VRA," 12 *Urban Law Annual* 311 (1976); Paul W. Bonapfel, "Minority Challenges to At-Large Elections—The Dilution Problem," 10 *Georgia Law Review* 353 (Winter 1976); Dennis J. Nall, "Multi-Member Legislative Districts: Requiem for a Constitutional Burial," 29 *University of Florida Law Review* 703 (Summer 1977); H. M. Yoste, Jr., "Section 5: Growth or Demise of Statutory Voting Rights," 48 *Mississippi Law Journal* 818 (September 1977); and Richard L. Engstrom, "Racial Vote Dilution: Supreme Court Interpretations of Section 5 of the Voting Rights Act," 4 *Southern University Law Review* 139 (Spring 1978).
7. *Baker* v. *Carr*, 369 U.S. 186; *Reynolds* v. *Sims*, 374 U.S. 533; *Avery* v. *Midland County*, 390 U.S. 474; etc.
8. 393 U.S. 544.
9. 400 U.S. 379.
10. 411 U.S. 526.
11. 425 U.S. 130 (1976).
12. 374 F. Supp. 363 at 393 (1974).
13. When the multimember district format invidiously discriminates against blacks, the Court has required that that segment of a reapportionment plan be excised and single-member districts be substituted. See *White* v. *Register*, 412 U.S. 755 (1973).
14. Only 1,557 people in the annexed territory were classified as black.
15. 403 U.S. 124 (1971). In *Whitcomb*, the Court upheld the power of the Indiana state legislature to restructure its electoral districts (by establishing multimember districts) against challenges that the primary purpose and result was to dilute black representation.

16. *Holt* v. *City of Richmond,* 334 F. Supp. 228 (1971); 459 F. 2nd 1093 (1972). The U.S. Supreme Court denied *certiorari.*
17. *Richmond* v. *U.S.,* 376 F. Supp. 1344 (1974).
18. *Perkins* v. *Matthews,* 400 U.S. 379 (1971).
19. *Richmond* v. *U.S.,* 422 U.S. 358.
20. Ibid., at 582.
21. 430 U.S. 144.
22. Ibid.
23. U.S. Commission on Civil Rights, *The Voting Rights Act: Ten Years After* (Washington, DC: The Commission, 1975).
24. With respect to affirmative action, consider the well-publicized decisions in *University of California* v. *Bakke,* 438 U.S. 265 (1978); and *Weber* v. *Kaiser Aluminum,* Sup. Ct. 443 U.S. 1973 (1979). The school busing decisions refer to Court action upholding busing plans of Columbus and Dayton as a method of achieving racial desegregation of the school systems.
25. See generally: Lucius J. Barker, "The Supreme Court from Warren to Burger: Implications for Black Americans and the Political System," (1973) *Washington University Law Quarterly* (Fall 1973), no. 4, 747; Robert Dahl, "Decision-Making in a Democracy: The Supreme Court as a National Policy Maker," 6 *Journal of Public Law* (1957); and Jonathan Casper, "The Supreme Court and National Policy Making," 70 *American Political Science Review* (1976): 50–62.

PART TWO

Black Political
Participation

FOUR

Black Political Progress in the 1970s: The Electoral Arena

Eddie N. Williams

Political participation is the means by which citizens share in the governance and governmental decisions over who gets what, when, and how. Citizens may participate in the political process in many different ways, but the most direct and influential forms of participation are voting and seeking and holding public office. These two forms provide useful reference points for a study of black political progress in the 1970s.

This chapter analyzes black political participation in terms of one of its most significant variables: the election of blacks to public office. It also touches on other significant and relevant factors, such as black political organizations and voting potential. The study is based largely on research conducted at the Joint Center for Political Studies.[1]

For black Americans, political participation has historically involved a struggle both to gain equal access to the political arena and to influence what goes on there. Although significant advances have come relatively recently, blacks are not strangers to politics.

During slavery, blacks were political objects as well as political actors. Author G. James Fleming and others have noted that black Americans affected political decisions long before they were citizens. For example, many laws and actions of the colonies and later by government bodies were influenced by the status and yearnings of blacks in the population.

Certainly black bodies hurtling off slave ships into the sea made a political statement more powerful than that of Patrick Henry. Nat Turner and John Brown and his followers (Sojourner Truth, among others) were all politicians in their day, using the resources and opportunities at their command to oppose slavery and oppression. Their political sparks ignited widespread black political participation during the Reconstruction period, but that participation was abruptly doused by the Hayes-Tilden Compromise of 1876, which created a new political slavery, a bondage from which attempts to escape met only limited success. The last quarter of the nineteenth century and the first half of the twentieth century were marked by legal and other efforts to assure the right of black Americans to participate equally in the political life of their country. In fact, it was not until the 1960s and, specifically, the passage of the Voting Rights Act of 1965, that blacks gained a lever powerful enough to pry loose a measure of political power. Especially in the South, black voters have used that lever to elect to public office persons—black and white—who represent their interests and to defeat those who oppose those interests.

The protest movement or "street politics" of the 1960s led to many new opportunities for black advancement, some of which foreshadowed the situation in black politics today. In 1967, for the first time, blacks were elected mayors of two major cities: Richard Hatcher in Gary and Carl Stokes in Cleveland. Also in 1967 Martin Luther King, Jr., made plans to politicize the movement he led. Historian David L. Lewis has written:

> King himself was aware (in 1967) that a rebirth of ideas and tactics was needed. . . . The new idea was to be "powerful enough, dramatic enough, morally appealing enough so that people of goodwill, the churches, labor, liberals, intellectuals, students, poor people themselves would begin to put pressure on Congressmen (politicians)." It was to be much more than a coalition of the dispossessed and disadvantaged. . . . This new approach was to be a Popular Front, a militant amalgam of the racially abused, the economically deprived, and the politically outraged, cutting across race and class. . . . The formula for success depended upon arousing what King called the "moral self-interest of the nation." . . . Racial compassion had to be reinforced by old-fashioned American political quid pro quo.[2]

While an assassin's bullet ended Dr. King's dream of coalition politics, his political legacy lived on, and many of his followers are now among the nation's 4,912 black elected officials.

As a footnote to this history, it should be pointed out that in 1967 and 1969, those blacks who held office called for the creation of a national nonpartisan organization to provide them with research, training, technical assistance, and information. That call was answered when in 1970 the Joint Center for Political Studies came into being.

Black political participation today is to the civil rights movement what the protest movement was in the 1960s: the dominant but not the exclusive thrust. Politics is widely viewed as a means of finally implementing what was legislated and litigated in the 1960s. Politics is the appropriate vehicle for implementation in a democratic society, and elected officials are the principal agents of implementation.

Black Elected Officials: An Overview

Among the several ways blacks have attempted to influence the political system and political decisions, none has been more dramatic and successful than the efforts to increase the number of blacks who seek and win elective offices. When the Voting Rights Act was passed in 1965, it was estimated that there were fewer than 500 black elected officials (BEOs) in the United States. In 1970 when the Joint Center for Political Studies began its annual survey of BEOs, there were 1,469 black officials. By July 1980 there were 4,912, an increase of 234 percent during the ten-year period.

The 1970–75 period was one of substantial increases in the number of black elected officials. Each year there was an increase of between 14.2 and 26.6 percent. Beginning in 1975, however, the annual rate of increase started to decline. In 1976 it was 13.6 percent—the lowest annual rate of increase since 1970—and in the following years it plummeted, reaching a low of 2.3 percent in 1979. Various reasons are given for this rapid decline:

- Between 1970 and 1974, blacks rapidly filled elected offices in jurisdictions with substantial black populations, thereby creating an artificial annual rate of increase (27 percent in 1971, 22 percent in 1972, 16 percent in 1973, 14 percent in 1974, and 17 percent in 1975). Thus, it is argued, as more and more predominantly black jurisdictions elected black officials, the number of newcomers declined. The annual increase was 14 percent in 1976, 8 percent in 1977, 4.5 percent in 1978, and 2.3 percent in 1979. (It should be noted, however, that this logic clearly cannot be applied to many predominantly black counties in the South where there are no black elected officials on county governing bodies.)
- Continuing political and economic barriers make it difficult for blacks to register and vote, or to run for and win public offices.
- The relatively low rate of black voter participation works against black candidates, who on the whole must rely more on black voters than on white voters to be successful.
- Blacks are also discouraged by the national disenchantment with politicians and by repeated allegations that black elected officials are harassed by media and law-enforcement authorities.
- In a sluggish economy, black interests may turn away from political participation toward personal survival.

Whatever the reason for the declining rate at which blacks were elected to office between 1975 and 1979, the factors may very well be transient. In 1980 there was a 6.6 percent increase in the number of black elected officials and an apparent reversal in the sharp decline that started in 1975. With the addition of 305 new officials in 1980, the total number of black elected officials for the first time represented one percent of all 490,200 elected officials in the United States.[3]

Several generalizations can be made about black elected officials during the past decade. A majority of them reside in the South, and their numbers have increased at virtually every level of government—federal, state, county, and municipal. Blacks have held office in every major category except the Presidency, vice-presidency, and governorship. There was a time during the last decade when there were two black lieutenant governors and one U.S. senator; all three left office in 1978.

Table 4.1 presents the numerical and percentage change in black elected officials by category of office from 1970 to 1980. For the six types of officials it shows:

- In 1970 there were 10 blacks in the U.S. Congress, including one senator. Despite attrition, including the defeat of Senator Edward W. Brooke, the number of black congressmembers increased to 17 in 1980, all in the House of Representatives. On November 4, 1980, 2 additional blacks were elected, bringing the total to 19 in 1981.
- In state legislatures the number of black members increased from 169 in 1970 to 323 in 1980, an increase of 91 percent. In 1970 there was a single black elected state executive; in 1980 there were 6.
- The number of black county officials rose from 92 in 1970 to 451 in 1980, a gain of 390 percent.
- Black elected officials in judicial/law-enforcement positions more than doubled between 1970 and 1980, rising from 213 to 526.
- Black municipal officials comprise the largest single category of black elected officials. In 1970, 42 percent of all BEOs were in this category; and in 1980, 48 percent were in this category. During this period the number of black municipal officials increased from 623 to 2,356, an increase of 278 percent. Included in this category are black mayors, whose numbers increased from 32 to 182, a gain of 149 percent.
- The next largest category of BEOs is in the education field. Here the number increased from 362 in 1970 to 1,214 in 1980, an increase of 235 percent.

Despite these increases over the last 10 years, black elected officials today represent only about 1 percent of all elected officials. To understand the significance of this figure, one must look at the ratio of elected officials to the total population. For every 100,000 nonblacks, there are 224

TABLE 4.1 NUMERICAL AND PERCENTAGE CHANGE IN BLACK ELECTED OFFICIALS BY CATEGORY OF OFFICE, 1970–80

Year	Total BEOs N	% Change	Federal N	% Change	State N	% Change	Regional N	% Change	County N	% Change	Municipal N	% Change	Judicial/Law Enforcement N	% Change	Education N	% Change
1970	1,469	—	10	—	169	—	—	—	92	—	623	—	213	—	362	—
1971	1,860	26.6	14	40.0	202	19.5	—	—	120	30.4	785	26.0	274	28.6	465	28.5
1972	2,264	21.7	14	0.0	210	3.9	—	—	176	46.6	932	18.3	263	-4.0	669	43.9
1973	2,621	15.7	16	14.3	240	14.3	—	—	211	19.8	1,053	12.9	334	27.0	767	14.7
1974	2,991	14.2	17	6.3	239	-0.4	—	—	242	14.7	1,360	29.2	340	1.8	793	3.4
1975	3,503	17.1	18	5.9	281	17.6	30	—	305	20.6	1,573	15.7	387	13.8	939	18.4
1976	3,979	13.6	18	0.0	281	0.0	33	9.1	355	16.4	1,889	20.1	412	6.5	994	5.9
1977	4,311	8.3	17	-5.6	299	6.4	26	-21.2	381	7.3	2,083	10.3	447	8.5	1,051	5.7
1978	4,503	4.5	17	0.0	299	0.0	25	-3.8	410	7.6	2,159	3.6	454	1.6	1,138	8.3
1979	4,607	2.3	17	0.0	313	4.7	25	0.0	398	-3.0	2,224	3.0	486	7.0	1,144	0.5
1980	4,912	6.6	17	0.0	323	3.1			451	13.3	2,356	5.9	526	8.2	1,214	6.1

SOURCE: *Joint Center for Political Studies.*

nonblack officials. For every 100,000 black Americans, there are only 19 black elected officials.

Black Elected Officials in 1980

As of July 1980 there were 4,912 black elected officials in the United States. This is 305, or 6.6 percent, more than there were in July 1979.

This increase was widely distributed geographically and by office. Altogether, 29 states experienced increases in the number of black elected officials, while 9 experienced declines. Increases continue to be greatest in southern states. The four states with the largest increases for the year—Mississippi (60), Alabama (30), Louisiana (29), and Texas (22)—are all in the South. As in 1979, seven states—Idaho, Montana, North Dakota, South Dakota, Utah, Vermont, and Wyoming—had no black officials (see Tables 4.2 and 4.3).

With few exceptions, blacks still must rely primarily on support from black voters to win elective office. Not surprisingly, therefore, the geographic distribution of black elected officials follows closely the distribution of the black population. Table 4.4 shows the regional distribution of the black population and black elected officials for 1980. With approximately 53 percent of all blacks residing in the South, that region has more than 60 percent of all BEOs, while the West, with only 8 percent of the black population, has 6 percent of all BEOs.[4]

Two southern states, Mississippi and Louisiana, now lead all other states in the number of BEOs, with 387 and 363, respectively. As Table 4.5 shows, the South continues to have an especially large proportion of

TABLE 4.2   NUMERICAL AND PERCENTAGE CHANGE IN BLACK ELECTED
OFFICIALS BY CATEGORY OF OFFICE, 1979–80

Level of Office	Number of BEOs 1979	1980	Numerical Change	Percentage Change
Federal	17	17	0	0
State	313	323	10	3.19
Regional	25	25	0	0
County	398	451	53	13.32
Municipal	2,224	2,356	132	5.93
Judicial/				
Law Enforcement	486	526	40	8.23
Education	1,144	1,214	70	6.12
TOTAL BEOS	4,607	4,912	305	6.62

SOURCE: Joint Center for Political Studies, 1980.

TABLE 4.3 BLACK ELECTED OFFICIALS IN THE UNITED STATES, JULY 1980

	Total	Federal		State			Regional		County			Municipal					Judicial and Law Enforcement						Education			
		Senators	Representatives	Administrators	Senators	Representatives	Members, Regional Bodies	Other Regional Officials	Members, County Governing Bodies	Members, Other County Bodies	Other County Officials	Mayors	Members, Municipal Governing Bodies	Members, Municipal Boards	Members, Neighborhood Advisory Commissions	Other Municipal Officials	Judges, State Courts of Last Resort	Judges, Other Courts	Magistrates, Justices of the Peace, Constables	Other Judicial Officials	Police Chiefs, Sheriffs, and Marshalls	Other Law Enforcement Officials	Members, State Education Agencies	Members, University and College Boards	Members, Local School Boards	Other Education Officials
Alabama	238				2	13			18		8	16	110	2		3		6	26	4	4				25	1
Alaska	3								1			1	1													
Arizona	14					2							5						2						5	
Arkansas	227				1	3			30			12	85			9					1			3	83	
California	237		3		2	6	10		5		1	5	35	5		3	1	57						17	86	
Colorado	15				1	1							4			1		4		1				1	2	
Connecticut	53				1	5							22	4					5		1				13	
Delaware	14				1	2							9												2	
D.C.	261		1									1	10		241										8	
Florida	109					4			2			7	76	1		1		6							12	
Georgia	249				2	21			20		3	7	139	4			1	4	3						43	2
Hawaii	1				1																					
Idaho	0																									

TABLE 4.3 (CONTINUED)

	Total	Federal		State			Regional		County			Municipal					Judicial and Law Enforcement						Education			
		Senators	Representatives	Administrators	Senators	Representatives	Members, Regional Bodies	Other Regional Officials	Members, County Governing Bodies	Members, Other County Bodies	Other County Officials	Mayors	Members, Municipal Governing Bodies	Members, Municipal Boards	Members, Neighborhood Advisory Commissions	Other Municipal Officials	Judges, State Courts of Last Resort	Judges, Other Courts	Magistrates, Justices of the Peace, Constables	Other Judicial Officials	Police Chiefs, Sheriffs, and Marshalls	Other Law Enforcement Officials	Members, State Education Agencies	Members, University and College Boards	Members, Local School Boards	Other Education Officials
Illinois	298		2	1	6	15	13		15	1		13	123	1		11		24						4	69	
Indiana	66				2	5			9		1	1	32		4			4	1					1	6	
Iowa	6										1							1							4	
Kansas	28				1	4			2				9	1		2		1							8	
Kentucky	71				1	3						2	41					2	6			2			14	
Louisiana	363				2	10			85	1		12	119					3	29	1	9		1		91	
Maine	2												1			1										
Maryland	85		1		6	14			4			6	42					7			1				2	
Massachusetts	27				1	5							9	2											10	
Michigan	284		2	1	3	12			28		3	13	62			17		31	4		1	1	2	11	94	
Minnesota	10					1							3					2							3	
Mississippi	387				2	15			27	19	8	17	143			4		2	67	5	4				67	7
Missouri	136		1		2	12			2			10	75	1		7		8			4				14	

State	Total																								
Montana	0																									
Nebraska	7		1	1					1																2	3
Nevada	6		1	2	1								1													1
New Hampshire	1		1										1				1								1	
New Jersey	151		1	4	7	1	5						63				3								67	
New Mexico	2		2										1													
New York	200		2	4	12	7	1						27	2				39							106	
North Carolina	247		1	4	18	2			13				136	3			7	1							62	
North Dakota	0																									
Ohio	186		1	2	10	1	1		8				93	3	5		20						2		40	
Oklahoma	77		1	3		8							29		13		2								21	1
Oregon	6		1	1		1							1		1	1									19	1
Pennsylvania	129		3	13		1	1						39	4	1		22	24	1						19	1
Rhode Island	7		1										5		1		1	16							65	1
South Carolina	238		14		34	1	3		13				86	1					3							
South Dakota	0																									
Tennessee	112		3	9		44							34		5		5	2				1			14	
Texas	196		1	13	2	5			5				68	2			5	13	3			1			77	
Utah	0																									
Vermont	0																									
Virginia	91		1	4		27	3		4				47		1				2	2						
Virgin Islands	22	1	1	12																		8				
Washington	14		1	1									6				3								3	
West Virginia	16		1	1			1						10		1		2	2							1	
Wisconsin	20	1	1	2		2							7				2								5	
Wyoming	0																									
Total	**4,912**	0	17	6	70	247	25	0	394	25	32	182	1,809	29	245	91	3	272	201	15	35	2	14	40	1,149	11

NOTE: *No Black Elected Officials Have Ever Been Identified in Idaho, Montana, North Dakota, South Dakota, Utah, Vermont, and Wyoming.*
SOURCE: *Joint Center for Political Studies.*

81

TABLE 4.4   DISTRIBUTION OF THE BLACK POPULATION AND BLACK ELECTED
OFFICIALS IN THE UNITED STATES BY REGION, 1980

Region	Percent of the Black Population	Number of BEOs	Percent of all BEOs
Northeast	18.4	570	11.6
North Central	20.7	1,041	21.2
South	52.7	2,981	60.7
West	8.2	298	6.1
Virgin Islands	85.0	22	.4
TOTAL		4,912	100.0

black county officials (80.3 percent) and municipal officials (67.7 percent). In viewing the current geographic distribution of black elected officials, the rapid gains in the South are especially noteworthy. One of the most important contributors to this rapid gain, of course, has been the Voting Rights Act of 1965, as amended in 1975. With removal of many barriers to voting, blacks have been able to participate extensively and to elect blacks to public office. Table 4.6 shows the change in southern states covered by the act between 1968, when the effects of the act were being felt for the first time, and 1980. In these seven states the number of black elected officials increased from 156 in 1968 to 1,813 in 1980.

In 1968 blacks held less than one-half of one percent of all elective offices in Alabama, Georgia, Louisiana, Mississippi, North Carolina, South Carolina, and Virginia (see Table 4.6). In 1980, fifteen years after passage of the Voting Rights Act, blacks held 5.6 percent of all elective offices in those states.[5] With 7.71 percent of its elective offices occupied by blacks, Louisiana boasts the largest proportion of black officeholders of the seven states. Virginia has the smallest proportion, with 2.99 percent of its elective offices held by blacks.

The rate of increase in BEOs in the South, including the states covered by the Voting Rights Act, tapered off substantially by the mid-1970s, even though the full potential of the black vote still has not been realized. Currently, unfavorable electoral arrangements, such as at-large elections and some racial gerrymandering, are major obstacles to further rapid gains by blacks in winning elective office in the South.

In the next section, we examine the growth and distribution of black elected officials at the federal, state, and local levels in the 1970s. We conclude this section by discussing the increases in black female elected officials at all levels of government (see Table 4.7).

Federal Officials

During 1979–80, 17 blacks were members of the House of Representatives.[6] No blacks have served in the Senate since 1978 when Edward W.

TABLE 4.5 NUMERICAL AND PERCENTAGE DISTRIBUTION OF BLACK ELECTED OFFICIALS BY REGION AND CATEGORY OF OFFICE, 1980

Region	Total N %	Federal Officials N %	State Officials N %	Regional Officials N %	County Officials N %	Mayors N %	Other Municipal Officials N %	Law-Enforcement Officials N %	Education Officials N %
Northeast	570 (11.6)	3 (17.6)	52 (16.1)	0 (—)	16 (3.5)	7 (3.9)	183 (8.4)	93 (17.7)	216 (17.8)
North Central	1,040 (21.2)	6 (35.3)	82 (25.4)	13 (52.0)	65 (14.4)	45 (24.7)	458 (21.1)	104 (19.8)	268 (22.1)
South	2,982 (60.7)	4 (23.5)	156 (48.3)	2 (8.0)	362 (80.3)	124 (68.1)	1,471 (67.7)	258 (49.0)	604 (49.8)
West	298 (6.1)	3 (17.6)	20 (6.2)	10 (40.0)	8 (1.8)	6 (3.3)	62 (2.9)	71 (13.5)	118 (9.7)
Virgin Islands	22 (.4)	1 (6.0)	13 (4.0)	0 (—)	0 (—)	0 (—)	0 (—)	0 (—)	8 (.6)
TOTAL	4,912 (100.0)	17 (100.0)	323 (100.0)	25 (100.0)	451 (100.0)	182 (100.0)	2,174 (100.0)	526 (100.0)	1,214 (100.0)

TABLE 4.6 NUMBER AND PERCENT OF BLACK ELECTED OFFICIALS IN SOUTHERN STATES COVERED BY THE VOTING RIGHTS ACT, 1968 AND 1980

State	Number of Elective Offices 1968	Number of Black Elected Officials 1968	Percent of Elective Offices Held by Blacks 1968	Number of Elective Offices 1980	Number of Black Elected Officials 1980	Percent of Elective Offices Held by Blacks 1980
Alabama	4,060	24	.59	4,151	238	5.73
Georgia	7,226	21	.29	6,660	249	3.74
Louisiana	4,761	37	.78	4,710	363	7.71
Mississippi	4,761	29	.61	5,271	387	7.34
North Carolina	5,504	10	.18	5,295	247	4.66
South Carolina	3,078	11	.36	3,225	238	7.38
Virginia	3,587	24	.67	3,041	91	2.99
TOTAL	32,977	156	.47	32,353	1,813	5.60

TABLE 4.7 NUMERICAL CHANGE IN BLACK ELECTED OFFICIALS BY STATE AND CATEGORY OF OFFICE, 1979 AND 1980

State	Federal Officials 1979–80		State Officials 1979–80		Regional Officials 1979–80		County Officials 1979–80		Municipal Officials 1979–80		Judicial and Law Enforcement Officials 1979–80		Education Officials 1979–80	
Alabama	—	—	16	15	—	—	22	26	109	131	39	40	22	26
Alaska	—	—	—	1	—	—	1	1	—	1	—	—	1	1
Arizona	—	—	2	2	—	—	—	—	4	5	2	2	5	5
Arkansas	—	—	4	4	—	10	30	30	106	106	1	1	85	86
California	3	3	9	9	10	10	5	6	48	48	55	58	97	103
Colorado	—	—	3	2	—	—	—	—	4	5	5	5	4	3
Connecticut	—	—	7	7	—	—	—	—	28	27	1	6	10	13
Delaware	—	1	3	3	—	—	—	—	9	9	—	—	2	2
Dist. of Columbia	1	—	—	—	—	—	—	—	238	252	7	6	8	8
Florida	—	—	4	4	—	—	2	2	69	85	7	6	9	12
Georgia	—	—	23	23	—	—	19	23	143	150	8	8	44	45
Hawaii	—	—	1	1	—	—	—	—	—	—	—	—	—	—
Idaho	—	—	—	—	—	—	—	—	—	—	—	—	—	—
Illinois	2	2	22	22	13	13	14	16	140	148	25	24	60	73
Indiana	—	—	7	7	—	—	6	10	36	38	5	5	8	6
Iowa	—	—	—	—	—	—	—	—	—	12	1	1	5	5
Kansas	—	—	5	5	—	—	2	2	12	12	1	1	8	8
Kentucky	—	—	4	4	—	—	—	—	47	43	11	10	14	14
Louisiana	—	—	10	12	—	—	76	86	121	131	39	42	88	92
Maine	—	—	—	—	—	—	—	—	3	2	—	—	—	—

TABLE 4.7 (CONTINUED)

State	Federal Officials 1979–80		State Officials 1979–80		Regional Officials 1979–80		County Officials 1979–80		Municipal Officials 1979–80		Judicial and Law Enforcement Officials 1979–80		Education Officials 1979–80	
Maryland	1	1	20	20	—	—	4	4	48	49	10	9	2	2
Massachusetts	—	—	6	6	—	—	—	—	3	11	—	—	8	10
Michigan	2	2	16	16	—	—	31	31	87	92	36	36	100	107
Minnesota	—	—	1	1	—	—	—	—	1	3	3	3	3	3
Mississippi	—	—	6	17	—	—	41	54	162	164	56	78	62	74
Missouri	1	1	15	14	—	—	2	2	90	93	12	12	12	14
Montana	—	—	—	—	—	—	—	—	—	—	—	—	—	—
Nebraska	—	—	1	1	—	—	—	—	1	1	—	—	5	5
Nevada	—	—	3	3	—	—	—	—	1	1	1	1	2	1
New Hampshire	—	—	1	1	—	—	—	—	—	—	—	—	—	—
New Jersey	—	—	5	5	—	—	9	8	68	71	—	—	61	67
New Mexico	—	—	—	—	—	—	—	—	2	1	—	—	1	1
New York	2	2	16	16	—	—	8	7	24	30	35	39	110	106
North Carolina	—	—	4	5	—	—	18	20	150	152	7	8	61	62
North Dakota	—	—	—	—	—	—	—	—	—	—	—	—	—	—
Ohio	1	1	12	12	—	—	1	2	99	109	20	20	44	42
Oklahoma	—	—	4	4	—	—	—	—	48	50	1	2	18	21
Oregon	—	—	1	1	—	—	1	1	1	1	2	2	1	1
Pennsylvania	1	1	16	16	—	—	1	1	44	44	44	48	23	19
Rhode Island	—	—	1	1	—	—	—	—	5	5	—	—	1	1

South Carolina	—	—	13	14	—	—	31	38	94	100	22	20	62	66
South Dakota	—	—	—	—	—	—	—	—	—	—	—	—	—	—
Tennessee	1	1	12	12	—	—	44	44	32	34	7	7	13	14
Texas	1	1	14	13	2	2	5	5	63	75	19	21	70	79
Utah	—	—	—	—	—	—	—	—	—	—	—	—	—	—
Vermont	—	—	—	—	—	—	—	—	—	—	—	—	—	—
Virginia	—	—	5	5	—	—	23	30	56	52	4	4	—	—
Virgin Islands	1	1	14	13	—	—	—	—	—	—	—	—	8	8
Washington	—	—	2	2	—	—	—	—	7	6	3	3	3	3
West Virginia	—	—	1	1	—	—	—	—	16	12	2	2	—	1
Wisconsin	—	—	4	4	—	—	2	2	5	7	2	2	4	5
Wyoming	—	—	—	—	25	25	—	—	—	—	—	—	—	—
TOTAL	17	17	313	323	25	25	398	451	2,224	2,356	486	526	1,144	1,214

NOTE: *The District of Columbia and the U.S. Virgin Islands are included.*
SOURCE: *Joint Center for Political Studies.*

Brooke served as the Republican senator from Massachusetts. Of the 17 black members of the House, 15 are U.S. representatives and 2, Walter E. Fauntroy of the District of Columbia and Melvin H. Evans of the Virgin Islands, are nonvoting delegates. All except Representative Evans of the Virgin Islands are Democrats. Blacks represent 3.9 percent of the 435 members of the House of Representatives. They come from all regions of the country with the largest number, 6, coming from the North Central region (see Table 4.5). As Table 4.8 shows, all black representatives are from urban districts, and all but three—Ronald Dellums, Julian Dixon, and Mickey Leland—represent districts where the majority of the population is black.[7]

A senior black member of the House, Charles C. Diggs, Jr., resigned his seat in June 1980. Diggs, a 13-term representative from Michigan's 13th District (Detroit), founded the Congressional Black Caucus and served as chairman of the House Committee on the District of Columbia and the African Subcommittee of the House International Relations Committee. In the November election his seat was filled by former Detroit Recorders Court Judge George Crockett. In addition, blacks won two House seats previously held by whites. Former California Lieutenant Governor Mervyn Dymally was elected in Los Angeles and publisher Gus Savage was elected in Chicago. Both Chicago and Los Angeles now have three black congressmen.

State Officials

Like the federal government, each of the fifty state governments has three major branches—executive, legislative, and judicial. At the executive or administrative level of state government, popularly elected officials typically include the governor, lieutenant governor, secretary of state, attorney general, treasurer, auditor, controller (comptroller), and members of boards of education. Of course, not all states have each of these executive positions, nor are all administrative positions filled by election. The terms of office for state administrators vary little from state to state. Most serve four years.

State senators and representatives, who comprise the legislative body, are elected from legislative districts within a state. The state legislatures vary in size. Minnesota has the largest number of senate seats (67), while Alaska and Nevada have the smallest (20 each). New Hampshire house, with 400 seats, is the largest. Alaska and Nevada have the smallest houses; each has 60 seats. In most instances, senators serve four-year terms, and representatives serve two years.

The courts of the state judiciary include the court of last resort, appellate courts, and major trial courts. Judges are selected by various

TABLE 4.8 CONGRESSIONAL DISTRICTS REPRESENTED BY BLACKS, JULY 1980

State Representative	Party	District	Central City	Percent Black	Percent Other Minorities
California					
Dellums	D	8	Oakland	21	7 Spanish origin
Dixon	D	28	Los Angeles	40	12 Spanish origin
Hawkins	D	29	Los Angeles	59	15 Spanish origin
District of Columbia					
Fauntroy	D	At-large	Washington, D.C.	71	2 Spanish origin
Illinois					
Collins	D	7	Chicago	55	17 Spanish origin
Stewart [a]	D	1	Chicago	89	1 Spanish origin
Maryland					
Mitchell	D	7	Baltimore	74	0.8 Spanish origin
Michigan					
Conyers	D	1	Detroit	70	0.8 Spanish origin
Diggs [b]	D	13	Detroit	66	2 Spanish origin
Missouri					
Clay	D	1	St. Louis	54	0.7 Spanish origin
New York					
Chisholm	D	12	Brooklyn	77	14 Spanish origin
Rangel	D	19	New York	59	17 Spanish origin
Ohio					
Stokes	D	21	Cleveland	66	0.8 Spanish origin
Pennsylvania					
Gray	D	2	Philadelphia	65	0.4 Spanish origin
Tennessee					
Ford	D	8	Memphis	47	
Texas					
Leland	D	18	Houston	44	19 Spanish origin
Virgin Islands [c]					
Evans	R	At-large	Charlotte Amalie	85	

[a] *Replaced on November 4, 1980, by former Illinois State Senator Harold Washington.*
[b] *Replaced on November 4, 1980 by former Judge George Crockett.*
[c] *Replaced by a nonblack official in 1980.*

methods; most are either elected to office or appointed by the governor. They usually serve six- to twelve-year terms of office.

In 1980, 32 blacks were in state-level elective offices, the largest number since Reconstruction. This number represents a net increase of 10 over the previous year's total of 313. These officials comprise 4 percent of the 8,061 elected state administrators and legislators in the United States. They serve in 39 states and in the territory of the Virgin Islands. There are 6 administrators, 70 senators, and 247 representatives. Black state legislators and administrators are most numerous in Georgia (23) and Illinois (21). The states with the most black senators are Illinois (6) and Maryland (6) where they constitute more than 10 percent of the upper house. Georgia has more black representatives than any other state (21, or almost 12 percent of Georgia's lower house).

Mississippi experienced the largest increase in black state legislators. The number rose from 6 in 1979 to 17 in 1980 with the addition of a black senator, Douglas Anderson, and 10 black representatives to its legislature. Other states that gained black legislators include Louisiana, North Carolina, and South Carolina. Losses occurred in Alabama, Colorado, Missouri, Texas, and the Virgin Islands.

While blacks comprise 11.8 percent of the total population of the United States, only 4.2 percent of the 7,497 state legislators in America are black. In three states—Alabama, Maryland, and Michigan—blacks make up at least 10 percent of the legislature. Although blacks make up over one-fourth of the total population in Georgia, Louisiana, Mississippi, and South Carolina, they hold less than one-tenth of the legislative seats in those states (see Table 4.9).

The number of black state administrators, including heads of state agencies, remained at 6 in 1980. They represent just over 1 percent of the 564 elected state administrators in the United States.[8]

Regional Officials

Regionalism, a collaborative approach among units of local governments within a specific geographical area to solve common problems, is now a prominent feature of government. It involves a wide variety of structural arrangements ranging from special-purpose regional or areawide bodies to unified regional governments. Every state except Alaska has formed special districts to provide to substate regions specific services such as fire protection, transportation, conservation, or recreation. In 1980 all major metropolitan areas were participants in regional governmental bodies.

While most members of regional councils, such as the Council of Governments, are nonelected representatives of their respective governments, members of most substate regional bodies are either appointed or elected to office. In 1977 the U.S. Census Bureau identified 25,962 special

TABLE 4.9   NUMBER AND PERCENT OF BLACK STATE LEGISLATORS AND
BLACK POPULATION BY STATE, 1980

State	Total State Legislators	Total Black Legislators	Percent Black Legislators	Percent Black Population
Alabama	140	15	10.7	24.5
Alaska	60	0	—	3.6
Arizona	90	2	2.2	3.1
Arkansas	135	4	3.0	15.9
California	120	8	6.6	.8
Colorado	100	2	2.0	3.7
Connecticut	187	6	3.2	6.1
Delaware	62	3	4.8	15.1
Florida	160	4	2.5	13.5
Georgia	236	23	9.7	26.2
Hawaii	76	1	1.3	.6
Idaho	105	0	—	.1
Illinois	236	21	8.9	14.6
Indiana	150	7	4.7	7.7
Iowa	150	0	—	17.0
Kansas	165	5	3.0	4.6
Kentucky	138	4	2.9	7.2
Louisiana	144	12	8.3	29.6
Maine	184	0	—	.2
Maryland	188	20	10.6	22.2
Massachusetts	200	6	3.0	4.2
Michigan	148	15	10.1	12.3
Minnesota	201	1	.5	1.1
Mississippi	174	17	9.8	35.1
Missouri	197	14	7.1	10.6
Montana	150	0	—	.4
Nebraska	49	1	2.0	2.9
Nevada	60	3	5.0	6.5
New Hampshire	424	1	.2	.2
New Jersey	120	5	4.2	11.9
New Mexico	112	0	—	1.6
New York	210	16	7.6	14.4
North Carolina	170	5	2.9	21.5
North Dakota	150	0	—	.3
Ohio	132	12	9.1	10.1

continued

TABLE 4.9   (CONTINUED)

State	Total State Legislators	Total Black Legislators	Percent Black Legislators	Percent Black Population
Oklahoma	149	4	2.7	7.4
Oregon	90	1	1.1	1.4
Pennsylvania	253	16	6.3	9.0
Rhode Island	150	1	.6	3.4
South Carolina	170	14	8.2	31.0
South Dakota	105	0	—	.1
Tennessee	132	12	9.1	15.4
Texas	181	13	7.2	12.5
Utah	104	0	—	.6
Vermont	180	0	—	.2
Virginia	140	5	3.6	18.7
Virgin Islands	15	12	80.0	45.3
Washington	147	2	1.4	2.4
West Virginia	134	1	.7	3.8
Wisconsin	132	3	2.3	3.3
Wyoming	92	0	—	.7
TOTAL	7,497	317	4.2	11.8

NOTE: *The District of Columbia and the U.S. Virgin Islands are included.*
SOURCE: *Joint Center for Political Studies.*

districts, 15,853 of which were authorized to elect their officials. These districts were served by 72,377 elected board members.

Very few blacks hold regional elective offices. The 25 who do comprise a mere .03 percent of all elected regional officeholders and are located in three states—Illinois (13), Texas (2), and California (10). Most black regional officials serve park and recreation districts (see Table 4.10).

County Officials

There are 3,042 organized county governments in the United States. The only states without county governments are Connecticut and Rhode Island. Officials elected to county offices typically serve as members of county governing bodies, county coroners, tax assessors, clerks, election commissioners, attorneys, judges, and law-enforcement officers. Of the 62,922 elected county officials in the United States, 20 percent (15,389) serve on county governing bodies; 2 percent (1,400) are school board members; 17 percent (10,579) serve on other county boards; and 57 percent (35,554) hold other county offices.

Over the past decade, the number of blacks holding county office has grown steadily. In 1970, 92 black county officials were identified. The number had more than tripled by 1975 to a total of 305. Between 1978 and 1979 there was a small decline. However, a gain of 53 black county officials in 1980 raises the total to 451 and reverses the decline. Louisiana and Mississippi experienced the largest increases, with gains of 10 and 13, respectively. Black elected county officials now make up .7 percent of all elected county officials.

County governing bodies gained 43 black members over the 1979 total of 351, with Mississippi and Louisiana gaining 10 each. Mississippi's gain is due largely to county reapportionment and redistricting to achieve greater racial parity among districts. Six of the 11 states that experienced increases in the number of black county legislators are in the South. In fact, southern states account for 80 percent of all black elected county officials. Louisiana has the most with 85, although South Carolina has the largest proportion of black county officials. Six percent of South Carolina's elected county office holders are black.

Of all categories of BEOs, county officials experienced the greatest increase in 1980.

Municipal Officials

In 1977, when the last census of governments was conducted, the U.S. Census Bureau identified 132,789 municipal officials elected to serve 18,862 municipal governments as administrators, members of governing bodies and municipal boards (excluding school boards), and judicial officials.[9] The 2,356 BEOs who served local governments in 1980 comprise 48 percent of all BEOs and 1.7 percent of all elected municipal officials.

Blacks have been elected to all categories of municipal office. There are 182 mayors, 1,809 members of municipal governing bodies, 29 members of other municipal boards, 245 members of advisory neighborhood com-

TABLE 4.10   BLACK ELECTED OFFICIALS ON REGIONAL BODIES, 1980

State	Regional District	Number of Black Officials
California	Hospital Districts	2
	Park and Recreation Districts	7
	Transit Districts	1
Illinois	Public Library Districts	2
	Park and Recreation Districts	11
Texas	Conservation Districts	2
TOTAL		25

missions, and 91 other municipal officials. Members of school boards and judicial officials are discussed below.

Since 1977, the rate of increase in black municipal officials has been declining. In 1980, however, there was a 5.9 percent increase over the 1979 total of 2,224, reversing that downward trend. The 132-member gain in black municipal officials was distributed over 23 states and the District of Columbia. Four southern states each had an increase of 10 or more municipal officials—Alabama (22), Florida (16), Louisiana (10), and Texas (12). One North Central state, Ohio, had an increase of 10 black municipal officials. The District of Columbia also elected 14 additional municipal officials. Seven states experienced losses: Kentucky (4), Virginia (4), West Virginia (4), Connecticut (1), Maine (1), New Mexico (1), and Washington (1).

The number of black elected municipal officials increased between 1979 and 1980. Local governments gained 13 new black mayors but lost 6, for a net increase of 7 over the 1979 total of 175 mayors. Alabama reported the largest increase, with 4 new mayors. Other states that gained black mayors were Colorado, Georgia, Kentucky, Louisiana, New York, Ohio, Oklahoma, South Carolina, and Texas. States that lost black mayors were Illinois, Michigan, Missouri, North Carolina, Virginia, and Washington. The state with the largest number of black mayors is Mississippi, with 17.

Black members of municipal governing boards increased by 113 in 1980 for a total of 1,809 members. Blacks comprise 1.8 percent of the 99,993 members of local governing boards across the nation. Nearly two-thirds of all black municipal governing board members serve in the South. The largest gains over the past year were also made in southern states. Mississippi has the largest number of black municipal governing board members, with 143, or one-third of all BEOs in the state.

Advisory Neighborhood Commissions represent a decentralized form of local government that brings govermental processes closer to the people. The neighborhood councils or commissions provide a structure for citizen participation in various governmental activities. In 1980, 245 blacks served on advisory neighborhood commissions, 14 more than in 1979. All but 4 are in the District of Columbia; the remaining 4 serve in Indiana.

Black elected administrative officials, such as city clerks, recorders, treasurers, and assessors, totaled 91 in 1980, 4 more than in 1979. A third of these officials are in Michigan (17) and Oklahoma (13).

Although the District of Columbia leads in the number of black elected municipal officials, with 252 incumbents, the overwhelming majority are advisory neighborhood commissioners. Nine states have 100 or more black municipal officials. Seven are in the South—Mississippi (164), North Carolina (152), Georgia (150), Alabama (131), Louisiana (131), Ar-

kansas (106), and South Carolina (100). Two are North Central states—
Illinois (148) and Ohio (101).

Judicial and Law-Enforcement Officials

Blacks elected to judicial and law-enforcement offices include 275 judges,
199 lower court officials (constables, justices of the peace, and magis-
trates), 15 officials who hold other judicial positions, 35 police officials
(police chiefs, sheriffs and marshals), and 2 other law-enforcement officials.

The number of black elected judicial and law-enforcement officials rose
from 486 in 1979 to 526 in 1980, an increase of 8.2 percent. The largest
increase, a gain of 29, occurred among lower court officials, while the
number of judges of appellate and major trial courts (8) and police officials
(5) increased slightly.

The South, which has elected more than half (52.7 percent) of all
black judicial and law-enforcement officials, experienced the greatest increase in 1980. Nearly three-fourths (73 percent) of the new black judges
and police officials were elected to offices in southern states. Mississippi
gained the most, 22 officials, and ranks first in the number of black judicial
and law-enforcement officials. Other states that had increases were Connecticut (5), New York (4), Pennsylvania (4), California (3), Louisiana (3),
Texas (2), Alabama (1), North Carolina (1), and Oklahoma (1). Losses
occurred in South Carolina (2), Florida (1), Illinois (1), Kentucky (1), and
Maryland (1).

Education Officials

Black elected education officials serve at the state, county, and municipal
levels of government. They hold office as administrators and members of
various education boards. There were 1,214 blacks in education offices in
1980, 70 more than in 1979, an increase of 6.1 percent. Although these
education officials comprise approximately one-fourth of all black elected
officials, they constitute only 1.3 percent of the 93,337 elected education
officials in the United States.

The distribution of black education officials among various offices is as
follows: Fourteen serve as members of state or territorial boards of education; 40 are members of university or college boards; 1,149 are local
school board members; and there are 11 other school officials who serve
as superintendents of schools.

Of the 14 state and territorial board of education members, 8 serve in
the Virgin Islands. The North Central region of the country has 4 members, with 2 in Michigan and 2 in Ohio. The remaining state board members are found in the South, one in Louisiana and one in Texas.

TABLE 4.11 BLACK ELECTED WOMEN OFFICIALS IN THE UNITED STATES, JULY 1980

	Total	Federal		State			Regional		County			Municipal					Judicial and Law Enforcement						Education			
		Senators	Representatives	Administrators	Senators	Representatives	Members, Regional Bodies	Other Regional Officials	Members, County Governing Bodies	Members, Other County Bodies	Other County Officials	Mayors	Members, Municipal Governing Bodies	Members Municipal Boards	Members, Neighborhood Advisory Commissions	Other Municipal Officials	Judges, State Courts of Last Resort	Judges, Other Courts	Magistrates, Justices of the Peace, Constables	Other Judicial Officials	Police Chiefs, Sheriffs, and Marshalls	Other Law Enforcement Officials	Members, State Education Agencies	Members, University and College Boards	Members, Local School Boards	Other Educational Officials
Alabama	44						1	1					28			2			6	2					3	1
Alaska	0																									
Arizona	1																								1	
Arkansas	27					3		4	2				9												9	
California	59			1		1			3			1	6	3		6		5						4	29	
Colorado	2					1																		1		
Connecticut	16					1							6	2					1						6	
Delaware	0																									
D.C.	105												5		97										3	
Florida	16								1			1	11			1									2	
Georgia	29					6					1	1	12					1							8	
Hawaii	0																									
Idaho	0																									
Illinois	54		1		1	3		2	4		1		14	1		4		1						1	21	
Indiana	15				2	1				1	1		5	1		1									3	
Iowa	1																							1		
Kansas	2																								2	
Kentucky	5				1	1							1												2	
Louisiana	45					1			5			2	14					1	3						19	

State	Total																								
Massachusetts	6											1						2						3	
Michigan	88				4			8			1	16		10	5	1						2	4	37	
Minnesota	1																							1	
Mississippi	62				1				7	1	2	19		4			12	2						14	
Missouri	31			3	1							18		4	1									4	
Montana	0																								
Nebraska	2																							2	
Nevada	1																							1	
New Hampshire	1				1																				
New Jersey	47				1			3			1	16		1			1							24	
New Mexico	0																								
New York	59			1	2			1				4		1	2									48	
North Carolina	38				1			4			2	13		1	2									15	
North Dakota	0																								
Ohio	38							1				16	2	1	5									13	
Oklahoma	30							1				15		9										5	
Oregon	2							1					1												
Pennsylvania	19							1				5		4	2		1							6	
Rhode Island	0																								
South Carolina	41							3			3	13		1	1		3							17	
South Dakota	0																								
Tennessee	12							4				1					1							6	
Texas	28							4				10			1		1							12	
Utah	0																								
Vermont	0																								
Virginia	14								2			10						2							
Virgin Islands	5			2																		3			
Washington	3				1																			2	
West Virginia	2											1					1								
Wisconsin	7							1			1	1					1							3	
Wyoming	0																								
TOTAL	976	0	2	10	49	0	6	46	8	6	13	279	10	98	50	1	25	26	7	0	0	5	11	322	1

NOTE: *The District of Columbia and the Virgin Islands are included. No black elected officials have been identified in Idaho, Montana, North Dakota, South Dakota, Utah, Vermont and Wyoming.*

SOURCE: *Joint Center for Political Studies.*

The 40 black university and college board members are distributed among western and North Central states, while local school board members are fairly evenly distributed among all regions of the country. Elected black superintendents of schools are only in the southern states of Alabama (1), Georgia (2), Mississippi (3) and South Carolina (1).

Between 1979 and 1980 the largest increase in black education officials was among local school board members. The number rose from 1,085 in 1979 to 1,149 in 1980, an increase of 5.9 percent. Illinois experienced the largest gain, with 12 additional school board members. States that lost members were Colorado (1), Indiana (2), New York (4), Ohio (2), and Pennsylvania (4).

Michigan leads all other states in the number of black education officials with 107, followed by New York (106) and California (103).

Black Women Officials

There are currently 976 black women holding elective office in the United States (see Table 4.11). In 1979 there were 882. While the annual rate of increase has declined steadily over the last five years, the 1980 gain of 94 black women reverses the downward trend (see Table 4.12).

The number of black female officeholders, comprising 20 percent of all BEOs, continues to increase at a faster annual rate than all BEOs combined. For example, between 1979 and 1980, the number of BEOs rose from 4,607 to 4,912, representing an annual increase of 6.6 percent. Women experienced a larger growth rate. Their number increased from 882 in 1979 to 976 in 1980, for an annual gain of 10.6 percent. The number of black female officeholders increased in every category of office except federal and regional offices (see Tables 4.13 and 4.14). The greatest numerical increase occurred among municipal officials. An additional 46 women were elected to office, raising the total from 404 to 450, an 11 percent increase. Most of the gains were made in the South. Alabama

TABLE 4.12   NUMERICAL AND PERCENTAGE CHANGE IN BLACK
ELECTED WOMEN OFFICIALS, 1975–80

Year	Number of Women BEOs	Percent Change
1975	530	—
1976	684	29.1
1977	782	14.3
1978	843	7.8
1979	882	4.6
1980	976	10.6

TABLE 4.13   NUMERICAL AND PERCENTAGE CHANGE IN BLACK ELECTED
WOMEN OFFICIALS BY CATEGORY OF OFFICE, 1979–80

Level of Office	Number of BEOs 1979	Number of BEOs 1980	Numerical Increase	Percent Change
Federal	2	2	0	0.0
State	57	60	3	5.26
Regional	6	6	0	0.0
County	49	60	11	22.44
Municipal	404	450	46	11.38
Judicial/Law Enforcement	51	59	8	15.68
Education	313	339	26	8.30
TOTAL WOMEN BEOS	882	979	94	10.65

and Michigan experienced the largest increases, with 6 new female municipal officials each.

Black women are represented in nearly every category of elective
office. Two are members of the U.S. House of Representatives. Sixty
hold state level offices, and 6 hold regional offices. At the county level, 60
black women hold elective offices, and there are 450 at the municipal
level. There are 59 black females serving in judicial and law-enforcement
positions and 339 in education offices.

For the most part, black elected women are distributed by region and
category of office in much the same way as all black elected officials (see
Table 4.15). Consequently, the South has the greatest number (53 percent)
and the West the least (7 percent). Washington, D.C., leads in the number
of elected black women with 105, followed by Michigan (88) and
Mississippi (62). Most black female officeholders serve in municipal and
education offices, as do the majority of black elected officials. Forty-six
percent now serve at the municipal level, including 13 mayors.

Agenda for the 1980s

The statistics on blacks in elective office suggest that 1979–80 was a
propitious year for BEOs. Substantial gains were made in virtually every
category of elective office and thus reversed the recent annual rate of
decline. Moreover, black women continued to make important gains as
elected officials. While these facts are encouraging, a more sobering reality is that blacks comprise a mere 1 percent of all elected officials in the
United States, even though they are more than 11 percent of the total
population. Clearly, blacks are still very far from being equitably represented among public servants. Correcting this inequity is essential if
blacks are to be a part of a genuinely representative system of govern-

TABLE 4.14 NUMERICAL CHANGES IN BLACK ELECTED WOMEN OFFICIALS BY STATE AND CATEGORY OF OFFICE, 1979–80

State	Federal Officials 1979–80		State Officials 1979–80		Regional Officials 1979–80		County Officials 1979–80		Municipal Officials 1979–80		Judicial and Law-Enforcement Officials 1979–80		Education Officials 1979–80	
Alabama	—	—	1	1	—	—	1	1	24	30	8	8	3	4
Alaska	—	—	—	—	—	—	—	—	—	—	—	—	—	—
Arizona	—	—	—	—	—	—	2	2	15	16	—	—	1	1
Arkansas	—	—	4	4	—	—	2	3	9	10	—	—	10	9
California	—	—	—	—	4	4	—	—	—	—	5	5	35	33
Colorado	—	—	1	1	—	—	—	—	—	—	—	—	2	1
Connecticut	—	—	1	1	—	—	—	—	10	8	—	1	4	6
Delaware	—	—	—	—	—	—	—	—	—	—	—	—	—	—
Dist. of Columbia	—	—	—	—	—	—	—	—	98	102	—	—	4	3
Florida	—	—	1	1	—	—	1	1	9	12	—	—	2	2
Georgia	—	—	6	6	—	—	1	1	15	13	1	1	8	8
Hawaii	—	—	—	—	—	—	—	—	—	—	—	—	—	—
Idaho	—	—	—	—	—	—	—	—	—	—	—	—	—	—
Illinois	1	1	4	4	2	2	5	5	19	19	1	1	19	22
Indiana	—	—	3	3	—	—	1	2	6	7	—	—	3	3
Iowa	—	—	—	—	—	—	—	—	—	—	—	—	1	1
Kansas	—	—	—	—	—	—	—	—	—	—	—	—	2	2
Kentucky	—	—	2	2	—	—	—	—	1	1	—	—	2	2
Louisiana	—	—	1	1	—	—	—	5	12	16	3	4	18	19
Maine	—	—	—	—	—	—	—	—	—	—	—	—	—	—
Maryland	—	—	4	4	—	—	2	2	9	10	1	1	1	1
Massachusetts	—	—	2	2	—	—	2	—	—	1	—	—	—	3
Michigan	—	—	4	4	—	—	8	8	21	27	6	6	39	43
Minnesota	—	—	—	—	—	—	—	—	—	—	—	—	1	1

Mississippi	—	—	—	—	—	8	9	24	25	10	14	10	14
Missouri	—	4	4	—	—	1	1	19	22	—	—	4	4
Montana	—	—	—	—	—	—	—	—	—	—	—	—	—
Nebraska	—	—	—	—	—	—	—	—	—	—	—	1	2
Nevada	—	—	—	—	—	—	—	—	—	—	—	2	1
New Hampshire	—	1	1	—	—	4	4	14	17	—	—	—	—
New Jersey	—	2	2	—	—	4	4	—	—	—	—	22	24
New Mexico	1	—	—	—	—	1	1	5	5	—	—	—	—
New York	1	2	2	—	—	3	4	14	16	1	2	46	48
North Carolina	—	—	1	—	—	—	—	—	—	1	2	13	15
North Dakota	—	—	—	—	—	—	—	—	—	—	—	—	—
Ohio	—	1	1	—	—	—	—	19	19	4	5	15	13
Oklahoma	—	1	1	—	—	—	—	22	24	—	—	4	5
Oregon	—	—	—	—	—	1	1	—	—	1	1	—	—
Pennsylvania	—	1	1	—	—	—	—	7	9	3	3	7	6
Rhode Island	—	—	—	—	—	—	—	—	—	—	—	—	—
South Carolina	—	1	3	—	—	2	3	14	17	1	1	17	17
South Dakota	—	—	—	—	—	—	—	—	—	—	—	—	—
Tennessee	—	1	1	—	—	4	4	1	1	—	—	5	6
Texas	—	4	4	—	—	—	—	7	11	2	1	5	12
Utah	—	—	—	—	—	—	—	—	—	—	—	—	—
Vermont	—	—	—	—	—	—	—	—	—	—	—	—	—
Virginia	—	2	2	—	—	2	2	9	10	2	2	—	—
Virgin Islands	—	2	1	—	—	—	—	—	—	—	—	3	3
Washington	—	1	1	—	—	—	—	—	—	—	—	2	2
West Virginia	—	—	—	—	—	—	—	1	1	1	1	—	—
Wisconsin	—	2	2	—	—	1	1	—	1	—	—	2	3
Wyoming	—	—	—	—	—	—	—	—	—	—	—	—	—
TOTALS	2	57	60	6	6	49	60	404	450	51	59	313	339

NOTE: *The District of Columbia and the U.S. Virgin Islands are included.*
SOURCE: *Joint Center for Political Studies.*

TABLE 4.15 NUMERICAL AND PERCENTAGE DISTRIBUTION OF BLACK ELECTED WOMEN OFFICIALS BY REGION AND CATEGORY OF OFFICE, 1980

	Total		Federal Officials		State Officials		Regional Officials		County Officials		Mayors		Other Municipal Officials		Law Enforcement		Education Official	
	N	%	N	%	N	%	N	%	N	%	N	%	N	%	N	%	N	%
Northeast	148	(15.1)	1	(50.0)	9	(15.0)	0	(0.0)	5	(8.3)	0	(0.0)	40	(9.1)	6	(10.1)	87	(25.7)
North Central	239	(24.5)	1	(50.0)	18	(30.0)	2	(33.3)	17	(28.3)	1	(7.7)	94	(21.5)	12	(20.3)	94	(27.7)
South	516	(52.9)	0	(0.0)	25	(41.7)	0	(0.0)	34	(56.7)	11	(84.6)	294	(67.3)	35	(59.3)	117	(34.5)
West	68	(7.0)	0	(0.0)	6	(10.0)	4	(66.6)	4	(6.7)	1	(7.7)	9	(2.1)	6	(10.1)	38	(11.2)
Virgin Islands	5	(.5)	0	(0.0)	2	(3.3)	0	(0.0)	0	(0.0)	0	(0.0)	0	(0.0)	0	(0.0)	3	(.9)
TOTAL	976	(100.0)	2	(100.0)	60	(100.0)	6	(100.0)	60	(100.0)	13	(100.0)	437	(100.0)	59	(100.0)	339	(100.0)

ment. Such an objective should therefore be a high priority for the country and particularly for blacks.

Of course, the reasons for the present underrepresentation are many and complex. They include deeply entrenched racial attitudes that make it extremely difficult for blacks to win elections in constituencies where they are a numerical minority; formidable structural obstacles such as racially gerrymandered electoral districts or at-large electoral systems; and in some cases, inadequate political participation by blacks. A major challenge now facing blacks and the entire country is to remove the remaining barriers to full black involvement in the political life of the country. The redistricting process to take place throughout the country in response to the decennial census offers one important opportunity for eliminating some of these barriers. Equally important is continued protection by the federal government of black voting rights in areas where they have been threatened historically.

The Black Vote

To review the gains made by blacks in elective offices is to underscore the importance of the black vote. The black vote is significant, especially in presidential politics, because of its size—10 percent of the electorate in 1976 and over 11 percent in 1980—because it is concentrated in major urban areas in states with sizable blocs of electoral votes, and because it is often wielded en masse. Therefore, in close elections, especially presidential races, the black vote could well hold the balance of power. This was true in 1948, 1960, and 1976. It was not the case in 1980. A review of black participation in the 1980 presidential election provides useful information on the black vote in the United States.

According to the U.S. Census Bureau, there were about 16,967,000 blacks of voting age in November 1980.[10] Various preelection estimates indicated that about 67 percent of these potential voters were registered. This would mean that about 11.4 million blacks were registered in 1980, or 3.7 million more than in 1976 when the voting-age population was 14 million.

Election results published by the Joint Center for Political Studies indicate that 7 million blacks, or about 40 percent of the voting-age population, went to the polls. This is about two percentage points higher than in 1976. What is striking in data produced both by the Joint Center and by the Census Bureau is that while there was a slight increase in the level of black voter participation in 1980 compared with 1976, the level of white participation remained about the same.

Looking at the election results another way, the Joint Center disclosed that about 61.3 percent of blacks who were registered went to the polls.

This is about three percentage points lower than the level reported by the Joint Center in 1976.

Taken together, these two sets of data—turnout of voting-age population versus turnout of registered voters—suggest that the massive voter registration drives undertaken by the National Coalition on Black Voter Participation (Operation Big Vote) and others increased black registration substantially, but that in 1980 a larger percentage of those who bothered to register failed to vote on election day. This phenomenon may be attributed to a combination of factors. There was relatively little in either the style or content of the 1980 presidential election to generate strong interest in voting among blacks. Perhaps reflecting the changed character of race in American politics, few explicitly racial issues were raised during the campaign. Moreover, in an election that emphasized use of the electronic media and massive public opinion surveys, the candidates rarely focused on black issues or black voters.

Regardless of what factors influenced black turnout, it is clear that the black vote could not have determined the outcome of the 1980 presidential race. Governor Reagan's winning margin was so great that the potential of the black vote paled in significance. Nevertheless, the black vote clearly had a presence in the presidential election.

The Joint Center's survey indicated that President Jimmy Carter won 91 percent of the black vote, about the same level that he won in 1976. Reagan won only 6 percent of the black vote, but blacks gave him enough support in several closely contested southern states to ensure his margin of victory. Independent John Anderson received only 1.5 percent of the black vote.

Although this pattern of voting held across all regions of the country, there were some noteworthy differences among regions. The Northeast and the South provided Carter's greatest support among blacks, while the North Central region was less supportive. Reagan's strongest black support came in the North Central region, and his lowest support was in the Northeast and South.

Indications are that although blacks were understandably dissatisfied with some aspects of the Carter administration's performance, they had little difficulty in choosing to support the President for a second term. One reason for this may have been the special relationship that existed between blacks and Carter in 1976. Another may have been a hesitancy to vote for an avowedly conservative Republican for President. In spite of their strong support for President Carter, however, there are signs that blacks were not particularly frightened by the prospect of a Reagan Presidency. Many in fact voted for Reagan; many others who were registered decided not to vote at all.

The outcome of the 1980 presidential election left blacks probably more conscious than ever of the limits of their ability to influence the outcome of presidential elections. On one level, black concern about the outcome of the election stems from the belief that support for the winning candidate confers some special advantages. Nevertheless, although some advantages probably accrue to segments of the electorate when the candidate they favor wins, it is easy to exaggerate these benefits. The political system is much too complex to permit a President to dispense either considerable rewards or penalties to any single segment of the electorate. Furthermore, Presidents, like all politicians, are as likely to seek to strengthen their base of support by courting the uncommitted as they are to reward the committed for past support. Thus, while blacks are likely to be disadvantaged by their limited ties to the new President and his position on some major issues, the results of the election might have substantial positive aspects.

Another potential benefit of the outcome of the 1980 election is that it may have freed blacks to think more independently, creatively, and pragmatically about the future. The Republican party, led by President Reagan, is in a good position to reach out to blacks, to demonstrate the party's capacity to respond to their interests, and to incorporate them to a significant degree into the structure of the party. In view of a long-standing uneasiness among blacks about the extent and persistence of their attachment to the Democratic party, such an effort might be welcomed by many blacks.

The election results also provide an unprecedented opportunity for blacks to play a leading part in restructuring and redirecting the Democratic party as it seeks to recover from the serious defeat of November 1980. Especially important in this regard is the need to evaluate the implications of the changing demographic scene for the future of party competition. The apparently increasing strength of the Republican party in the South and West, the regions experiencing rapid population growth, will undoubtedly require imaginative responses by the Democratic party. In addition, the need to strengthen party organization from the grass roots up, and to formulate fresh, widely acceptable approaches to the major problems facing the country in the decades ahead, is urgent and requires contributions by blacks. These are not easy tasks, but they are exciting and challenging.

Another potential benefit of the outcome of the 1980 election is that it challenges blacks to a new and perhaps more sophisticated style of politics. Undoubtedly a Reagan administration will seek different approaches to some of the chronic national problems that blacks have sought to address for the past several decades. Blacks will need to formulate some of their specific objectives and modify some of the strategies they have advocated in seeking to protect their interests. Moreover, blacks may be forced to make much stronger substantive contributions than they have in the past to the development of national policies in areas where extensive changes are contemplated.

Still another likely benefit for blacks might derive from the need to reemphasize self-help. The tendency to focus on the government for solutions to many of the pressing problems blacks face sometimes overshadows the clear and urgent need for a more vigorous effort by blacks to achieve social and economic advancement for themselves, despite continuing obstacles to such advancement. There are many areas in which government can only be a partner—and, for blacks, a reluctant partner.

To emphasize the likely benefits of a Reagan Presidency is not to ignore or underestimate the actual and potential problems it poses for blacks and other disadvantaged minorities. Many commentators have hastened to interpret the outcome of the election as representing a fundamental ideological shift by the electorate, one conferring a mandate for sweeping retrenchment and retreat from much of the social progress of recent years. The available data on the attitudes and perceptions of the electorate provide no conclusive evidence for such an interpretation. On the contrary, those data suggest that the electorate sought mainly a change in leadership and an improvement in the country's economy, military strength, and international standing. An assumption by the administration that it is mandated to implement sweeping conservative reforms could indeed be devastating for blacks, other minorities, and all the poor and disadvantaged in American society.

There is no doubt that Ronald Reagan as a campaigner criticized a number of social programs and national policies that have been especially beneficial to blacks. He also criticized the alleged growth and increasing intensity of the federal government and advocated further devolution of authority and resources to state and local governments. Such policies, thoughtlessly pursued, would seriously threaten the well-being of blacks and other disadvantaged minorities.

The history of racial discrimination in this society and efforts to combat it indicate that the federal government has been vital to the survival of blacks. Furthermore, while blacks are not the only, nor even the principal, beneficiaries of the major social programs of the past two decades geared to assist the low-income and the otherwise disadvantaged, a large proportion of the black population is especially dependent on them and thus highly vulnerable to any major cutbacks. Anything but the most cautious moves toward reforming social programs or further sharing resources and power with state and local governments could be extremely detrimental to blacks and require them to struggle relentlessly for their survival.

Conclusion

For blacks, as indeed for the nation as a whole, a new presidential administration and a new decade signify a time of considerable speculation—of high optimism for some and apprehensiveness for others. Blacks, on the whole, are apprehensive about some of the policies of the Reagan administration, but the polls showed that they have not given up on the future.

There is both optimism and momentum in the political arena. Black political participation is not only the cutting edge of the civil rights movement but it is accelerating the push for greater economic empowerment. Black leaders are continuing their search for unifying strategies to galvanize the disparate political, economic, social, and civil rights elements in the black community. They recognize the importance of electing blacks to offices at all levels, of making black concerns felt in elections in which there are no black candidates, and of becoming more involved in the formulation and implementation of public policies that affect their lives.

There is every reason to believe that the number of black elected officials and the impact of the black vote will continue to grow in the 1980s. The pace and extent of that growth will be influenced by several factors:

1. Black registration and voting patterns
2. Demographic changes in the population as a whole
3. White attitudes toward new forms of racism and discrimination.

These and other factors help to explain why, even fifteen years after passage of the Voting Rights Act, blacks are not yet equal in the political arena.

Notes

1. Much of the material in this paper is drawn from JCPS publications or from contributions JCPS has made to volumes published by others.
2. David L. Lewis, *King: A Critical Biography* (Urbana: University of Illinois Press, 1970).
3. The figures for the number of elected officials in the United States are from U.S. Department of Commerce, Bureau of the Census, *1977 Census of Governments*, vol. 1, no. 2; *Popularly Elected Officials* (Washington, DC: Government Printing Office, 1973).
4. The figures for the black population in the United States are cited from U.S. Department of Commerce, Bureau of the Census, *Current Population Reports*, series P-20, no. 334, *Demographic, Social, and Economic Profile of States: Spring 1976* (Washington, DC: Government Printing Office, 1979); and U.S. Department of Commerce, Bureau of the Census, *Current Population*

Reports, series P-25, no. 976, *Illustrative Projections by Age, Race, and Sex: 1975 to 2000* (Washington DC: Government Printing Office, 1979).

5. The figures for BEOs in southern states covered by the Voting Rights Act are from U.S. Commission on Civil Rights, *The Voting Rights Act: Ten Years After* (Washington, DC: Government Printing Office, 1975).

6. The figures for the number of congressional districts represented by blacks are from Michael Barone, Grant Ujifusa, and Douglas Matthews, *The Almanac of American Politics, 1980* (New York: Dutton, 1979).

7. The figures for the black and minority populations within congressional districts are cited from U.S. Department of Commerce, Bureau of the Census, *Congressional District Data, 94th Congress* (Washington, DC.: Government Printing Office, 1974).

8. The figures for the numbers of state administrators, legislators, and judicial officials are from Council of State Governments, *The Book of the States, 1980–1981,* vol. 23 (Lexington, KY: Council of State Governments, 1980).

9. The figures for the number of local governments are from U.S. Department of Commerce, Bureau of the Census, *1977 Census of Governments,* vol. 1, no. 1, *Governmental Organization* (Washington DC: Government Printing Office, 1978).

10. The figures for voting-age population are from U.S. Department of Commerce, Bureau of the Census, *Current Population Reports* series P-25, no. 879, *Projections of the Population of Voting Age for States, November 1980* (Washington, DC: Government Printing Office, 1972); and U.S. Department of Commerce, Bureau of the Census, *1970 Census of the Population,* Supplementary Report, *Age and Race of the Population of the United States, by States: 1970* (Washington DC: Government Printing Office, 1972).

FIVE

Fear, Apathy, and Other Dimensions of Black Voting

Douglas St. Angelo and Paul Puryear

Blacks and poorly educated whites participate less in politics and have a much lower voter turnout rate than those who have secured greater economic and social benefits.[1] Until recently, racial discrimination was regarded as the cause of lower black participation and, to a lesser extent, the lower level of participation among less educated whites. Contrary to accepted mythology, this legally and racially enforced discrimination existed in the North as well as the South for much of the twentieth century.[2] The civil rights activities of the early 1960s did much, although at great cost, to halt the use of legal devices to block black voting. Mississippi was literally a battlefield in the struggle for black political rights. Thousands of dedicated persons from all parts of the nation put their lives on the block—and far too often, those lives were taken—but by the late 1960s the spine of legal political discrimination had been broken. To racial activists who paid the price and made the sacrifice to fight for the right of full black political participation, the discovery that blacks still do not participate or vote in the political process to the same extent as other social groups has been a bitter pill to swallow.

Many scholars and other observers have said that apathy is the reason that blacks do not engage in political activities at the same level as whites. This argument suggests that blacks vote less often because they are not as interested in politics as whites are. It implies that blacks have a low sense of civic obligation—the basic argument is that one has a duty to engage in public affairs. An additional reason offered is that blacks do not have as clear an understanding as whites of the impact that politics has on their lives.

Some scholars and almost all black activists reject the idea that apathy is the major reason that blacks have lower political participation rates than whites. These observers have been far more likely to argue that fear has been a major reason why blacks participate less than whites. This has been particularly true of activists and scholars with a knowledge of black politics in the deep southern states. In 1973 this conflict broke into print when two scholars, Salamon and Van Evera, published an article that offered evidence to support the argument that fear of voting, rather than apathy, was more important in keeping blacks from voting in Mississippi.[3]

To demonstrate the importance of fear as a barrier to political participation among blacks, they analyzed the twenty-nine counties in Mississippi that had, by the 1960 census, a majority black voting-age population. Their index of participation was the average county vote for Hubert Humphrey in 1968 and the two leading local black candidates in each county. Two indexes were used to measure fear. Both were indirect measures drawn from county census data. Occupations that these authors deemed to be most subject to white control were used as indicators of the degree of fear present in each county. The ratio derived from the number of persons in the least economically dependent occupations was divided by the black voting-age population and the derivative served as the county index of fear. They gauged the part played by black political organization on a score based on the judgment of a panel of political activists in Mississippi that estimated the degree of outside political and civil rights organizational support each of the twenty-nine counties received.

Salamon and Van Evera found that black economic dependence (fear) accounted for just under 20 percent of the explanation of political participation, that the outside assistance score accounted for just over one-fifth of the black political participation, and that the percentage of the non-white voting-age population accounted for 17 percent of the variation. Together, these three factors accounted for just under 70 percent of their measure of black voting participation. Contrary to county censuses, they did not find education or income important to black voting. Since earlier studies had concluded that lack of income and education went hand in hand with apathy, Salamon and Van Evera decided that apathy could not be a major reason for nonvoting among Mississippi blacks. Their report ends on its major strain: Fear, while not alone, accounts for a large portion of the explanation why blacks participated less heavily in the political process than they had a potential to do.

It is not astounding that Salamon and Van Evera discovered fear to be one important reason why many blacks did not participate in the Mississippi elections of 1967 and 1968. Following the intensive individual, organizational, and legal efforts at extending registration and voting rights for Mississippi blacks from 1964 to 1966, white resistance in the state grew so strong that by 1966 the number of blacks permitted to register or vote was still less than one-third of the state's black voting-age population.[4] According to Salamon and Van Evera, numerous written accounts by participants and observers of the registration and voting effort on the behalf of blacks in Mississippi refer to the conscious threat, intimidation, and economic reprisal directed against blacks who attempted to register and vote in the state. The 1967 election was the first to follow the intervention by federal referees acting under the Department of Justice to observe and sometimes correct voting and registration practices in Mississippi. It should be noted that even this was a partial effort and that these observers were only stationed in the state on a temporary basis. We can hardly be surprised then, one year after the departure of the federal officers, to find fear was a major force in reducing the degree of black political participation in the voting process. What is surprising is that Salamon and Van Evera were able to offer such an imaginative empirical demonstration, based on aggregate data, of the relationship between fear and nonvoting. Nonetheless, the same issue of the *Review* carried a commentary rejecting the idea that fear was related to nonvoting.[5]

Sam Kernell, in that commentary, attempted what was described as a replication of the study summarized above and concluded that fear does not play a major role in black nonvoting. He did not, as has been the case in the past, revert to the concept of apathy among black voters as an explanation of nonvoting. Instead, he found a positive relationship between black voting and the age of black voters in the Mississippi counties. This finding is limited to counties where 60 percent of the voting-age population is black. When he looked at all eighty-two counties, he deduced that of the variables tested, education had the strongest positive relationship to black voting.

Readers of these two pieces are confronted with a credibility dilemma. The dilemma is compounded by the fact that Kernell did not use the same data bases as did Salamon and Van Evera. The first study used only the 29 counties that had a black majority, whereas the second study used all 82 counties. The census data utilized in the first article were based on the 1960 and, to a lesser extent, 1964 information; Kernell used the 1970 census. Kernell used the presence of federal registrars as an indication of civil rights activity, whereas Salamon and Van Evera utilized the judgments of a panel of participants. Even the elections analyzed differed. To make matters worse, Kernell's article was followed by a "rejoinder" from Salamon and Van Evera,[6] which offered a refutation for each point raised by Kernell and reaffirmed the position that fear was an important determinant in black nonvoting, at least in Mississippi and, in all likelihood, in similar political environments elsewhere in the nation and the world.

The only synthesis that seems to emerge from these three articles is an agreement about a positive relationship between county black voting-age population and black voting. This agreement, at least, would seem to update the precivil rights struggle studies, which found that black political participation in the South decreased as the black population increased.[7] This encouraging note of agreement strongly suggests that the civil rights movement did succeed in minimizing the worst of the white suppression of black political activity.

Neither of these studies had survey data available to them, and thus they were forced to deal only with countywide aggregate information and indirect measures of fear. A project under the direction of the authors of this article provided considerable survey information on black political participation in Mississippi and directly on the point of black fear as it relates to political participation.[8]

Another Measure of Fear and Black Political Participation

In the summer of 1972 a survey was conducted asking respondents, "Did you vote in the November election last year?" At a later point in the questionnaire, respondents were asked whether they felt any harm would come to them for voting or undertaking some other acts of political participation. These questions were preceded by an introduction that required the interviewers to say, "Now, going back over some of these different things we have been talking about, do you think it is likely or unlikely that whites in this county or area would make trouble for you nowadays for voting?" The responses offered were "likely" and "unlikely," although any other response, including "don't know," was recorded and coded. These two questions provide the basis for the present examination into the influence of fear in black voting behavior in some Mississippi areas.

Four areas in Mississippi were surveyed as part of this project. The first was the state's most urban area, the capital city of Jackson and the surrounding standard metropolitan statistical area, which included all of Hinds and Rankin counties. Surveys were also conducted in Bolivar, Claiborne, and Noxubee counties, each of which had more than 60 percent black population. In each, a subsample of blacks was drawn from the entire population (a complementary white sample was also drawn but is not dealt with in this discussion), and all black respondents were interviewed by native black interviewers.

An analysis of the survey data indicates that some fear of voting existed among blacks in the counties studied. In Bolivar County, more than one out of five persons told interviewers that they felt some harm might come to them from whites if they attempted to vote in that area. About one in seven persons in Claiborne County indicated that whites might harm them for attempting to vote. By weighting the four county samples, to equalize the effect of differing black populations, we found 18.2 percent of the blacks gave a fearful response to the thought of voting. Two immediate conclusions can be drawn from these results.

First, many Mississippi black citizens did find voting a frightening prospect. Second, these survey reports did not indicate that feelings of fear about voting were sufficiently high in the four areas sampled to support the Salamon and Van Evera conclusion that fear could account for as much as 20 percent of the variation explaining nonvoting in Mississippi.

We make no claim that these survey data are more accurate than Salamon and Van Evera's aggregate data. It is possible that respondents underreported their feelings of fear. A male interviewee might well have been reluctant to express any such feelings to a reasonably attractive female interviewer. It must also be noted that the Salamon and Van Evera effort was related to 1968 voter turnout. Our survey data came along four years and three statewide elections later. We can easily understand how feelings of fear about voting might have been much higher four years earlier and how they might have been dissipated somewhat by the actual, and less threatening than expected, experience of voter participation. This view is supported by turnout reports: 21.4 percent of our respondents reported voting in 1968, 40.0 percent in 1971, and 44.9 percent in 1972.

We must also indicate that the most threatening items of political action, according to the black respondents, were running for and holding public office. Responses to these two activities indicated nearly twice as much fear as responses to voting. Between 1968 and 1972, many local black candidates offered themselves for political office, and there were no dramatic instances of harm befalling them. More important, in 1971 Charles Evers ran for governor. Evers and his campaign caravan traveled extensively throughout Mississippi over a long period of time. They fully expected and were fully prepared for serious trouble—including assassination attempts. Many blacks in Mississippi also expected serious trouble in the Evers campaign. Another portion of our survey asked the respondents, "Did you sometimes wonder if Charles Evers was going to be killed in 1971 while he was running for governor?" Weighting all the respondents together, we find that 60.1 percent had thought Evers might be killed.[9] Therefore, it may well be that the four-year time span, the additional experience with elections, and the fact that Evers and other candidates had not been harmed by their efforts had done much to alleviate the fears of black Mississippi citizens with respect to voting. Consequently we do not feel that a 30 percent estimate relating fear to voting was unrealistic for 1968. At the same time, we found sufficient professions of fear regarding voting, four years later, to subject the phenomenon to further investigation.

In our quest we turned first to the proposition that fear of voting is related to occupational status. Readers will recall that occupation was the substitute Salamon and Van Evera utilized for a measure of fear. They combined the census occupations they considered least controlled by whites into a category called "least vulnerable" and those they considered most subject to white control into a category designated "most vulnerable," with the remainder designated as "uncertain." We attempted to replicate this from the occupations given by our respondents. It should be noted that we asked respondents occupational information about a second related member of the household as well as about the respondent; in unclear cases we used the second stated occupation. For example, when a housewife indicated that she was a private household worker but that her husband was a proprietor, we listed them as "professional" and consequently among the least vulnerable in respect to fear of voting. Others reclassified in this manner were students, retired persons, and unemployed persons. Following the Salamon and Van Evera scheme, we placed professionals (including teachers and clergymen), managers, and proprietors in the least vulnerable category. Students were also categorized in this way unless they could be reclassified on the basis of a second occupation in the household. In the uncertain category we placed clerical and salesworkers, craftsmen, foremen, and operatives, as well as service workers such as policemen, waiters, janitors, and so on. That categorization also followed the scheme of the previous authors. In the most vulnerable category, we placed private household workers, farm laborers, general laborers, and others whose work is largely of a manual nature. Salamon and Van Evera placed farm owners in the least vulnerable category and tenant farmers in the most vulnerable category. Unfortunately, we did not have a distinction between farm owners and tenant farmers; consequently, we designated farmers with an income of over $4,000 annually as in the least vulnerable group, and farmers who reported income of less than $4,000 in the most vulnerable group.

Table 5.1 shows the results of relating occupation to fear of voting. Persons who had nonvulnerable positions also reported that they were not intimidated by voting. Beyond that, the data are not so clear. The findings indicate that, at a minimum, those who had the most vulnerable occupations reported they were *unafraid* to vote by better than a four-to-one

TABLE 5.1 FEAR OF VOTING AND OCCUPATIONAL VULNERABILITY

Fear Level	Least Vulnerable		Uncertain		Most Vulnerable	
	N	%	N	%	N	%
Afraid	12	11.4	52	18.6	56	19.1
Unafraid	96	88.6	227	81.4	239	80.9

$X^2 = .173; g = .121$

NOTE: *County samples weighted to equalize the effect of differing black populations.*

margin. Moreover, there is no meaningful difference between the category listed as uncertain regarding vulnerability and the category listed as most vulnerable.

Since Kernell offered education as an alternate explanation for fear as a retardant to voting, there was some justification for relating education to fear, even though he had concluded that this was true only in those counties that were less than 60 percent black. Three of the four counties from which we have survey data are over 60 percent black, but weighting the four samples tends to overrepresent the urban minority black area—thus minimizing the impact of the over 60 percent black counties to some extent. Data on this relationship are presented in Table 5.2. The table shows that voting fear is less prevalent among blacks at the highest level of education than at the two lower levels of education. The relationship appears to possess curvilinear qualities as persons with a high school education reported more voting fear than either the higher or lower educational groups. More will be said on this subject when we present the regression analysis, but at this point, the findings seem to suggest that occupation is more important to voting fear than education. Moreover, the relationship between education and professionalism, the least vulnerable occupational category, suggests that occupation accounts for the relationship obtaining between voting nonfear and the highest level of education.

TABLE 5.2 FEAR OF VOTING AND EDUCATION

Fear Level	Years of Education Completed							
	0–4		5–11		12		Over 12	
	N	%	N	%	N	%	N	%
Afraid	24	17.7	65	18.6	25	23.8	12	11.5
Unafraid	111	82.2	285	81.4	80	76.2	92	88.5

$X^2 = <.001; g = -.057$

NOTE: *County samples weighted to equalize effect of differing black populations.*

This indefinite relationship between education and fear of voting is important because so much has been written about nonvoting and apathy, particularly in the case of black nonvoting. According to these studies, as education decreases, apathy increases.

One of the benefits of survey research is that it provides a more direct measurement of psychological variables such as apathy. This project included eight questions on apathy that have been combined into a scale measuring the degree of apathy verbalized by respondents. Four of the questions concerning apathy were general and would be applicable to any respondent; four of the questions were specifically designed to measure political apathy among black respondents. The general questions ask whether the respondent had talked about politics within the last two years, whether the respondent paid much attention to politics, and whether the respondent thought that voting was important. The four questions specifically designed for black respondents asked whether the respondent had talked to another black person about politics in the past two years, how badly the respondent had wanted Charles Evers to be elected governor in 1971, how much attention the respondent paid to elections in which black candidates ran, and whether the respondent paid more attention to elections when black candidates were running than when just white candidates were.

Table 5.3 gives the frequency of apathy among these respondents where low apathy is defined as two or less apathetic responses to the eight questions; mid-range apathy is defined as three to five apathetic responses to the eight questions; and high apathy is defined as six or more apathetic responses to the eight questions. The most notable thing about this distribution is that apathy was extremely low among these respondents. Nearly two-thirds of the respondents were classified as low in apathy, while less than 10 percent were designated as highly politically apathetic. It should be noted that when just the four questions related to black political apathy were scored, apathy among these black respondents was even lower than when the general apathy questions were included. The difference between these two designations is about 10 percent. With

TABLE 5.3   APATHY AMONG MISSISSIPPI BLACKS

Group	Overall Apathy	Black Apathy	General Apathy
Low	64.0%	76.2%	66.6%
Mid	28.0	14.5	14.2
High	8.1	9.4	19.2
N = 694			

NOTE: *County samples weighted to equalize effect of differing black populations.*

apathy at this low level it is hard to see how it could be a significant contributor to nonparticipation among blacks, at least for the blacks represented by this sample.

In order to provide some generalized statistical procedure for the phenomenon of voting fear, a multiple regression analysis was performed utilizing voting fear as the dependent variable and education, occupational vulnerability, income, black political apathy, and general political apathy as the independent variables. The results were confirmed by probit analysis performed on the same variables for each of the individual county samples. These procedures let us look at the impact of all these forces at the same time. Under either form of analysis the outcomes were considerably less than stunning. The overall equation resulted in a multiple regression coefficient of .156, which explains less than 2.5 percent of the total variance relating to the fear of voting. All this really enables us to say is that, as far as these variables were concerned, fear was clearly independent and unrelated to any of them; at this point, perhaps that is saying a good deal.

Summarizing to this point, we can now say that voting fear did exist in the combined samples questioned for this survey. Its presence, while extensive, was not overwhelming; however, it was sufficiently great to suggest the possibility that it could affect nonvoting. We have also found that the presence of the fear of voting cannot be explained by the income of the respondents, the degree of political apathy, their occupational vulnerability, or educational attainments. Having presented this much by way of background, it is now proper that we look at voting—the central measure of this study and the preceding two studies.

Relationship Between Fear of Voting and Nonvoting

To place matters in perspective, we begin this discussion by noting that these surveys measured black voter participation over three election periods. Black respondents were asked whether they had voted in the 1968 presidential election, the 1971 gubernatorial election, and the 1972 presidential election. As is usually true in voting research, we are dealing with recalled or remembered information. Questions concerning voting in 1968 and 1971 were asked in the summer of 1972; the question concerning voting in 1972 was asked in the weeks following the 1972 election. Consequently, respondents were asked to recall voting acts that were three years previous, one year previous, and a few weeks previous. Responses indicate an increasing pattern of voting participation in Mississippi elections. Only 31.4 percent of the blacks questioned indicated that they had voted in the 1968 general elections; 40.0 percent of the black respondents reported voting in 1971; and more than 44.9 percent of the respondents recalled having voted in the 1972 presidential election. To the extent that these reports are accurate we can say that the five-year period being tested here demonstrated an almost 14 percent increase in black voter participation in Mississippi.

Turning to the interaction between voting and the fear of voting (see Table 5.4), we find that those persons who were afraid to vote were less likely to participate in all three elections than those who stated no such fear. In 1968 those reporting that they did not have any fear of voting were just a little more than twice as likely to vote as those who reported they did fear voting. The pattern persisted for 1971 and 1972 but was not quite as strong. This suggests that with the passage of time fear remained a barrier to voting but was no longer as strong a barrier as it had been in the first election open to mass black political participation. The chi squares for these three distributions are all significant at the .001 level and the gammas are moderately high. However, a conservative analysis would require us to note that the absence of the relationship occurring by chance does not establish a causal relationship, and it does not rule out the assumption that the relationship is spurious. For this reason, we placed the key variables normally used to explain nonvoting into a multiple regression equation with voting as the dependent variable in order to provide a more stringent test of the relationship between fear and nonvoting.

The independent variables entered into the multiple regression equation were fear of voting, income, education, occupational vulnerability (as defined in the Salamon and Van Evera article), overall apathy, general apathy, and black political apathy. Table 5.5 presents the results of the multiple regression equations for each of the three elections. For 1968 and 1971, the seven independent variables produced a multiple regression coefficient of only .343 and .337, respectively. These results explain only 12 percent and 11 percent of the variance. For 1972, the multiple regression coefficient was .447, an increase in explanation to 20 percent of the total variance. Thus the equation explains only a limited part of the

TABLE 5.4   VOTING AND VOTING FEAR

Political Participation	1968 Election Afraid		Unafraid		1971 Election Afraid		Unafraid		1972 Election Afraid		Unafraid	
	N	%	N	%	N	%	N	%	N	%	N	%
Voters	21	16.7	197	34.7	32	25.3	245	43.2	36	28.6	276	48.6
Nonvoters	105	83.3	371	65.3	94	74.7	323	56.8	90	71.4	292	51.4
			N = 694				N = 694				N = 694	
			X^2 = >.001				X^2 = >.001				X^2 = >.001	
			g = −.454				g = −.384				g = −.406	

NOTE: *County samples weighted to equalize the effect of differing black populations.*

TABLE 5.5 VOTING MULTIPLE REGRESSIONS

| | 1968 Voting | | | 1971 Voting | | | 1972 Voting | |
Variables	R^2 Change	Cumulative R^2	Variables	R^2 Change	Cumulative R^2	Variables	R^2 Change	Cumulative R^2
General apathy	.081	.081	Overall apathy	.084	.084	General apathy	.148	.148
Voting fear	.025	.106	Voting fear	.020	.103	Voting fear	.028	.176
Job vulnerability	.005	.112	Income	.008	.111	Job vulnerability	.016	.192
*Education	.004	.116	*Job vulnerability	.003	.114	Income	.008	.200
*Income	.001	.118	*General apathy	.000	.114	*Education	.000	.200
*Black apathy	.000	.118	*Education	.000	.114	*Overall apathy	.000	.200
Overall apathy	**		Black apathy	**		Black apathy	**	

* Not significant at the .05 level.
** Variable did not enter the equation.

variance in the first two years and a very small portion of the variance in the third year.

Looking at the individual independent variables in the equations, we see that in 1968 the measure of general apathy accounted for the largest percentage of the explanation given by the regression. This measure accounted for almost 10 percent of the total 12 percent explained by the regression in 1968. In second place for the 1968 election was the voting-fear variable, which accounted for almost all the remainder of the explanation given, although it lagged far behind general apathy in its power in the regression. The general apathy measure consisted of the four questions that asked the respondents their feelings about politics when the questions were devoid of any specific black political context. In 1971 the overall apathy measure replaced the general apathy measure and provided about the same degree of explanation as the general apathy explanation had provided for 1968. The overall apathy measure, it will be remembered, combines the general apathy measure with the black apathy measure and thus provides an estimate of apathy when the black contextual questions are added. The variable coming in second in 1971 once again was fear of voting, and it dropped only slightly in its ability to relate to the dependent variable. As in 1968, all the other variables failed to indicate any significant relationship to the voting dependent variable. In 1972 we find general apathy returning to its position of preeminence in the equation, and in that year it accounted for almost 15 percent of the variance. This was the highest percentage of variance that any variable reached in the entire three years measured. Again in second place, the voting-fear variable once more accounted for almost 3 percent of the relationship of the voting dependent variable. Actually, 1972 was the year of the highest strength for the voting-fear independent variable.

The major implication of this section of the analysis seems to be that apathy accounts for more nonvoting among the sampled Mississippi blacks than any of the other normally investigated variables. The second implication is that following apathy, voting fear accounts for more nonvoting than any of the other independent variables normally found to explain that phenomenon.

Thus apathy, the traditional explanation for nonvoting among blacks, does seem to be a major factor in nonvoting, despite the findings presented by Salamon and Van Evera as well as the commentary by Kernell. Before we dismiss the qualifications placed on apathy by those authors, however, we should look at the cross-tabulations produced by relating apathy to voting. Table 5.6 presents the relationship between voting and apathy; the latter is the overall apathy measure, which combines all apathy items, both those from the general apathy scale and the black political apathy scale. It produced the highest gammas of the three and the

TABLE 5.6 VOTING AND OVERALL APATHY

Political Participation	1968 Election						1971 Election						1972 Election					
	Low Apathy		Mid Apathy		High Apathy		Low Apathy		Mid Apathy		High Apathy		Low Apathy		Mid Apathy		High Apathy	
	N	%	N	%	N	%	N	%	N	%	N	%	N	%	N	%	N	%
Voters	183	41.1	29	15.1	6	10.9	222	50.0	49	25.3	6	10.7	260	58.6	50	25.8	1	1.8
Nonvoters	262	58.9	165	84.9	49	89.1	222	50.0	145	74.7	50	89.3	184	41.4	144	74.2	55	98.2

1968 Election: N = 694, $X^2 < .001$, g = .591

1971 Election: N = 694, $X^2 < .001$, g = −.557

1972 Election: N = 694, $X^2 < .001$, g = −.698

NOTE: *County samples weighted.*

most extreme distributions in the directions expected. This cross-tabulation makes clear that blacks with high political apathy were far less likely to vote than blacks classified as moderate or low in political apathy. Also, the trend across the three elections indicates that new voters coming into Mississippi politics from the black sector were more likely to come from the low apathetics than from the moderate or the high apathetics. From this we must conclude that blacks, like other citizens in the United States, are far less likely to vote if they are apathetic. To that extent, these findings sustain the traditional position that relates apathy to nonvoting. But if we review the facts presented in Table 5.3, we must also conclude that the most important finding is that at least in Mississippi, apathy had not contributed heavily to low turnout. For if the statistics presented in the cross-tabulation analysis in Table 5.6 tell us that black apathetics were very unlikely to vote, the statistics in Table 5.3 tell us that in Mississippi there were very few black apathetics. With low apathy ranging from two-thirds of the respondents to three-fourths of the respondents, depending on which measure we use, and high apathy ranging from less than 10 percent to less than 20 percent of the respondents, it is clear that a great deal more could be accomplished by way of voter turnout without even confronting the problem of black apathy.

While we would not want to generalize upon these data, we must point out there is no current evidence to the contrary. So much current political research depends upon nationwide samples, in which the number of blacks must necessarily be small because of costs; consequently, by the time one or two controls are introduced into a black subsample it is no longer possible to find out anything very significant about that voting group.

Returning to the multiple regression analysis, it is also useful to look at the negative findings produced by that set of statistics. For some, it may come as a surprise that the SES characteristics carry so little weight in these statistics. Political scholars explain voting and nonvoting in terms of such characteristics as education, income, and occupational status and have usually explained black nonvoting in terms of low education, low income, and low occupational status among blacks in comparison to whites. Such scholarship has generally added, with a somewhat patronizing air, that when controls for these SES factors are introduced, the voting rate difference between blacks and whites disappears.[10] The findings reviewed here suggest that for these blacks, distinctions disappear before the controls are introduced. The neutral loading of the SES variables in multiple regression analysis suggests that they vote at pretty much the same rate regardless of their income, their education, or their occupational status. In 1968 none of the gammas on the relationship between voting and SES characteristics reached .20. In 1971 only one of these relationships exceeded .15 and that was income, which obtained a .31. In 1972 all three were under .30 with income again going to the highest gamma of .297. The trend toward traditionally expected behavior is there, and it is emerging more clearly in the later elections than in the earliest election. Income appears to be the first of the traditional variables to begin to show any kind of relationship with voting, and by 1972 that slight relationship was beginning to appear along with occupational vulnerability and with education. It must be asserted, however, that in spite of these trends, the SES characteristics do not go very far in the direction of helping one to predict black voter turnout in the Mississippi areas surveyed in this project.

Black Political Organizational Effectiveness and Voter Turnout

Salamon and Van Evera found that black organizational effectiveness helped explain black voter turnout.[11] Kernell also attempted to measure political effectiveness and used the presence of federal registrars as a substitute measure of political effectiveness. The first authors stated that political organization did contribute to black voter turnout, whereas Kernell did not find nearly as significant a contribution from this source.

We also had a measure of black political organizational effectiveness. Our measure differs from that of Salamon and Van Evera and Kernell. The counties to be surveyed in our sample were chosen on the basis of their black organizational strength. In the Salamon and Van Evera situation the judgment of organizational effectiveness was made by a panel of local Mississippi activists. In our study the activists making up the panel did more than a study of the active statewide campaign workers for Charles Evers. They were asked to designate two counties that had political organizations at the beginning of the black activist movement of the 1960s. Of these counties, one was to be effectively organized and well united. The other two were to be chosen from among those not effectively organized. The panel was asked to designate a third county that had not had a political organization in the 1960s but had developed a strong and effective political organization in more recent years. The final county was to be urban but not particularly effectively organized. The panel then ranked these counties in terms of effectiveness. The county ranked most effective was the well-organized and highly united county; the county ranked second was more recently organized and united; the county ranked third most effective was disorganized and least united; and the county ranked least effective was the urban county.

When organizational effectiveness was entered into the regression equation, very interesting things happened. First, the regression coefficients increased sufficiently so that they were significant for each of the three elections. The 1968 regression accounted for almost 13 percent of the variance, while the 1972 regression accounted for almost 21 percent of the variance. Still more interesting was the discovery that organizational effectiveness ranked above all other variables in the last two elections and was second in the first election, providing that we exclude apathy on the grounds that apathy was too low among Mississippi blacks to be a significant factor in nonvoting. We found that the organizational effectiveness accounts for 33.5 percent of the 1963 voting variance (see Table 5.7), 53.5 percent of the 1971 voting variance, and 31.8 percent of the 1972 voting variance. Let it be understood that those percentages are of the variance explained and not of the total variance to be explained. The R^2 change attributed to the organizational effectiveness variable was not overwhelming. In 1968 that figure was .018, in 1971 it was .043, and in 1972 it was .025. One thing clearly suggested by these numbers is that organizational effectiveness varies from election to election. The variable had less effect in 1968, suggesting perhaps that the organizational strength had not yet sufficiently taken hold. We should probably have expected this because of the much heavier emphasis placed by the black political leaders on Mississippi in the 1971 election. That was the year in which Charles Evers ran for governor and some two hundred other candidates made a fairly united effort for local election throughout the state. By the same token, the presidential election was about the only matter of broad interest to Mississippi black leaders in 1972 since there were no statewide black candidates and very little in the way of local elections to be contested during that year.

It is not surprising that organizational effectiveness has an impact on black voter turnout. A "rule of thumb" that emerges from most studies indicates that political organizational effectiveness will add at least a 5 percent difference in voter turnout.[12] So the finding that organizational effectiveness has an impact on turnout is not surprising. When we look at the differences in turnout in Mississippi and compare them to their ratings for black political effectiveness, however, the results are indeed stunning. Taking the 1971 election as an example, respondents in the county rated as the most effectively organized reported voting at a 70.7 percent rate. Respondents in the county judged to be the second most effectively organized county reported voting at a 54 percent rate. Respondents in the county rated as the third most effectively organized voted at a 47 percent rate, and those in the least effectively organized voted at a 32.2 percent rate. These figures indicate a major impact on black voter turnout. Organizational influence on black turnout is considerably greater than its influence on white turnout. Regardless of the cause of lower black voting rates, this is convincing evidence about the usefulness of organizational efforts to increase black voting.[13]

TABLE 5.7 VOTER TURNOUT EXPLANATIONS WITH A TEST FOR EFFECTIVENESS OF BLACK POLITICAL ORGANIZATION

1968 Black Voting			1971 Black Voting			1972 Black Voting		
Variables	R^2 Change	Cumulative R^2	Variables	R^2 Change	Cumulative R^2	Variables	R^2 Change	Cumulative R^2
Apathy	.075	.075	Apathy	.084	.084	Apathy	.131	.131
Voting fear	.022	.097	Organization	.043	.127	Organization	.025	.156
Organization	.018	.115	Income	.021	.148	Income	.025	.181
Occ. vulnerability	.006	.121	Voting fear	.014	.163	Voting fear	.018	.199
*Education	.004	.125	*Occ. vulnerability	.002	.165	Occ. vulnerability	.017	.209
*Income	.004	.129	*Education	.000	.165	*Education	.000	.209

* Not significant at the .05 level.

Black Voter Participation in Recent Elections

There is no question that blacks can affect the outcome of many electoral contests. The presidential election of 1976 provided one clear illustration of this point. Black spokespersons, media analysts, and others often point to the black vote as essential to Carter's presidential victory. The postelection issue of *Time* magazine declared, "Without the overwhelming support for Carter among blacks . . . Gerald Ford would have been elected." *Newsweek* said, "He [Carter] did smashingly with black voters. . . ." And *Focus,* more reservedly, said, "Black voters provided Carter with the crucial margin of victory in several closely contested states without which he could not have been elected."[14] Various surveys placed the percentage of black voters favoring Carter between 82 percent and 93 percent across the nation. A survey by the Joint Center for Political Studies found that in a number of southern cities, black support ran as high as 95 percent.[15] Carter's popular vote margin was a razor-thin 50.1 percent, and a shift of just 8,000 votes to Ford in two states would have given Ford an electoral college victory. Countless state and local elections have also been determined by black voters. Without doubt, black voting is a significant force in American politics.

In spite of the demonstrated power of black voting, a nagging irony has stalked the issue: Blacks consistently vote at lower rates than whites. The Bureau of the Census has provided convincing evidence on racial turnout differentials.[16] Since 1964 the bureau has reported postelection survey results in its series of *Current Population Reports.* The reports note, as in virtually all survey studies, that there is a tendency among respondents to overreport voting activities. The bureau notes that this inflation of voting rates is fairly constant over time and appears to be free of any racial bias.

In the four presidential elections from 1964 through 1980, the average black turnout across the nation was 11.6 percent (standard deviation .9) behind that of whites. The lowest black-white lag occurred in 1980 when it was measured at 10.4 percent. The decrease has not been steady, for 1972 and 1978 provided the highest turnout differences during these four elections. In each of these years since 1968, when the federal voting and registration regulations first come into effect, the average lag in the South has been 1.6 percent (sd 1.05) lower than in the rest of the nation. This is attributable to lower white southern turnout rather than higher southern black voting. Throughout the sixteen years for which we have Census Bureau figures, southern blacks have voted less heavily than nonsouthern blacks. In the beginning of the period, the regional voting differences between blacks were very great—28.8 percent in 1964 and 13.2 percent in 1968. The drop between those two elections almost certainly reflects the intervening electoral reforms. Over the next three elections this difference steadily decreased, so that by 1980 southern blacks were voting at a rate only 4.6 percent less than that of northern and western blacks.

The census reports do not give specific information on Mississippi; however, in 1976 and 1978, figures were given for divisions. Mississippi was listed with a four-state division that also included Alabama, Kentucky, and Tennessee. Those reports show that blacks in this east south central division voted at a higher rate than blacks in the remainder of the South. The evidence from those two elections did not indicate that the rates of change varied between the division and the rest of the South, but little can be said on this point without similar breakdowns from earlier years.

Implications of Recent Turnout on Apathy and Fear

Black turnout rates have been remarkably stable since the 1972 national election. In the absence of new data on these issues, this suggests that little has changed on these matters in the last ten years. Had turnout dropped, it could have been argued that fear had abated and that blacks were responding to apathy. Had turnout increased, the argument would be no clearer than before: Who could say whether the rise was due to a decrease in apathy or fear? As it is, we feel comfortable in maintaining that black turnout operates relatively independently of those forces.

In 1976 black voter turnout lagged about 12 percent behind white turnout, a situation that has persisted since 1964, and the percentages for both blacks and whites has been dropping—at almost the same rate—for the past four national elections. White turnout was 60.9 percent in 1976, the lowest since 1948, and black turnout dropped to 48.7 percent, going below 50 percent for the first time in many elections. Since the difference between white voting and black voting has remained stable, however, and the dropoff in turnout is the same for each race, it seems clear that increased black apathy cannot be blamed for the difference. It should also be noted that between 1976 and 1980 black voting rates increased slightly (1.8 percent), while white rates did not change. Moreover, there is some evidence from 1976 to suggest that our finding about the importance of political organization in overcoming differences between white and black voting rates was true of the 1976 election as well. That evidence comes from an analysis conducted by the Joint Center for Political Studies estimating that black voter registration had increased by about 1 million persons from 1972 to 1976 and that "massive voter registration campaigns conducted in the black community by Operation Big Vote, the Voter Education Project, labor unions, and the Democratic National Committee, proved successful in stemming the tide of black voter apathy that had been predicted." [17]

Conclusions and Speculations

Our data document more directly than have earlier studies that fear of voting was present in the minds of a large number of blacks. We found that blacks who feared voting were less likely to vote than those who did not report such fear. Nevertheless, we could not attribute extensive non-voting to fear.

Along with more recent research on blacks and political activity, we found that the normal socioeconomic variables associated with low political activity did not explain voting or nonvoting among the blacks sampled in this research. Higher levels of education, income, and occupation were not related to voting. It was found that in the last of the three elections reviewed, income appeared to have a greater association to voting than in the first two elections. However, the increased association was not strong enough to suggest even more than the most meager beginnings of a possible trend.

We did find a relationship between black political organizational effectiveness and black voting. The statistics of this relationship were not large, but did confirm that black voting increased as the black political effort in a county was judged stronger. The statistics regarding this variable reflect the manner in which the variable was operationalized. Thus we felt we could only say that County A was better organized than County B, and so on, but not that County A was better organized by a ratio that might more clearly describe the real difference in organizational effectiveness. We feel that the organizational variable had greater impact than reflected in the statistics. The vote difference between the counties and the attitude sensed by visits to the counties add support to our conviction that a good political organization, run by blacks, can make much more difference than the 5 percent turnout gain normally assigned to organizational effectiveness.

In spite of the strong multiple regression coefficients found by the conflicting aggregate data studies by Salamon and Van Evera and by Kernell, we also feel that something is still missing in the traditional models used to explain black voting. We are not satisfied that the full answers are contained in some mix of the fear, SES, apathy, discrimination, and organizational explanations. A further line of research that needs to be tested is black perceptions of black electoral gains in various election situations, and the relationship of those perceptions to black voting. That is, do blacks vote more heavily when they feel the outcome of the election will make more difference in their lives than when those feelings are not present?

Finally, we conclude, as did both Salamon and Van Evera and Kernell, that apathy among blacks does not meaningfully account for black nonvoting. Although black apathetics, like others, do vote less than those less apathetic, our samples produced so few politically apathetic that we feel this explanation is without merit.

Notes

1. Harry Halloway, "The Texas Negro as a Voter," *Phylon* 24 (Summer 1963): 137; Lyman A. Kellstedt, "Race and Political Participation: A Reexamination" (paper delivered at the Southern Political Science Association, New Orleans, Louisiana, November 7–9, 1974); Everett C. Ladd, Jr., *Negro Political Leadership in the South* (New York: Atheneum, 1969), p. 86; Donald Matthews and James W. Prothro, *Negroes and the New Southern Politics* (New York: Harcourt, Brace and World, 1966), pp. 52–54; Lester W. Milbrath, *Political Participation* (Chicago: Rand McNally, 1965), p. 138; Joe R. Feagin and Harlan Hahn, "The Second Reconstruction: Black Political Strength in the South," *Social Sciences Quarterly* 51 (January 1970): 42–56; Lester Salamon, "Mississippi Post-Mortem: The 1971 Elections," *New South* 27 (Winter 1972): 46.

2. Hanes Walton, Jr., *Black Political Parties* (New York: Free Press, 1972), pp. 20–21.

3. Lester M. Salamon and Stephen Van Evera, "Fear, Apathy, and Discrimination: A Test of Three Explanations of Political Participation," *American Political Science Review* 67 (December 1973): 1288–1306.

4. Report of the United States Commission on Civil Rights, *Voting in Mississippi* (Washington, DC: Government Printing Office, 1965), p. 8.

5. Sam Kernell, "Comment: A Rejoinder of Black Voting in Mississippi," *American Political Science Review* 67 (December 1973): 1307–18.

6. Lester M. Salamon and Stephen Van Evera, "Fear Revisited: Rejoinder to 'Comment' by Sam Kernell," *American Political Science Review* 67 (December 1973): 1319–26.

7. Others have also found that since 1965 black political participation has been directly related to high concentrations of black population. See Johnnie Daniel, "Negro Political Behavior and Community Political, Socioeconomics Structural Factors," *Social Forces* 47 (March 1969): 274–80; F. Glenn Abney, "Factors Related to Negro Voter Turnout in Mississippi," *Journal of Politics* 36 (November 1974): 1057–63. The pre-1965 pattern was just the opposite; political participation rates among blacks declined as the black percentage of the population increased. See Matthews and Prothro, *Negroes and the New Southern Politics,* pp. 52–54.

8. The authors express their gratitude to the Russell Sage Foundation for its support of the project that made this paper possible.

9. Evers' brother, Medgar, had in fact been assassinated in 1963 while leading civil rights activities in the state for the NAACP. In the decade from 1961 to 1971, the murders of 41 Mississippi blacks can definitely be attributed to the struggle for black equality.

10. Joel D. Aberback and Jack L. Walker, *Race in the City* (Boston: Little,

Brown, 1973), p. 207; Everett Cataldo and Lyman Kellstadt, "Conceptualizing and Measuring Political Involvement Over Time," *Proceedings of the American Statistical Association,* 1968, pp. 81–94; Thomas R. Dye, *The Politics of Inequality* (Indianapolis: Bobbs-Merrill, 1971), p. 145; Oscar Glantz, "The Negro Voter in Northern Industrial Cities," *Western Political Quarterly* 13 (December 1960): 1107; Marvin E. Olsen, "Social and Political Participation of Blacks," *American Sociological Review* 35 (August 1970): 682–96; Anthony M. Orum, "A Reappraisal of the Social and Political Participation of Negroes," *American Journal of Sociology,* July 1966, pp. 32–46; Sidney Verba and Norman H. Nie, *Participation in America* (New York: Harper & Row, 1972), p. 170.

11. Black organizational effectiveness was operationalized by asking a panel of "persons with long experience in the Movement in Mississippi" to estimate the amount of "outside organizer" assistance the 29 heavily black counties had received. See Salamon and Van Evera, "Fear, Apathy, and Discrimination," p. 1299.

12. John C. Blydenburgh, "A Controlled Experiment to Measure the Effects of Personal Contact Campaigning," *Midwest Journal of Political Science* 15 (May 1971): 365–81; William J. Crotty, "Party Effort and Its Impact on the Vote," *American Political Science Review* 65 (June 1971): 439–50; Phillip Cutwright and Peter Rossi, "Grass Roots Politicians and the Vote," *American Sociological Reivew* 23 (April 1958): 171–79; Samuel Eldersveld, "Experimental Propaganda Techniques and Voting Behavior," *American Political Science Review* 50 (March 1956): 154–65; Daniel Katz and Samuel J. Eldersveld, "The Impact of Local Party Activity Upon the Electorate," *Public Opinion Quarterly* 25 (Spring 1961): 1–24; Gerald H. Kramer, "The Effects of Precinct-Level Canvassing on Voting Behavior," *Public Opinion Quarterly* 34 (Winter 1971): 560–72; David E. Price and Michael Lupter, "Volunteers for Gore: The Impact of a Precinct-Level Canvass in Three Tennessee Cities," *Journal of Politics* 35 (May 1973): 410–38; Raymond E. Wolfinger, "The Influence of Precinct Work on Voting Behavior," *Public Opinion Quarterly* 27 (Fall 1963): 387–98.

13. See note 10.

14. *Time,* November 15, 1976, p. 19; *Newsweek,* November 15, 1976, p. 25; *Focus,* November 1976, p. 4.

15. *Focus,* November 1976, pp. 4–5.

16. The turnout information in this section is from the U.S. Bureau of the Census, *Current Population Reports,* series P-20: nos. 143 (1964), 174 (1966), 192 (1968), 228 (1970), 230 (1972), 253 (1972), 293 (1974), 322 (1976), 334 (1978), and 359 (1980) (Washington, DC: Government Printing Office).

17. *Focus,* November 1976, p. 4.

SIX

Black Independent Politics in Mississippi: Constants and Challenges

Mary Coleman and Leslie Burl McLemore

The Independent race in Mississippi's Fourth Congressional District began as early as 1890, after the enactment of the post-Reconstruction constitution that effectively disfranchised black and poor Mississippians.[1] It was still in progress in 1980 when the state Democratic party, in an effort to strengthen party unity, dampened the uncertain but long-standing hopes of black party loyalists.

Litigation, organized protest, and political activism characterize black Mississippians' long-range strategies. Some Mississippians, both black and white, have a real compulsion to "crack Mississippi"; their strategy, therefore, focuses on an intelligent use of the franchise. The long denial of the vote from 1890 to 1970 has made a real impression on young and senior black Mississippians who have observed and struggled through racial hatred and political exclusion. A brief history is instructive: In 1940, 60 of the state's 82 counties were more than 30 percent black; 35 were more than 50 percent black; 17 were more than 70 percent black. In 1970, 56 counties were more than 30 percent black; 24 were more than 50 percent black; and 3 were more than 70 percent black.

The 1970s ended in Mississippi with 17 black legislators and well over 400 county, municipal, and city officials. Political participation is now a more realistic and practical prospect as state district lines have been redrawn to more nearly reflect the state's biracial composition.

This chapter traces the historical development of black Independent congressional races from 1968 to 1980. First historical antecedents and their varying outcomes are briefly described; special attention is given to the dynamics that gave rise to the 1980 congressional Independent race. Second, the campaign's organizational structure and its attendant weaknesses and strengths are analyzed. Third, voting behavior in the Fourth Congressional District is presented and analyzed in the aggregate. Two counties, one majority black and the other less so, are analyzed in somewhat more detail. Precinct-level data are used to examine office salience in the only 98 percent black district in Claiborne County. Furthermore, theoretical questions concerning racial neutrality within the party system are pondered. Finally, black electoral behavior is examined, first as political scientists have treated it over the last two decades, and second as we have observed it in Mississippi over the last decade. In sum, we provide a theoretical foundation that includes political mobilization and education as primary variables affecting the future of black congressional success in Mississippi politics. A fundamental conclusion derived from the study is that party allegiance is too fluid to neutralize the race question. What we need is the mass mobilization of Mississippi's most economically and educationally deprived black underclass. Moreover, a new politics is called for, one that is based on more than promises.

If increases in black political representation in Mississippi are to become a reality, the black middle class must become more active in politics, and lower-income blacks must be educated to the efficacy of voting (or shown the linkages between voting and improvements in their lives). Only if this is done can mass mobilization and structured party politics rise above white prejudice.

Precursors to Contemporary Politics

Congressional Elections in Historical Perspective

McLemore's race in the Fourth Congressional District was one of a long line of Independent and party-related candidacies. In fact, one of the first blacks to run for the U.S. Congress since Reconstruction ran in the Fourth Congressional District. In 1962 two black ministers—the Reverend Merrill Winston Lindsey and the Reverend Robert L. T. Smith—ran in the Democratic primary. Dr. Lindsey ran in the Second Congressional District, and Dr. Smith ran in the old Third Congressional District, now comprising most of the Fourth.[2] The Lindsey and Smith campaigns laid the foundation for subsequent political campaigns in Mississippi. Their significance was described by one political scientist in the following terms:

> Smith had no hope of winning but wanted to challenge the system and thereby bolster Negro morale. For the Mississippi Negro, long locked into a system of segregation and subordination, it was important to prove that such a challenge could be made. He also hoped to encourage Negro registration and make a stab at reaching whites. He carried on most of his campaigns through radio and T.V. To do so required a struggle with local managers of these medias, who were not accustomed to giving equal time to a Negro. Smith persisted and was successful enough to feel later that one of the great gains of his campaign was establishing a Negro candidate's right to use local media.[3]

Smith waged a heated campaign, but was unable to overcome the many years of black exclusion from the ballot box. He carried ten Jackson precincts and lost to his opponent, Representative John Bell Williams, by approximately 13,000 votes. Smith received nearly 2,000 votes, and Williams garnered 15,000.[4]

Two years later, four congressional seats and one senatorial seat were sought by blacks. James Houston of Vicksburg, the Reverend John Earle Cameron of Hattiesburg, Mrs. Fannie Lou Hamer of Ruleville, and Mrs. Annie Devine of Canton were the congressional candidates. Mrs. Victoria Jackson Gray of Hattiesburg, a housewife and civil rights activist, ran for the U.S. Senate against Senator John C. Stennis, of DeKalb. Mrs. Gray had tried to register to vote as early as 1959 and was finally able to do so after the Fifth Circuit Court of Appeals ruled in her favor in 1963. Mrs. Gray waged a statewide campaign urging blacks to register and vote. Her campaign was the first opposition that Senator Stennis had during his long tenure in the Senate. Mrs. Gray and others lost, but they laid the foundation for successful local campaigns all across the state.[5]

James M. Houston challenged Representative John Bell Williams of the Third Congressional District. Houston, a seventy-four-year-old retired machinst and furniture dealer from Vicksburg, had been active in the civil rights movement since the New Deal era.

Thirty-one-year-old John Earle Cameron, a minister from Hattiesburg, challenged Representative William Colmer of Pascagoula in the Fifth Congressional District. Dr. Cameron's campaign was primarily conducted from the Hattiesburg jail, for he had been arrested during a civil rights demonstration for "disturbing the peace."

Supported by the Council of Federated Organizations (COFO), a coalition of civil rights groups in the state, Mrs. Fannie Lou Hamer ran for Congress in the Second Congressional District. Mrs. Hamer, a former plantation timekeeper from Sunflower County, the home of Senator James O. Eastland, opposed Representative Jamie Whitten of Charleston.

The second woman to run for Congress was Mrs. Annie Devine of Canton, a Congress of Racial Equality (CORE) field secretary, who had been active in her community for several years.

The 1965 Voting Rights Act enabled several blacks to run and win local offices in 1967. In fact, until the election of Robert George Clark, Jr., in 1967, no black had served in the Mississippi legislature since 1890. Seventy-seven years had elapsed since a black person had participated in the governmental process in Mississippi. Clark, a native of Holmes County and a public school teacher, was elected from Holmes and Yazoo counties. He defeated a long-term state representative who had been extremely hostile toward blacks and poor people.[6]

The 1968 congressional campaign of Charles Evers was the first systematic and well-organized congressional campaign since Reconstruction. Evers' campaign was of signal importance in bringing together divergent forces in the state. These eventually formed the Loyal Democrats, who successfully unseated Mississippi's lily-white delegation at the 1968 Democratic National Convention in Chicago.

Evers ran in the Third Congressional District, now called the Fourth District. The incumbent, Congressman John Bell Williams, had decided to run for governor after the Democratic leadership had stripped him of his seniority for supporting Republican Senator Barry Goldwater in the 1964 presidential election. A special election was called to fill Williams' position, and Evers did not have to run under any particular party label.

The opposition candidates were Charles Griffin of Utica, former administrative assistant to John Bell Williams; District Attorney Joe N. Pigott of McComb; Troy Watkins, a former two-term mayor of Natchez; State Senator Ellis Bodron of Vicksburg; David L. Perkins of Jackson, an avid anticommunist and a frequent candidate for public office; and Hogan Thompson of Jackson, a former radio and television newsman and the only Republican in the contest.[7]

Charles Evers polled more votes than his opposition but was not able to garner a majority in the first election. Evers received 33,173 votes; his nearest competitor, Charles Griffin, received 28,806. In the runoff, Evers did not fare as well. He lost to Charlie Griffin by nearly 45,000 votes. Griffin had 87,761 votes, and Evers received 43,083. Evers' total increase throughout the district was accounted for by a heavier black vote and a handful of white liberals, for on the last day of the campaign Evers was endorsed by the Mississippi Young Democrats, an integrated group.[8]

The Evers campaign and first runoff victory proved, in the words of *Newsweek*, "that with stouthearted leadership Mississippi Negroes could turn their recently acquired franchise into a bludgeon that could give deep pause to the rampant segregationist tides that have prevailed so long in the state."[9]

The next major attempt by a black to capture the Fourth Congressional District seat was made by the Reverend Eddie McBride of Vicksburg in 1972. McBride ran as an Independent and was opposed by State Representative Ellis Bodron. In the 1968 special election Bodron had opposed Evers and attorney Thad Cochran, the Republican nominee who eventually won the election. McBride received approximately 8 percent of the vote.

Several blacks and other Independents have run in the Fourth Congressional District. Nearly 40 percent of its voters are black, so it is generally assumed that an attractive black candidate can win. This has not happened because the black candidates have not been able to marshall the necessary forces—the proper organization, financial resources, and the like—to mobilize the mass turnout that is needed.

The last black Independent to run prior to McLemore's effort was Tax Assessor and Collector Evan Doss of Claiborne County. Doss opposed Jon C. Hinson of Tylertown and the Democratic nominee, State Representative John Hampton Stennis of Jackson, in 1978. In this particular election the combined votes of Doss and Stennis did not equal the total vote of Jon Hinson, the eventual winner. Hinson, the administrative assistant to Representative Thad Cochran, ran for Cochran's seat after he decided to run for the vacated U.S. Senate seat of Senator James O. Eastland. Cochran was elected to the Senate in the fall of 1978.

The 1980 Democratic Primary: Its Aftermath

The summer of 1980 had been hot and eventful. The state parties were readying themselves for the congressional and presidential races, and the state Democratic party was determined to form a new leadership since the presence of blacks in authoritative positions seemed an affront to its efforts. William Winter, the Democratic governor of the state, suggested to the party that it abolish the four-year cochairmanship then shared by a white and a black male. Black Democrats, who had most often benefited symbolically from party identification, were infuriated by such a suggestion, but William Winter carried the day for his party and subsequently, Aaron Henry, a loyal black Democrat, was no longer chairman of the party. Meanwhile, Henry Jay Kirksey, a one-term state senator and father of the state's successful reapportionment effort, called a news conference to discuss the future of blacks in the state Democratic party.

Amid continuous political frustration and black political impotence, Kirksey announced his intention to run as a Democratic candidate in the June 3, 1980, primary for the Fourth Congressional District. A diverse group of citizens gathered in Kirksey's headquarters to exchange views on his candidacy. Three central themes characterized that meeting and

the subsequent campaign efforts and final outcome. Only six months earlier Senator Kirksey had been elected as one of two black state senators in
the Mississippi legislature. In his senate bid, Kirksey had faced a white
opponent, and he and his supporters had had to work, day in and day out,
to fashion a winning campaign strategy; in the end they were successful.
Kirksey's efforts as a primary litigant in state reapportionment resulted in
a 60 percent black district from which he was elected state senator.

Results on the morning of June 4 showed that Senator Kirksey had won
43 percent of the votes cast, or about 11,000 votes.[10] Britt Singletary, a
thirty-year-old white lawyer, finished with 7,000 votes.[11] A candidate
receiving 50 plus 1 percent of the vote could have proceeded directly to
the November 4 general election against the Republican incumbent Jon
Hinson.

The second primary was June 24, 1980. The Kirksey for Congress
Committee managed to raise well over $20,000 for this second try.[12] De-
spite the availability of funds and the desire to keep up the fight, Kirksey
had to struggle against a divided black leadership, a lack of countywide
organization, inadequate media exposure, and his own inability to
motivate enough black and white voters. The campaign effort ended in
defeat for the sixty-five-year-old warrior in Mississippi politics.

Events had barely begun to unfold before loyal black Democrats
gathered to discuss their collective future in the party. The discussions
resulted in a request for nominees for the Independent ticket. From that
process arose black Independent Leslie McLemore.[13] Black Democrats
in attendance reasoned that they had given their loyalty to the party but
that the fruits of party victories had rarely, if ever, been enjoyed by them.
They were angry with and frustrated by the party. This public anger and
frustration gave rise to a relatively unified nonpartisan effort.

The hopes created by twenty years of black Democratic party participation had been dashed, and compensation would be hard to come by and
even harder to maintain, but the challenge was launched and the black
Independent effort was begun with support, albeit sometimes tacit support, from a myriad of black leadership sources.

Campaign Organization

The Advisory Committee

The McLemore campaign was begun with a sober assessment of the organizational moves required for the independent candidate's ultimate victory. The organizational structure and subsequent campaign efforts reflected an extensive knowledge of campaign needs and the availability of
resourceful but unexpected full-time volunteers.

An Advisory Committee made up of professional and nonprofessional people was formed to reflect a general cross-section of people in the Fourth Congressional District. Most of its members were elected officials—ranging from county supervisors to state representatives and state senators. Several students, as well as educators, were also on the list. In fact, the McLemore campaign staff worked very closely with educators and students from throughout the district, since a great deal of McLemore's support emanated from the academic community.

The Advisory Committee was cochaired by six individuals from across the district; one of these, A. A. Alexander, was even from outside the state. He was a retired public school principal and long-time educator who had been involved in Fourth District politics for nearly fifty years.

Dr. Margaret Walker Alexander, former director of Jackson State University's Black Studies Institute and a world-renowned author of poetry and fiction—best known for her novel, *Jubilee*—was the second cochair. Dr. Alexander was perhaps the most outspoken cochair and frequently reminded others of the need for black representation throughout the district.

Bishop Frank C. Cummings of the African Methodist Episcopal Church, a resident of New Orleans, also cochaired the Advisory Committee. Bishop Cummings is head of the A.M.E. churches in the Fourth District. In 1978 he played a pivotal role in the U.S. Senate campaign of Mayor Charles Evers of Fayette.

The fourth and most politically active cochair was State Representative David Green of Amite County. Green directed the McLemore campaign activities in the southern part of the district, although he campaigned on a regular basis in other sections of the district as well. Representative Green made most of the political contacts in Amite, Wilkinson, and Franklin counties.

The Reverend W. C. Mazique of Natchez, a person with several Baptist churches in the district, was the primary contact with the ministers outside Hinds County. Dr. Mazique proved invaluable in helping the campaign staff identify sources of support in a number of the rural areas.

The sixth cochair of the Advisory Committee was Bobbie Jean Walker of Walthall County. Ms. Walker, a community activist, had not participated in a political campaign prior to the McLemore effort. She worked on a fairly full-time basis in Walthall and in eastern Pike County. She was most effective in developing grass-roots involvement among ordinary citizens. Ms. Walker constantly spoke of the need to involve black people in the political process. She felt very strongly that no compromise with the Democratic party in any form or fashion was possible until the party learned to appreciate the black voter in Mississippi.

Campaign Manager

The key staff position in the campaign was held by Calvin Fraley, a native of New Jersey, a fifteen-year veteran of the U.S. Army and a Jackson State mass communication graduate, who served as campaign manager and press person. This was the first time that a full-time manager had been employed by an Independent congressional candidate. He worked with a full-time secretary, Ann Holmes, who, like Fraley, was a veteran of several statewide campaigns. Both had worked with Charles Evers in his bid for the U.S. Senate and with several gubernatorial candidates between 1975 and 1979.

Fraley's value to the campaign is hard to describe, for he was more than a campaign manager. In addition to press responsibilities, Fraley was the chief scheduler and transportation person during the early stages of the campaign. During the campaign, he was responsible for its day-to-day operations. Fraley used his managerial skills at all levels of the campaign, coordinated the varying committees as well as the county chairpersons, and was extremely effective when it came to persuading local committee persons to perform selected tasks. Fraley's prior experience as a press person turned out to be one of his chief assets, since he was able to focus more than usual national attention on the campaign, despite the fact that McLemore was not widely known outside the city of Jackson. Fraley helped to portray McLemore as a dynamic person who was knowledgeable about Mississippi and national politics. He tried to project McLemore as the candidate of all the people—black and white, rich and poor.

Fraley, working with a mostly volunteer staff, experienced occasional difficulty trying to coordinate the various elements. Some of the difficulty occurred because some of the volunteers—the old political pros—had never before dealt with an efficient full-time campaign manager. In the final analysis, however, Fraley was able to deal with the entire staff in a very professional manner, and it was his involvement that made clear what a black candidate had to do to succeed at the district level: It is essential that he or she employ a full-time efficient and competent campaign manager.

Finance Committee

Central to any effective campaign is a well-run Finance Committee. The McLemore campaign Finance Committee consisted of twenty persons from across the Fourth District. Dr. James Anderson, a Hinds County physician and active Democratic party enthusiast, served as its chair. Dr. Anderson, a veteran of several local and statewide political races, proved to be a top-flight finance chairperson. He organized several effective fund raisers as well as a fairly effective direct mail appeal in the district and throughout the state.

Dr. Anderson and attorney John L. Walker, Jr., the campaign treasurer, also emphasized the national import of the campaign by pointing out the need for a black representative from Mississippi at the national level. An effort was made to persuade people from across the nation—especially native Mississippians—to identify with and contribute to the campaign. As a result, Dr. Anderson and the Finance Committee members worked very closely with Calvin Fraley in organizing fund raisers in several places outside Mississippi, including Amherst, Massachusetts; Chicago; Washington, D.C.; and Atlanta. While this overall strategy did not work as well as expected, it did help tremendously during the waning days of the campaign.

In spite of the very active campaign committee, and the fact that it raised about $35,000, it became clear to the Finance Committee and campaign staff that a professional fund raiser should have been part of this district-wide campaign. Raising money was by far the most difficult and nerve-racking aspect of the total effort. Of course, if one calculated the in-kind service, that $35,000 figure would more than double, since a number of professional persons volunteered their time and effort to the campaign.

County Chairpersons

The twelve county chairpersons constituted the heart of the campaign organization and worked directly with the campaign manager. They were selected or elected during countywide meetings called by the McLemore campaign staff. The county chairpersons were responsible for day-to-day county coordination. One great weakness in the overall campaign organization was the absence of someone to work with the county chairs on a full-time basis.

Volunteer Committee

Several hundred volunteers worked very closely with the McLemore campaign. They were relied upon to conduct surveys, mobilize voters, conduct door-to-door canvassing, develop policy statements, and do whatever was necessary to make the campaign run smoothly.

The volunteers were coordinated by the campaign manager with the assistance of Hinds County Chairperson Dr. E. C. Foster, a professor of history at Jackson State University who had worked in several local campaigns. The majority of the volunteers were students from local high schools, Alcorn State University, and Jackson State University. Frankly speaking, the student volunteers were the heart and soul of the campaign. They served as foot soldiers from beginning to end.

As was true in the case of the county chairpersons, the army of volunteers suffered from a lack of coordination. In fact, an overall assessment of the campaign would have to conclude that its primary deficiency was the absence of a full-time paid staff person to coordinate the various volunteer forces. A campaign manager simply cannot do his own job and at the same time oversee a disparate group of eager but inexperienced workers, especially when one considers that without those workers, the campaign would be doomed to failure.

Voting Behavior in the Fourth Congressional District

Trends and Challenges

The years 1970 and 1980 marked a watershed in the political life of black Mississippians, a watershed because black Mississippians, learned and unlearned, turned out to vote for the black Independent in record numbers. This phenomenon does not, in and of itself, convey the significance of the 1980 congressional race. Its full significance is suggested by the fact that while record numbers voted on November 4, 1980, black Mississippians did not appear in sufficient numbers to elect a black congressman; in order to ensure future black congressional success, black Mississippians will have to defy their socioeconomic standing and years of nonparticipation and do for themselves what no one else has done or can do for them. The alternative is far less challenging and far less rewarding. All of this will require an enormous effort.

The late V. O. Key, Jr., wrote that "so far as the outside world is concerned the Negro fixes the tone of Mississippi politics." [14] Much has occurred within and outside Mississippi since Key's vintage analysis in *Southern Politics* was copyrighted in 1949. For example, in 1940, 35 counties in Mississippi were more than 50 percent black; today 25 of the state's 82 counties are more than 50 percent black. In 1940, 8 percent of the black voting-age population in Mississippi was registered to vote; today at least 70 percent of the black voting-age population is registered to vote. In 1940, Mississippi had no black representation in the state legislature; today, black Mississippians are 12 percent of the House chamber and 2 percent of the Senate chamber. In 1940, Mississippi had fewer than 40 county and city officials; today, there are well over 400 county, municipal, and city officials. In 1981, black Mississippians still have no representation in the U.S. Congress. Table 6.1 presents figures for the November 1980 election in all Mississippi congressional districts, while Table 6.2

TABLE 6.1   CONGRESSIONAL DISTRICTS IN MISSISSIPPI BY REGISTERED VOTERS
AS OF NOVEMBER 4, 1980

	Registered Voters	Voter Turnout	Percentage
District 1	299,206	165,561	55
District 2	262,372	139,050	53
District 3	326,219	128,000	39
District 4	301,423	177,896	56
District 5	296,319	177,975	60

SOURCE: Number of registered voters: Secretary of State's Office, State of Mississippi,
October 15, 1980–November 3, 1980. Voter turnout data compiled by the author.

shows voter turnout in the Fourth Congressional District from 1970 to
1980.

These aggregate data illustrate two important trends: First, presidential
election years garnered the better voter turnouts, and second, competitive
black presence in congressional races tended to increase voter turnout at
rates close to presidential election years. Thus, black voters in the district
turn out to vote in presidential races and in races that pit competitive
black candidates against the Democratic and Republican candidates.

The 1980 Independent congressional race could not have been won
with the usual black voter turnout. It required either a successful coalition
of white and black Democrats or optimal black political participation
during the campaign and on election day. Crude estimates of previous
black voter turnout in the district totaled 50 percent. If black registered
voters on the registrar's books really existed, they would have to have
been identified and persuaded to vote for a black Independent rather than
a Democrat. Thus, if 70 to 80 percent of the black registered voters had
bothered to vote, a black man would have gone to Congress on January 5,
1981.

TABLE 6.2   VOTER TURNOUT IN THE FOURTH CONGRESSIONAL DISTRICT,
1970–80

Election Year	Voter Turnout
1970	79,168
1972	141,374
1974	89,209
1976	132,991
1978	132,132
1980	177,896

SOURCE: Secretary of State's Office—official election returns.

Several black Independents have sought congressional office over the last two decades. In 1972 and 1978 two entered the race for the House of Representatives and one entered the 1978 Senate race; the House candidates received 8 percent and 19 percent of the votes cast, respectively, while the candidate in the Senate race garnered 25 percent.[15] The black Independent in 1980 received 30 percent of the votes cast in the Fourth Congressional District race (see Table 6.3).[16]

The conservative incumbent, who in 1976 had been charged with sexual misconduct, defeated the black Independent candidate by nine percentage points.[17] Voters in the Fourth Congressional District preferred their parties' candidates to a black candidate. The one-party South, about which so much has been said and written, was clearly not operational during this congressional race; at the same time, black Mississippians deviated from partisan politics and voted almost 100 to 1 for the black Independent candidate. Let us take a closer look at black voting behavior in the fall 1980 Fourth District congressional race. The Senate race of 1978 offers a point of comparison. The findings indicate that while McLemore received more votes than Evers did in 1978 (see Table 6.4), he did not do as well in Claiborne and Wilkinson counties (see Figure 6.1); these counties (along with Jefferson) have the largest percentage of registered black voters in the district (68, 69, and 60 percent, respectively).

The counties having the largest percentage of blacks are the ones where the 1980 candidacy did not reach the 1978 voter turnout rates.[18] In 1978 Mayor Evers' strength lay in Claiborne, Jefferson, Adams, and Amite counties. Fayette is located in Jefferson County, and neighboring Claiborne and Adams counties lie to the north and south of Fayette, respectively. Perhaps, in the 1978 race, the aforementioned counties could have been considered Evers' home counties. McLemore, a resident of the state for forty years and a resident of Hinds County for ten years, was based in the capital city, and his primary strength lay in the surrounding areas. While the home county theory is plausible, it leaves much unexplained. Did more black voters in District One of Claiborne County

TABLE 6.3   ELECTION RETURNS IN THE FOURTH CONGRESSIONAL DISTRICT RACE, 1980

Candidate	Votes	Percent
Britt Singletary (D)	52,303	29
Jon Hinson (R)	69,321	39
John McInerney (I)	3,313	2
Leslie Burl McLemore (I)	52,959	30
TOTAL	177,896	100

SOURCE: *Secretary of State's Office, January, 1981.*

TABLE 6.4   VOTER TURNOUT FOR BLACK INDEPENDENTS IN THE FOURTH CONGRESSIONAL DISTRICT BY COUNTIES, 1978–80

County	Evers in 1978	McLemore in 1980	Difference
Adams	5,008	4,997	− 11
Amite	1,439	1,349	− 90
Claiborne	2,557	2,137	− 420
Copiah	2,753	3,106	+ 353
Franklin	873	968	+ 95
Hinds	18,630	25,941	+7,311
Jefferson	2,452	2,064	− 388
Lincoln	1,596	2,053	+ 468
Pike	2,401	3,732	+1,331
Walthall	1,078	1,013	− 65
Warren	3,535	4,014	+ 479
Wilkinson	1,753	1,585	− 168
TOTAL	44,075	52,959	8,884

SOURCE: *Secretary of State's Office, Jackson, Mississippi, 1981.*

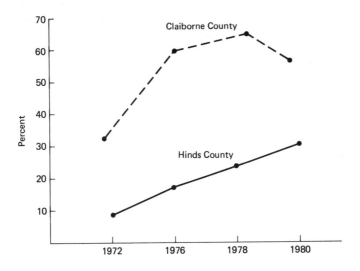

FIGURE 6.1 Percent of vote received by black independents in congressional races in Claiborne County and Hinds County, 1972–80.*

* *During the years 1974 and 1976 there were no black independent candidates seeking House or Senate seats.*

vote for local candidates than voted for congressional candidates, presidential electors, and the black Independent in the congressional race? This calls for a closer look at the recapitulation data for this 98 percent black district and an analysis of specific election returns.

Local political participation, it would seem from Figure 6.2, may offer opportunities to become involved in an alternative political arena when leadership symbols of a normal election do capture the popular fancy. Congress may be regarded as a less accessible forum, however. What seems clear is that voters in District 1 were less likely to vote for congressional candidates than they were to vote for county officials. A seat on the County Board of Education may well have been viewed as a much more tangible and concrete decision-making position than one in the U.S. Congress. However ironic the above statement seems, these findings are generally consistent with voting behavior in national elections.[19]

The problem of nonparticipation is particularly relevant for the study of state politics in Mississippi. As select majority black precincts in Hinds County indicate, black voters who live in rental areas, characterized by prostitution, low levels of education (i.e., less than 8.3 years), and relatively low levels of income, vote less than 46 percent of their actual registered voter strength. This, of course, does not reflect the voting-age population data. In contrast, Precinct 27, which contains the semblance of a political machine, a locus of state and city officials, and a permanent residential area of middle- and high-income blacks, consistently votes at three-fourths of its registered voter strength. While fewer blacks turned out to vote in Precinct 02, a larger proportion of the voters in this precinct voted for the black Independent than did the proportion of voters in the

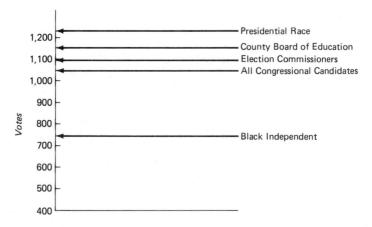

FIGURE 6.2   District 1 Claiborne County, Mississippi. (Recapitulation data returns for Claiborne County as compiled by Claiborne County Circuit Clerk, December, 1980).

more stable and politically active precinct. The difference between the congressional votes received and the votes cast for the black Independent in Precinct 27 is 6 percent, while the difference between congressional votes received and votes cast for the black Independent in Precinct 02 is only 1 percent.

There are 113 precincts in Hinds County, 40 of which are majority black. Table 6.5 shows that in only one of the six select precincts did presidential and congressional votes show absolute equality. Precinct 02, the precinct with the highest percentage of absentee congressional voting, is also the most disadvantaged precinct shown in Table 6.5. Fourteen percent of those who voted in the presidential race from Precinct 02 failed to vote in the congressional race. Furthermore, only 46 percent of the registered voters in Precinct 02 voted for a congressional candidate, and 56 percent of the registered voters in Precinct 02 voted for a presidential candidate.

Table 6.5 indicates a number of trends: First, in all precincts except one, the presidential votes are higher than the congressional votes; second, voters in precincts 19, 58, 27, and 31 voted at percentages higher than the state and the national averages (according to the Federal Election Commission, 53.9 percent of the registered voters across the nation voted in the fall general election of 1980). The black Independent in the Fourth Congressional District race received only 17 percent of the registered-voter vote. Jon Hinson, the reelected congressman, received only 23 percent of the vote in the Fourth Congressional District.[20] Surely, these data give rise to questions concerning representative democracy and non-participation. Moreover, these data are striking because they show that even though a majority of the precincts listed in Table 6.5 had relatively high rates of voter participation at the presidential level, and to a lesser extent at the congressional level, in neither case was their choice victorious. Accordingly, these voter preferences were clearly marginal in relation to the preferences of the voting majority.

TABLE 6.5   PRESIDENTIAL VERSUS CONGRESSIONAL VOTES IN SELECT MAJORITY BLACK PRECINCTS IN HINDS COUNTY, MISSISSIPPI, 1980

Precinct	Percent Black	Registered Voters	Percent for President	Percent for Congress	Percent for McLemore
(02)	98	1,160	56	47	46
04	98	1,083	57	55	53
31	98	1,767	68	66	63
(27)	98	1,629	75	73	69
58	98	1,789	63	63	50
19	98	912	67	63	60

Party Politics, Accommodation, and Political Mobilization

So far, this analysis has presented a microscopic view of black electoral behavior. A few words about party loyalty and the black Independent movement at the state level are now in order. Mississippi's two-party system seems more a masquerade in which blacks are continually frustrated and relatively powerless. These frustrations are present amid symbolic concessions such as serving as chairpersons and committee members on the various county executive committees. Currently, Democrats, black and white, have a problem—each other.[21]

Black demands for political acceptance on their terms must eventually be given a forum, and some major concessions must be made. If major concessions are not forthcoming, the Democratic party may be forced to move farther to the right to attract defecting Republicans. The 30 percent Independent bloc characteristic of the nation is silent in Mississippi, if indeed that bloc of voters is present at all.[22] Consequently, a middle-of-the-road stance for the state Democratic party is hardly appropriate at this time. The other possibility, of course, is to awaken the nonparticipant.

Let us explore two of the abovementioned possibilities. Arend Lijphart's study of the Netherlands provides one of the best theoretical rationales for the politics of accommodation.[23] Lijphart reasons that at the level of the nation-state, primary groups must agree that the nation-state is to be maintained. The implicit assumption here is that the entity should be maintained. The consensus on nation-state persistence provides a forum for concessions. Lijphart refers to the process as consociational democracy.[24] Consociational democracy is meant to explain the process by which ethnically, religiously, and/or racially plural societies reach agreement on fundamentals, thereby rendering cleavages secondary to nation-state persistence.

The Mississippi Democratic party must first be committed to its maintenance. Accordingly, blacks and whites in the party must feel that it is worthwhile for the party to remain competitive and viable. Ostensibly, party maintenance requires agreement on the fundamentals. Furthermore, the primacy of party maintenance requires proper displacement of tensions and conflict; otherwise, racial voting is likely to deny *Democratic* victories in congressional and gubernatorial races.[25] Moreover, shared consensus on the desirability of party maintenance requires a recognition of black concerns and their legitimacy within a viable party organization.

Can meaningful concessions be granted within the Democratic party ranks? Will black political leadership acquiesce to party loyalty without adequate insurance on jointly agreed concessions? Is the black Independent movement ever to realize its political leverage in a state containing erstwhile Democrats? Can nonparticipants come to feel an immediate need to participate in perceived remote issues, activities, and candidate selection? If the Independent movement remains alive, and indicators do not point in that general direction, will that participation be loyal and/or blind? Are there any collective benefits that are likely to accrue to black Mississippians who look with favor toward the state Republican party? Can a state that ranks twenty-fourth in the number of millionaires [26] and last in years of education completed by the citizenry [27] come to terms with economic development in a way that stimulates the nonparticipant and the disinterested? When will the citizenry elect legislators who in the main will not drag their feet on bills of enormous import to black and middle-income citizens? In a state where compulsory education is nonexistent and where kindergartens are few in number, future voting behavior that proceeds from adequate knowledge and an independent spirit seems unlikely.[28]

Events of great moment are not enough to sustain an Independent movement. Monetary resources and an anger based on an assessment of short- and long-term benefits and costs to Mississippi's disadvantaged and underrepresented are desperately needed. Meaningful access to the benefits of politics has invariably been associated with a degree of mobilization and with effective organization.[29] Black political mobilization must occur before party politics in Mississippi can "take on the trappings of a real contest over scarce resources."[30]

The minimum requirements for political mobilization are (1) citizenship and representation rights; (2) effective organization; (3) the ability to make use of representation and citizenship rights through available mechanisms acceptable to the group seeking access as well as to those occupying positions and key points of decision open to those interests; and (4) the economic resources and political skills to make demands upon fellow blacks and sympathetic whites.

Mobilization requires moral conscience and group commitment. It may be that without a party label and its attendant resources, black Mississippians will need to unite and forge a grass-roots mobilization effort; such a move is absolutely indispensable to black electoral success in congressional politics.

The Voting Rights Acts, state reapportionment, and spasms of black political mobilization (i.e., the Mississippi Freedom Democratic party, the Independent Coalition, and the more recent independent campaign) have not sparked the interest of more than 50 percent of the black voting-age population in the Fourth District. Furthermore, less than 1 percent of the black electorate in the Fourth District actively campaigned during the 1980 congressional race. McLemore's campaign staff and ardent supporters totaled appoximately twelve in number.

Fourth District blacks, rich and poor alike, may feel that congressional politics probably will not improve their life styles. Consequently, the well-to-do black may feel that he or she can be reasonably comfortable no matter who represents the district; and poor blacks may feel despair. Voting is such a simple mechanical act. It is one that fewer and fewer Americans, not just blacks, are willing to perform. Clearly, this malaise must be overcome if blacks of influence who want to represent the under-represented are to succeed.

Let us turn now to conventional literature and its treatment of black political participation. We shall, in turn, provide our own theory of black electoral behavior.

Black Political Participation: Threads and Loose Ends

Black political participation has usually been studied as an aggregate of political behavior in the United States.[31] Political participation is conventionally defined as voting behavior, campaign activity, and contacts with political officials. Though this general outline of political participation is more an index of politically defined behavior, in reality political participation literature has largely centered on voting behavior. More recently, political behavioralists have pointed to the need to ask more revealing questions about participants and nonparticipants.[32] Thus, the why of political participation has been ascertained by asking respondents to explain why they engage in political activity.[33] In addition to seeking answers to political motivation, a few political scientists have broadened the participatory modes to include protest and litigation as political acts. Both directions are to be applauded, but they portend some complexity and make it necessary to draw boundaries between the political and the nonpolitical.

Political behavior studies generally illustrate that participation is influenced by attitudes, that is, by what people think about themselves in relationship to others in their environment.[34] Political participation and political efficacy are positively correlated. Campbell et al. defined efficacy as the belief that individual political action does have, or can have, an impact upon the political process, that it is worthwhile to perform one's civic duty. The civic duty response is probably not as prevalent among black voters as it is among white voters.[35] However, underlying efficacy is the personal sense of political effectiveness that meshes self-confidence with routine and socially expected political behavior. One interesting source of evidence on political behavior is Almond and Verba's *Civic Culture*,[36] a cross-cultural study of individual political attitudes and behavior covering five countries: the United States, Great Britain, Germany, Italy, and Mexico. The authors state that in all countries, a positive relationship held between the sense of political efficacy and political participation, though the sense of competence was higher at the local than at the national level.[37] Almond and Verba also investigated the effects of participation in voluntary organizations. They found that in all five countries the sense of efficacy was higher among members of organizations than among nonmembers and that it was highest among active members.[38] Political efficacy seems to be a generalized feeling that develops as a result of having participated in nongovernmental as well as governmental authority structures.[39]

Efficacy correlates well with socioeconomic status; low-socioeconomic-status citizens tend to be low in a sense of political efficacy (and to participate less).[40] Middle- and upper-socioeconomic-class citizens are most likely to score high on the efficacy scale. Similarly, the higher one's educational level, the greater the regularity of political participation. Do all these findings support the theory that political participation is a useful exercise only for those who have developed an understanding of and an appreciation for the decision-making process? In short: Are the requisites for political participation found in upwardly mobile jobs and high levels of education? Is economic disadvantage related to psychological disadvantage? One conclusion rises above all others: The way people perceive themselves is probably just as politically relevant as the objective facts concerning income, education, and job prestige. This admission is made rather tacitly by Milbraith and Goel when they suggest that a high sense of group consciousness correlates with political participation.[41] Others have rarely drawn the nexus between group consciousness and political participation.[42] If this nexus is not clarified, those in the citizenry who do not have high income, occupational status, high levels of education, and organizational activity seem forever destined to the category of nonparticipant. More important, since the late 1970s it has become fashionable to lament the bygone years when group consciousness, at least among the young and blacks, was visible and politically potent.

The waning of group consciousness inevitably retards the intensity of racial voting. In like manner, the waning of group consciousness among the highly educated reinforces individual poltical interest. Consequently, it is probably among the least educated and the least wealthy that the greatest hope for developing group consciousness lies. Viewed from a nation-state perspective, the absence of group consciousness will contribute to nationalism and render parochial ties obsolete—or at least render them inconsequential. Herein lies the irony of democracy: Parochialism, or group consciousness, if you will, contributes to the representative character of nationalism and makes more meaningful the nation-state concept. Whatever the plausibility of the matter, political facts remain. There is a large stratum in America that is regularly inactive—it includes blacks, whites, women, and the psychologically disadvantaged.

Amundsen, in *A New Look at the Silenced Majority*,[43] reports that gender-based differences, which are socially learned and sometimes legally and socially supported, prepare most men and women for dissimilar political behavior. Gender-based personality traits tend to reinforce and distinguish political roles for men that differ markedly from the political roles of women. Political behavior becomes those innate and learned traits expressed in a decision-making environment. Political behavior studies consistently conclude that men generally participate in politics at higher rates than women do. These same studies indicate that whites generally have higher rates of participation than blacks do.[44] It is generally agreed that high socioeconomic status, organized activism, and group consciousness are highly correlated with political participation.[45]

Goel and Milbraith, two eminent political scientists, have pointed to the importance of the environment and the individual in shaping behavior and attitudes towards participation: "Political roles, or modes, are shaped by the social milieu in which persons live, by their personality and most importantly by their own conception of themselves and their responsibility to society." [46]

Milbraith and Goel's conclusions are somewhat interesting in that while high socioeconomic status and organized efforts correlate well with high rates of participation and perhaps a variety of participatory postures, political roles, they surmise, are shaped by the environment in which persons live and by their own conception of themselves and their responsibility to society. The notion of self-concept implies that the concept is not a relative formulation. In relationship to others in different environments it would be comparatively futile to engage in the least cumbersome mode of participation. Furthermore, nonparticipants would probably expect more and receive less than participants. The important point is that participation is purposeful.

The vote, it has been said, is an imprecise instrument that conveys very little in the way of specific information on the needs and problems of voters.[47] While the needs of voters cannot be superficially discerned by noting whether and how often one votes, it is possible to determine the importance of candidate and office salience for voters. Similarly, it is plausible that one's perceived salience of a political office is related to the perceived and objective ability to understand and participate in it.[48] Office and issue salience are often considerations of great moment to voters, but knowledge and motivation are a prerequisite for political activity.

Toward a Theory of Black Electoral Behavior

American black politics can be defined as a systematic struggle to acquire equal formal and informal access to and effective shared control of the available political and economic resources of this country. The primary participants in black politics have been the black middle-income group; those with a virtual monopoly on economic and political resources have been whites. The major modes used to achieve equal access to and effective shared control of political and economic resources have been litigation, demonstrations, and electoral politics. The primary beneficiaries of black politics have been middle- and upper-income blacks. The lower-income black has received little from, and has given relatively little to, black politics.

Acquiring political access means getting an arena in which demands may be authoritatively decided upon through the political process. Control is the ability to have one's way with policies, programs, and goals that would not otherwise have been favorably acted upon. Do blacks in Mississippi have equal access and effective shared control of electoral politics? Given our earlier definition of access, it seems clear that blacks are not a monolithic group of people in search of a means to participate in the decision-making process. Access is acquired individually, and sometimes vicariously, through black spokesmen. Although individual blacks may have access to politics, they have not been able to infiltrate the decision-making enterprise. Furthermore, individual access to the party does not automatically translate into group access for black Mississippians. Moreover, access requires resources internal to the group seeking to make political inroads. Money, maximum voter mobilization, attractive candidates, psychological maturity, and actual voter turnout figure prominently as resources needed by black Mississippians.

Where do blacks have congressional representation in America? Table 6.6 shows that representatives from the deep southern states are noticeably absent. In 1976 the states containing the largest percentage of voting-age blacks had 0.6 percent of the U.S. Representatives. Black U.S. representation comes primarily from major urban centers in the eastern and midwestern United States. Obviously, these urban centers and their black majority concentrations reflect the historical migration patterns of newly freed American blacks during the 1890–1920 period.[49] Present black representation in Congress is relatively recent. In fact, the elections of a majority of the past and present black U.S. congresspersons date back only to 1965. Moreover, the civil rights movement during the 1954–64 decade and the assassinations of President Kennedy in 1963, black leader Malcolm X in 1965, civil rights advocate Martin Luther King, Jr., and Senator Robert F. Kennedy in 1968 provide the scenario from which black electoral successes began (see Table 6.7).

The House of Representatives consists of 435 voting representatives, each state being entitled to at least one representative and the actual number from each state being determined by population. The size and shape of congressional districts are determined by the states themselves; however, the Supreme Court has ruled that such districts must be "sub-

TABLE 6.6   VOTING AND NONVOTING BLACKS IN THE U.S.
HOUSE OF REPRESENTATIVES

U.S. Representative	Party	State
Cardiss Collins	Democratic	Illinois
Parren Mitchell	Democratic	Maryland
Shirley Chisholm	Democratic	New York
Charles Rangel	Democratic	New York
William Gray	Democratic	Pennsylvania
Harold Ford	Democratic	Tennessee
Julian Dixon	Democratic	California
Augustus Hawkins	Democratic	California
John Conyers	Democratic	Michigan
Louis Stokes	Democratic	Ohio
William Clay	Democratic	Missouri
Mickey Leland	Democratic	Texas
Ronald Dellums	Democratic	California
Walter Fauntroy[a]	Democratic	District of Columbia
Harold Washington	Democratic	Illinois
Mervyn Dymally	Democratic	California
Gus Savage	Democratic	Illinois
George Crockett	Democratic	Michigan

[a] *Nonvoting member.*

stantially equal'' in population and must be equally redefined when they
fail to meet this requirement.[50] During the last decade, Alabama, Georgia,
and Mississippi have undergone litigation to equalize the voting strength
of the black electorate in their respective states. State redistricting has
brought about significant increases in the number of black state legislators. The Supreme Court has moved less reluctantly in congressional
districting, and in 1964, in *Wesberry* v. *Sanders,* the Court held that there
existed a basic right to have one's legislative representative apportioned
according to population. The decision was based on a straightforward
motion: "One man's vote . . . is to be worth as much as another's" (376
U.S. at 8).

TABLE 6.7   BLACK CONGRESSIONAL REPRESENTATION IN THE
DEEP SOUTHERN STATES, 1980

	Percent Voting-Age Black	Percent Black Elected Officials	Number in Congress
Alabama	23.0	3.7	0
Georgia	22.9	1.9	0
Louisiana	26.6	3.1	0
Mississippi	31.4	4.0	0
South Carolina	26.3	3.8	0

Black candidates bidding for congressional office in Mississippi have learned through numerous defeats that one man's vote is worth as much as another's only when others are cast. Legal and legislative victories have improved the potential of black electoral politics, but these victories, perhaps in part because they have come about only recently, have not produced maximum participation.

In a recent study, Hill and Luttbeg note that "researchers generally agree that American electoral behavior is changing, but they have not reached a consensus as to the degree of change in recent elections. On the whole, evidence as to whether the electorate is in a state of stability or change has been inconclusive." [51] Hill and Luttbeg's notion of the American electorate more than likely applies to the electoral behavior of blacks. To be sure, there is no general consensus regarding the change or stability of the black electorate.

How is it possible to factor in regional and sectional differences pertaining to the voting behavior of Americans? What impact, if any, do regional differences have upon blacks? It has been documented, for instance, that northerners vote more than southerners and that southern blacks vote less than any other segment of the population. [52] What steps should be taken to mobilize blacks to participate in the electoral process? What can be done beyond the commonplace? What is the relationship between political participation and economic incentives? Conversely, does one have to be threatened economically before he or she is motivated enough to engage the political system?

The answer to these queries is not simple and immediately forthcoming. Political scientists have pondered these issues for a number of years. Of course, one of our overriding concerns has been how one mobilizes black voters on a consistent and systematic basis. We have not provided the definitive answer, but it is clear that black voters have to see some relationship between their voting and the possibility of improving their life chances. Thus, black electoral behavior assumes a survival posture when economic and social survival are clearly in focus.

Voters are surely significant participants in electoral politics, and this activity, though critical to campaign outcomes, is not very time-consuming nor does it tax one's leisure and monetary resources. Additionally, a voter may come from any economic stratum. Certainly, the low-income black who is without much formal education and whose environment does not stimulate positive external participation is disproportionately represented in the nonvoting population.

Forty-six percent of the black voting-age population in the nation did not vote in 1972. Similarly, in 1976, 52 percent of the voting-age population in Mississippi did not vote. It is estimated that in 1980, 48 percent of the black voting-age population in Mississippi did not vote. The 1980 black vote in the Fourth Congressional District lacked the participation of

45 percent of the black registered vote. Although the 1980 independent race garnered 55 percent of the black vote in the district, electoral behavior in majority black counties fell short of previous voter turnout. Moreover, from 1968 to 1980 the black voter turnout in majority black Claiborne County has largely held constant; the exception was in the 1978 black Independent congressional race of Charles Evers.

Why vote and participate in the political process? This is, indeed, an age-old question. The question in Mississippi is answered simply: Traditional party candidates have not and probably will not represent the interests of the vastly unrepresented poor black and poor white. Could a sensitive and knowledgeable black have done better for this group of people? If the people "who get less" do not complain, why should black candidates complain? Poor blacks in Mississippi have a resource that black middle-class candidates desperately need in an environment where white registered voters outnumber blacks by about two to one. Black citizens of voting age have a collective resource only when it is mobilized and maintained.

There is no "affirmative action" in politics unless the disintegration of the party is viewed as too high a price to pay for the elimination of racial prejudice. There is no gainsaying the fact that interests are served through politics. The black and white economic and educational underclass has not been reached in Mississippi's Fourth Congressional District. Black Mississippians can alter the future that historical and contemporary politics portend. When and how it shall be done remains to be seen.

Notes

1. Mississippi Economic Council, *Mississippi's Constitution* (Jackson, MS: 1974), p. 24.
2. Leslie Burl McLemore, "The Effect of Political Participation upon a Closed Society—A State in Transition: The Changing Political Climate in Mississippi," *Negro Educational Review* 23 (January 1972): 5.
3. Harry Holloway, *The Politics of the Southern Negro: From Exclusion to Big City Organization* (New York: Random House, 1969), p. 42.
4. Ibid.
5. "Three Women Challenge House Seating," *Student Voice* (SNCC), December 1964, p. 3.
6. John Pearch, "Negro Winner Gives Reasons for Running," *Jackson Daily News*, November 9, 1967.
7. "Mississippi Seat Sought by Evers," *New York Times*, January 26, 1968.
8. "Evers Will Be in Runoff on March 12," *Mississippi Newsletter*, March 1, 1968; Douglas E. Kneeland, "Defeat of Evers in Runoff Likely," *New York Times*, February 29, 1968; Ben A. Franklin, "Evers Defeated in Mississippi Bid," *New York Times*, March 13, 1968.

9. "Mississippi: Forward March," *Newsweek,* March 25, 1968, p. 36.
10. "Democratic Primary Results," *Clarion Ledger,* June 4, 1980.
11. Ibid.
12. Henry J. Kirksey, *Secretary of State, House of Representatives—4th District* (Federal Report, 1980).
13. There were two nominees for the Independent ticket. McLemore received about 75 of the 100 votes cast for the nominees.
14. V. O. Key, Jr., *Southern Politics* (New York: Vantage Books, 1949), p. 229.
15. Secretary of State, *Official Recapitulation Data: Senate Race, 1978* (Jackson, MS: 1978).
16. Secretary of State, *Official Recapitulation Data: Congressional Race* (Jackson, MS: 1980).
17. Cliff Treyens, "Hinson Backers Demand Resignation," *Clarion Ledger,* February 5, 1981, p. 1; see also David Bates, "Hinson to Officially Open Campaign Headquarters Today," *Clarion Ledger,* August 15, 1980, p. 1.
18. Claiborne, Jefferson, and Wilkinson counties have the largest percentage of black registered voters in the district. The black registered voter's percentages are 68, 69, and 60 percent, respectively.
19. Richard Rose, ed., *Electoral Behavior: A Comparative Handbook* (New York: Free Press, 1974), p. 242.
20. Secretary of State, *Official Recapitulation Data* (Jackson, MS: November 8, 1980).
21. Black elected officials who have been party loyalists for the last 15 to 20 years do not show much public consternation with the party and its decisions. But a growing independent black citizenry seems to have the stamina and leverage to publicly criticize the party.
22. Independent candidates have received little motivation in Mississippi. John Anderson received 2 percent of all votes cast in the state in 1980. Governor Wallace, the Independent presidential candidate in 1968, received 64 percent of the votes cast. Black independents in congressional and state races convolute one's ability to gauge independent voting except as a reflection of racial voting. There may be reason to believe that the "undecideds" in presidential and congressional races are the potential independent voters in the state. Two days before election eve, 23 percent of the voters had not yet decided the congressional candidate for whom they were likely to vote.
23. Arend Lijphart, *Democracy in Plural Societies: A Comparative Exploration* (New Haven: Yale University Press, 1977), p. 181. See also Clifford Geertz, "The Integration Revolution: Primordial Sentiments and Civic Politics in New States," in *Old Societies and New States: The Quest for Modernity in Asia and Africa,* ed. Geertz (Glencoe, IL: Free Press, 1963).
24. Lijphart, *Democracy in Plural Societies,* p. 184.
25. Competitive black candidates and their white Democratic counterparts amassed 60 percent of the votes cast, thereby giving the race to a Republican. One should note that only when the black Independent candidate has wide appeal will this split occur; otherwise Democrats manage to win with about 40 percent of the votes cast.
26. Mississippi Research and Development Center, Data Bank Information for Mississippi, Jackson, Mississippi, January 9, 1981.

27. *Social and Economic Characteristics of the Black Population* (1976), Bureau of the Census, *CPR,* series P-60, no. 85 (December) and series P-60, no. 87.
28. "Senate Takes Gordon's Lead, Kills Kindergartens for Now," *Clarion Ledger,* February 15, 1981.
29. Murray Edelman, *The Symbolic Uses of Politics* (Urbana: University of Illinois Press, 1964), p. 174. See also Murray Edelman, *Politics as Symbolic Action* (Chicago, Markham, 1971).
30. Edelman, *The Symbolic Uses of Politics,* p. 177.
31. The best treatment of black political participation to date has been analyzed by Lester Milbraith, *Political Participation: How and Why Do People Get Involved in Politics* (Chicago, Rand McNally, 1977); see also William Flanigan, *Political Behavior of the American Electorate* (Boston: Allyn and Bacon, 1968); and finally see Lucius Barker and Jesse J. McCorry, Jr., *Black Americans and the Political System* (2nd ed.; Cambridge, MA: Winthrop 1980), esp. chap. 4.
32. Milbraith, *Political Participation.*
33. Ibid.
34. Gabriel A. Almond, "The Political Attitudes of Wealth," in *Politics and Social Life,* ed., Nelson W. Polsby et al. (Boston: Houghton Mifflin, 1963), p. 278.
35. Milbraith, *Political Participation,* p. 171.
36. G. A. Almond and S. Verba, *The Civic Culture* (Boston: Little, Brown, 1965).
37. Ibid., p. 118.
38. Ibid., p. 122.
39. Robert A. Dahl, *Polyarchy* (New Haven: Yale University Press, 1971), p. 82.
40. Almond and Verba, *Civic Culture,* p. 110.
41. Ibid.
42. Traditional studies on political participation and black Americans have rarely examined group consciousness as a variable in political activity.
43. Kirsten Amundsen, *A New Look at the Silent Majority: Women in American Democracy* (Englewood Cliffs, NJ: Prentice-Hall, 1977).
44. Milbraith, *Political Participation.*
45. Ibid.
46. Ibid., p. 217.
47. Sidney Verba and Norman Nie, *Participation in America: Political Democracy and Social Equality* (New York: Harper & Row, 1977). See their chapter on Black Political Participation.
48. Please refer to Figure 6.2 and Table 6.5.
49. Floretti Henri, *The Black Migration: Movement North 1900–1920* (Garden City, NY: Anchor, 1975).
50. *Wesberry* v. *Sanders,* 376 U.S. 8 (1964).
51. David B. Hill and Norman R. Luttbeg, *Trends in American Electoral Behavior* (Itasca, IL: F. E. Peacock, 1980), p. 1.
52. Angus Campbell, *The American Voter* (New York: Wiley, 1960); see also Walter D. Burnham, "The Changing Shape of the American Political Universe," *American Political Science Review* 59 (1965): 7–28.

PART THREE

Urban Politics
and
Public Policy

Black Politics and Public Policy in Chicago: Self-Interest Versus Constituent Representation

Michael B. Preston

The most striking thing about the study of black politics is the changes that have taken place since the 1960s. In the 1960s, the primary thrust of the civil rights movement led to the enactment of several key laws: the Civil Rights Acts of 1957, 1960, and 1964; the Voting Rights Acts of 1965, 1970, 1975, and 1978; and the Housing Act of 1968. Today, the emphasis has shifted from policy formulation to policy implementation. The key actors are no longer civil rights leaders but black politicians.

In the 1970s, the emphasis shifted from protest to politics. There is general agreement among black politicians that "politics is now the cutting edge of the civil rights movement." To be sure, civil rights organizations still exist, but they no longer form a movement with widespread appeal. Indeed, the increase in black elected officials nationwide is ample proof that electoral politics is currently the dominant game in the black search for equality.[1]

It is important to note that the new focus on electoral politics represents a new strategy for blacks and has some important policy implications: (1) Electoral politics can be used to improve the social and
economic positions of black Americans; and (2) blacks currently seem to
believe that more can be gained from working within the system than
outside it. In other words, blacks have come to believe that "political
power" is better than "street power." Whether they will continue to
believe that "politics is the new cutting edge of the civil rights movement" may well depend less on what black politicians say and more on
what they are able to produce.[2] Thus, the new black politics offers both
opportunities and challenges.

The emphasis on "ballot power" has other important implications. It
assumes that there is power in numbers and that where numbers are large
enough, blacks can elect officials who will use their influence to achieve
policy goals for the black community. A second assumption is that black
leaders share a community of interest, and this should lead to a collective
effort on behalf of their constituents. A third assumption is that the vote
should be used to reward friends and punish enemies. That argument
assumes that party is less important than the interests they represent. If,
for example, the Democratic party or organization fails to address black
interests and concerns, black voters will respond in an appropriate manner at the ballot box.

Chicago, in many respects, represents an important test for many of
the assumptions of the new black politics. In some ways, though, Chicago
is unique: It is one of the few cities left with a political machine, and it is
also a city that has had for many years a sizable number of black elected
officials—indeed, more than any other city of its size in America. On
closer inspection, however, we find that black politics in Chicago is not as
unique as it appears. It offers, on the one hand, a direct challenge to some
of the assumptions of the new black politics; on the other hand, it illustrates how changes in black voting behavior can lead to the election of
more responsive officials.

The latter point is important because it means, in most cases, that new
black politicians must run and be elected outside the regular party apparatus. Thus, they are likely to be more independent and more accountable to their constituents. Yet, the very fact that they are independent
creates a different set of problems. First, they are likely to be few in
number and limited in resources. Second, but more important, they seldom develop the kinds of political organizations needed to sustain them or
their predecessors in office in the long-run. Third, it leads to fragmented
black leadership, which in itself is not necessarily bad but is certainly not
desirable given the many obstacles already confronting the black community. These problems are as evident in Cleveland, Atlanta, New York

City, and to some degree, Detroit, as they are in Chicago. Thus Chicago, the most political city in America, offers an excellent illustration of the advantages and disadvantages of the new black politics.

The purpose of this chapter, then, is to examine and analyze how black politics in Chicago illustrates the effectiveness or ineffectiveness of the key assumptions surrounding the new black politics. We begin by describing the changes taking place in Illinois and Chicago politics and their likely impact on black political influence in the future.

The Decline of the Democratic Machine in Chicago

Political power is fragile and illusive. To get it is one thing; to keep it is another. To get it one needs several things: a majority of the voters, resources, and political organization. To keep it, one needs to develop a political organization that is responsive to the needs of most of the people, an economic base from which to draw resources, and some form of incentive system that rewards the members of the organization for their individual and group efforts on behalf of the organization. In Chicago, especially during the years of Mayor Richard Daley, the Democratic machine sought and achieved an enormous amount of political power in the city, the state, and the nation. Yet, during Daley's last term in office, it was clear that the machine was losing some of its force as internal and external forces began to erode the power that was once taken for granted. There are three significant events taking place now that are likely to have a critical impact on Chicago politics in the future.

One of the most striking political developments in Illinois and Chicago politics in the 1980s may be the decline of Chicago as a "sovereign city-state." While the city will remain the economic center of the state, neither the city nor its present and future mayors are likely to be the dominant forces in state politics they were in the past. The power center in Illinois is likely to shift from Chicago to the state capital; the dominant political forces will not be the mayor and the Chicago City Council but the governor and the state legislature. How does one account for a possible decline in Chicago's dominance of state politics?

There are, no doubt, many possible answers. Basic Talbott of the *Sun-Times* has offered what I think are some of the most compelling reasons for the decline. He argues that outside forces are likely to reduce the mayor's power regardless of who is in the mayor's office. These factors are decreasing resources, decreasing patronage opportunities, and decreasing population. The city relies on the real estate tax, which lags behind the economy when reassessment occurs every four years, while the state relies on the sales tax, which increases steadily with the economy. Second, the city's leverage over other elected officials rests on its ability to give city jobs or take them away, and this power has diminished because of the two *Shakman* decisions (*Shakman I* barred the firing of public employees for political reasons; *Shakman II* restricted the hiring of employees for strictly political reasons). Third, the 1980 census registered a drop in Chicago's population. By law, the legislature must redraw legislative boundaries to reflect the shift. Chicago probably will lose 4 state senators, 12 state representatives, and at least 1 seat in the U.S. House of Representatives to the burgeoning suburbs.[3]

In brief, then, the state's ability to increase its revenues and the city's loss of revenue plus its loss of representation to the suburbs and loss of patronage will all act to reduce the city's influence. To make matters worse, the city needs money for its schools and for the Regional Transportation Authority (RTA). The city already has a Finance Board to oversee the schools, and the governor is proposing a restructuring of RTA, which will give the state more control.

The second major change in Chicago politics is the loss of the machine's dominance over black voters. The sharp decline in black support for local machine candidates began with the 1975 primary and general elections, the last elections in which Daley ran. The decline continued in the special mayoral primary and the general election in 1977, in which Michael A. Bilandic was elected mayor of Chicago. It accelerated in 1979 when Jane Byrne defeated the regular Democratic mayoral candidate, Michael A. Bilandic. Blacks voted antimachine with a vengeance; they gave Byrne over 63 percent of their votes. In the year that followed, black voters were disappointed to see Jane Byrne embrace the very politicians they had helped her defeat in the primary. In the 1980 Illinois primary, black voters defeated almost all of Mayor Byrne's candidates for political office.[4] Black voters are becoming a potent force in Chicago politics.

The trend seems clear: Blacks are seeking alternatives to machine candidates and policies. Black voters are no longer the loyal, predictable, controllable, deliverable voters they once were; since 1975 they have become increasingly more unloyal, unpredictable, uncontrollable, and undeliverable. In fact, one of the most important changes in black voter behavior is not its *antimachine* posture but its *more pro-independent inclinations,* especially among middle-class black voters.

The decline in black support for the machine is becoming more significant because of the demographic changes taking place in the city. In 1970 Chicago had a population of 3,362,825, which included 1,098,569 blacks. The 1980 census shows that there are 1,197,000 blacks in Chicago. Of this number, an estimated 950,000 are eligible voters, and 550,000 are registered.[5] In 1980, then, blacks made up 34.7 percent of the city population.

The third significant development in Chicago politics is the return of the black middle class to politics. They are not yet large enough to be a dominant force, but they are growing. More important, they are in large part more independent and more demanding of the machine than non-middle-class voters. They are more interested in substantive than symbolic representation. Thus they seek public policies that improve the quality of life in the black community—the desegregation of schools, more and better housing, improved employment opportunities, and better services. Along with a growing number of non-middle-class blacks, they also seek political representation that is responsive and accountable to the black community. In the 1979 and 1980 elections, they proved that they will no longer support black or white machine candidates that are unresponsive to their needs. This raises the question of what kind of representation blacks actually have in the city and whether these politicans actually represent black policy concerns. As Leon Finney, executive director of the Woodlawn Association, explains:

> There are two sources of power: money and people. Either one, unorganized, remains merely a source of power . . . There is no black cartel working as a disciplined force in an organized way . . . The regular Democratic Organization is not going to concede anything unless there's an organization to force it to.

Black Political Representation and Public Policy

There are two important things to note about black political representation in Chicago. First, it is fairly large, yet ineffective; second, it is divided rather than unified. If Robert Lineberry is correct that "politics shape policy and that the choices we make about the future are produced by the politics of today," [6] then blacks in Chicago have great cause for concern. Their problem is not the quantity of representation (though they are still underrepresented given their numbers), but the lack of quality.

From a quantitative standpoint, there are 5 blacks in the state Senate and 17 in the House. In 1969–70, black House membership was 11. Blacks have gained only one more Senate seat in the last ten years, though this may change with reapportionment as whites leave and the senate districts become predominantly black. But while black representation is increasing, black political unity is not. Black politicians are composed of regular machine loyalists and independents. This produces splits in the ranks and a loss of influence. If blacks can unite, and there have been a few attempts to do this in the city, though most have been unsuccessful or have not lasted long, then they can wield some influence over policies at the state level. This is especially true given the closeness of the parties in the state Senate, where the Democrats have a one-vote edge. Indeed, as Ken Watson has pointed out, blacks can demand and win concessions from the

Democratic leadership in return for their votes in key fights with the Republicans. They proved this when they produced a deadlock over the Senate's presidential election. Black votes were the key to the Democratic takeover of the Senate.[7]

The big issues that blacks are concerned with at the state level are (1) the support for RTA, on which large numbers of blacks depend for transportation to jobs and recreation; (2) aid to public schools, welfare standards, unemployment compensation, and law enforcement. If blacks were unified, they would be in an excellent position to influence action on these and other public policies that would be beneficial to the black community in Chicago.

In Chicago, blacks had 16 black aldermen and 15 black committeemen as of 1980.[8] This is the largest single bloc of any ethnic group in the council. But, like their state legislative brethren, they too are divided. Black regular Democrats put loyalty to the machine over loyalty to their constituents. Indeed, the system of influence in Chicago under Daley was designed to keep power blocs from forming. Loyal committeemen controlled aldermen, and machine leaders controlled them all by dispensing patronage and rewards in such a manner that they were applied personally and not collectively. Cohesive action was viewed as disloyal (the most serious offense a machine politician could commit), especially if it was not cleared and sanctioned by the top leadership. Black politicians were especially subject to individual control, given the increase in the black population and the growth in their numbers on the council.

Since the death of Mayor Daley, the machine's control has not been as tight. As different groups have struggled to gain the upper hand, a cohesive black group might have been in a position to influence the future direction of the machine. More important, black politicians could now get the multitude of problems facing the black community on the political agenda and demand that something be done about them. The problems of poor housing, lack of jobs, poor police-community relations, segregated schools and poor instruction, as well as getting more appointments to top-level jobs in the city bureaucracy, are all important problems facing the black community. It is clear that individual action will not be effective; a fragmented machine is still more powerful than an unorganized group of individuals. If black machine regulars and black independents remain fragmented, then they are also likely to remain relatively powerless.

Black politicians, in their roles as committeemen and aldermen, put the interest of the regular Democratic organization first and end up being merely officeholders rather than representatives of their constituents. This point is reinforced by Alderman Cousin in an interview with the *Chicago Reporter:*

> Most black aldermen do not provide political leadership or deal with issues which are of interest to black people. . . . There has been more control over

the black community than over the white. The administration has been able to select people to represent the interests of the administration who have been very effective. They've been given the patronage they needed to keep the people in line, to engender fear in the community of reprisals or of not receiving any consideration.[9]

Most black aldermen and committeemen counter by saying that their power is undermined because blacks don't vote. It should be remembered that patronage and other rewards in Chicago are based on the size of the vote that each alderman and committeeman can deliver for the party. That is, the higher the vote for machine candidates, the higher the rewards and level of influence.

For example, the power to influence who gets slated for federal, state, and city political offices is based partially on the number of votes that individual committeeman and alderman produce from their wards. In addition, vote size per ward is supposed to determine the number and quality of patronage positions allocated per ward. Stated differently, influence depends on productivity.

The *Chicago Reporter* ranked black committeemen on the size of the vote they were able to produce in the primary elections of 1978 and 1979. In the February mayoral primary they assert that while blacks comprised 28 percent of the city committee, they had only 21.7 percent of the total weighted votes. They go on to say that the average registration in black committeemen's wards is 25,629, 10 percent lower than the average in all wards. And they conclude that the average turnout of registered voters was 63.4 percent for white committeemen's wards in the last primary, while the figures for black committeemen's wards was 51.2 percent (see Table 7.1).[10]

The lack of black voter turnout and the loss of political power is discussed by one current and one former alderman:

> *Alderman Marian Humes* (8th Ward): Blacks don't have political power in Chicago . . . you get power through the exercise of the vote and blacks are not voting in significant numbers. My ward had 38,000 registered voters but only 11,000 came out to vote. Alderman Patrick Huel (11th) got 20,000 out of 30,000 registered voters in his ward—now that's political power.

> *Alderman Bennett Stewart* (21st Ward): Until blacks start going to the polls and voting, we can forget about any kind of power in Chicago's political structure. The basis of political power is in the vote—that determines our influence. What kind of demands can I make with 39,000 registered voters in my ward and only 10,000 coming out to vote? [11]

What accounts for the lack of voter support in black committeemen's wards? Milton Rakove, a student of Chicago politics, is quoted as arguing that low voter turnout in black wards can be attributed to three related factors: weak ward organizations, floating or transient populations, and

TABLE 7.1   RANK OF FOURTEEN BLACK COMMITTEEMEN, PRIMARY ELECTIONS, 1979 AND 1978

Ward	Committeeman	1979 Primary					1978 Primary				
		Democratic Voters	Rank (of 14)	Rank in city [a]	Percent Voters [b]	Rank in city [a]	Democratic Voters	Rank (of 14)	Rank in city [a]	Percent Voters [b]	Rank in city [a]
21	Bennett M. Stewart	19,391	1	14	55.7	35	8,212	2	32	24.1	49
8	John H. Stroger, Jr.	17,707	2	19	52.5	42	8,956	1	26	27.1	43
34	Wilson Frost	17,088	3	21	52.0	43	7,977	4	35	24.8	46
6	Eugene Sawyer	15,045	4	28	51.4	45	7,116	8	43	24.7	48
7	Joseph G. Bertrand	12,623	5	37	48.7	47	6,330	12	47	24.9	45
2	William Barnett	12,407	6	39	53.0	39	8,094	3	34	34.9	29
17	William H. Shannon	12,256	7	40	51.5	44	6,333	11	46	27.0	44
4	Timothy C. Evans	11,415	8	41	50.5	46	7,294	7	42	31.2	37
16	James C. Taylor	11,332	9	42	52.6	41	7,841	6	38	35.7	26
3	Tyrone T. Kenner	11,256	10	43	56.7	33	6,500	10	45	33.6	30
20	Cecil A. Partee	11,144	11	44	47.8	48	7,861	5	37	33.4	31
24	Walter Shumpert	9,507	12	48	52.7	40	7,112	9	44	39.6	17
29	Willie Flowers	9,430	13	49	46.6	49	4,995	14	50	24.8	47
28	William Carothers	8,864	14	50	45.7	50	5,353	13	48	28.8	42
	Average 50 wards	16,581			60.0		9,949			37.5	

SOURCE: *Board of Election Commissioners of Chicago, analyzed by the Chicago Reporter.*
[a] *Among 50 Democratic committeemen.*
[b] *Percentage of registered voters who cast ballots.*

poor registration.[12] While I agree with Rakove that these factors are important, I do not agree that these are the only or most important factors.

I would cite for example, first, that 36 percent of the black population in Chicago in 1975 were in or near poverty.[13] In 1980, an estimated 600,000-plus Chicagoans were in poverty, and 85 percent were nonwhite.[14] The impact of poverty and low education on voting is well documented in the political science literature.[15] Second, a large part of the black middle class withdrew from politics but now seems to be returning. Third, the machine has not been and is not interested in registering blacks who they feel will not vote the "right way." But perhaps the most important reason why a large percentage of blacks do not register and vote is because they see few or no linkages between their votes and the political outcomes of the system. This is reinforced when they see the people they supported voting against, or being silent on, issues that are important to them. Put differently, black representativeness in Chicago does not equal responsiveness.

Journalist Lu Palmer's statement of why blacks don't register and vote in Chicago illustrates my point:

> Blacks have voted and voted and voted in this town, but the more they vote, the worse things get. It doesn't matter if they vote for a white or a black. . . . Sometimes I think black people who don't vote are more sophisticated than those who do, because the black voter has to choose between the lesser of the two evils. If a person decides not to choose any evil, he's more sophisticated.[16]

A classic case of how machine loyalty overrides black community interest is the case of two new school appointees suggested by Mayor Byrne, about whom we will deal in the next section.

Loyalty, Self-Interest, and Public Policy

The current school board in Chicago is composed of 11 members, 5 of whom are black. However, two of the black appointees, Leon Davis and Michael Scott, have one-year terms and will not be reappointed by Mayor Byrne. She proposes to replace them with two white females. This will mean that while the black school population is going up (currently 61 percent black), its representation on the board will drop from 45 to 27 percent. The appointments are even more controversial because one of the nominees, Betty Bonow (southwest) has a history of opposition to racial integration of the public schools in the Bogan community. Rosemary Janus (northeast side), on the other hand, is not as controversial; she simply represents the mayor's insensitivity to the black community.

The appointees must be confirmed by the City Council Education Committee and then the full council. Before the subcommittee vote, the

NAACP conducted a poll of black aldermen to see how they would vote. Some aldermen were furious at the NAACP for conducting the poll and the publicity it created.[17] According to Vernon Jarrett, the loyalists are looking for a way out of the dilemma:

> Seven of Chicago's 16 black aldermen are "trapped," as one alderman put it this week. Another alderman said: "They are trying to keep in tight with Miss Boss Byrne while trying not to appear as out and out Uncle Toms to the voters in their wards. . . ."
>
> The remaining nine blacks are still silent or have decided to wait until after the hearings. There is speculation they are trying to convince the mayor to permit them publicly to look good to the black community while maintaining private loyalty to her. The fact there are nine blacks on a Northern city council who have remained silent about a drastic reduction of black school board members explains much about political enslavement in Chicago.[18]

To add fuel to the fire, William Frost, the most powerful black alderman, chairman of the Council's Finance Committee, and a Byrne loyalist, is scheduled to be this year's chairman of the NAACP's freedom dinner. What if he votes for Bonow and Janus?

On March 25, 1981, the controversial appointments were approved by the City Council's Education Committee by a 9-5 vote. Alderman Allan Streeter (17th), a black appointed by Mayor Byrne to replace Tyrone McFolling, who had resigned, voted with most of the white aldermen for the appointment; and according to Robert Davis of the *Chicago Tribune*, another black alderman, Tyrone Kenner (3rd), didn't attend the meeting and did not vote. The blacks on the subcommittee that voted against Byrne's choices included Marian Humes (8th), Clifford Kelley (20th), Niles Sherman (21st), and Danny Davis (29th). Martin Oberman, a white independent, also voted against the two women.[19] The full council is expected to vote and approve the choices.* If black machine regulars run true to form, loyalty and self-interest will win out over the interest of their constituents; if they can persuade the mayor to take the "heat off," they might well vote no to save face. In either case, it becomes obvious why more and more machine incumbents (aldermen and committeemen) are being defeated at the polls. Black voters have moved from loyal supporters to exit, as we shall discuss this in the next section.

Black Electoral Support: Loyalty-Voice and Exit

Jane Byrne's defeat of the regular machine candidate for mayor, Michael A. Bilandic, in the 1979 mayoral primary election was one of the major

---

* The council, as expected, approved the choices.

political upsets in the nation's history. Black voters gave Byrne over 63 percent of their votes in the primary and a much larger percentage during the general election. If there ever was any doubt that a new black voter had emerged in Chicago, it has been dispelled by this and subsequent elections.

One of the most consistent patterns in black wards since 1975 has been the increasing size of the antimachine vote. Table 7.2 shows a continuation of this trend: A majority of black voters rejected the regular Democratic candidate in the 1979 mayoral primary. In fact, *since 1975, black voters have voted in greater percentages against the machine than all other wards combined.*[20]

Black voter dissatisfaction with regular machine candidates in 1979 was not due solely to the Bilandic administration's act of closing the "El" (rapid transit) stop in black neighborhoods during the "blizzard of 1979." Its roots were planted long before this event, some preceding Bilandic by many years. Among them one could include Daley's attempt to punish Ralph Metcalfe by slating cabinet member Erwin A. France to run against Metcalfe in the primary; there were the issues of police brutality and the shooting death of Black Panther leader Fred Hampton by police assigned to State's Attorney Edward V. Hanrahan; the total disrespect shown Alderman Wilson Frost (34th Ward) when, as president pro tem of the city council, he was passed over as acting mayor after Daley's death; and the disregard and disrespect shown the black community with the slating of Bennett Stewart for Metcalfe's seat in Congress. Of course, large groups of white voters were also dissatisfied with the Bilandic administration over the breakdown in city services (read snow removal), cronyism in city government, corruption, and the fact that the administration seemed to support the condominium hustle by real estate interests that tended to

TABLE 7.2   ANTIORGANIZATION VOTE IN BLACK WARDS[a]

	Votes for Organization Candidate	Votes Against Organization Candidate	Percent Against	Percent Against Organization: All Wards
1955	73,366	17,775	19.5	51.0
1975	85,668	92,090	51.8	42.2
1977	71,427	74,757	51.1	48.9
1979	74,805	110,683	59.7	51.0

SOURCE: "Chicago Board of Election Commissioners," Chicago Reporter 8, no. 4 (April 1979): 8.

[a] *In 1955: wards 2, 3, and 20, which were more than 80 percent black in 1950, and wards 4, 6, and 24, which were racially mixed in 1950 and more than 85 percent black in 1960. In 1975–79: wards that were more than 80 percent black in 1970 (2, 3, 4, 6, 16, 17, 20, 21, 24, 27, 28, and 29); and wards 8, 9, and 34, which were more than 80 percent black by 1975.*

drive up rents in many areas. This combination of factors led to Bilandic's defeat.

Another interesting aspect of the 1979 election was the defeat of three incumbent machine aldermen by black independent candidates (voters also elected two former regular Democrats who had been dumped by the machine over two machine candidates). The three new black independent aldermen are Danny Davis (29th), Niles Sherman (21st), and Robert Shaw (9th). Whether these three will remain independent is an open question. If they do, it may signal to black voters in other wards that it is possible to elect people who will be responsible to them and not some external source. Indeed, this may well be a more significant victory for black voters than the election of Jane Byrne as mayor. Black voters may now realize that they can "beat the machine."

According to Vernon Jarrett, Richard Barnett, the campaign manager for Danny Davis, explained their strategy on beating the machine this way: "We discovered that Cross (the incumbent in the 29th Ward) had around 3,200 votes that he could depend on . . . that meant to us that there were nearly 17,000 registered voters waiting for the right movement—not to mention the thousands not registered." [21] This statement is signficant for several reasons. First, it points out the weakness in the machine's strategy of relying on low-turnout elections. When the voters are given a viable alternative, and the candidate is serious and well organized, the regular machine candidate is vulnerable. Second, this statement suggests a more fundamental flaw in machine strategy in black wards—the weakness of the ward organization. Most black aldermen do not have the resources (or if they do, they do not use them) to build strong ward organizations. Moreover, black aldermen are not encouraged to build too strong a base in their wards because it would lessen their dependency on the machine leader. Thus the reliance on low but controlled turnout means that black aldermen may win the election battle in their wards but lose the war at the city level. That is, the small turnout means that they have little power in the organization and that they get the most menial patronage jobs the machine has to offer. Third, this statement points out a gap between "leaders" and "followers"; it suggests that most black leaders have only a few followers and that a large segment of black voters are not led by and do not follow regular machine candidates.

Another significant development was the return of the black middle class to local politics. In 1977 these wards had the lowest voter turnout in both the primary and general elections. In 1979 they showed the greatest percentage increase in voter turnout over the 1977 elections in both the general and primary elections. If we look at just the black lower-class, the ethnic middle-class, and the black middle-class wards, the latter group was the only one to have an increase in voter turnout from the primary to the general election in 1979. In 1977 they had shown the greatest decrease (down 11 percent) in voter turnout from the primary to the general election. The other two groups still had a decline in voter turnout in 1979, although it was less than that of 1977.

It is important to note that Jane Byrne won all but two (the 24th and 27th) of the predominantly black wards in the primary. In addition, she won five other wards (7th, 9th, 10th, 15th, and 37th) that have a black majority.[22] Nonetheless, in 1979 each had a white alderman and four of the five had white Democratic committeemen. If we add Ward 5, with its estimated black majority (57 percent), there were, in 1979, 20 black wards but only 16 black aldermen and 14 black committeemen. It has been suggested by Don Rose, a journalist and Jane Byrne's former campaign manager, that a ward has to be 70 percent black before the machine lets it have a black representative.[23] These figures indicate that while the black population is expanding, its representation is not.

The 1979 mayoral primary election also provided a clear picture of the gap that has developed between black political leaders and the majority of black voters. Although all the black politicians supported the regular Democratic candidate, only 2 of the 14 predominantly black wards and none of the majority black wards voted for the regular machine candidate for mayor. This is a clear signal that black machine leaders have lost touch with their followers. And it also seems clear that leaders that lack followers are not likely to be leaders very long.

The 1980 Primary

If the Democratic organization was surprised by the large antimachine vote by blacks in the mayoral election of 1979, they must have been astounded by the results of the 1980 Illinois primary. Jane Byrne, who only one year earlier had received overwhelming support by black voters, saw her choices for political office soundly defeated by those same black voters. Her betrayal of their trust may well mean that the relationship of black voters to the machine has suffered a permanent rupture; if not permanent, certainly it is one that will take a major effort to repair.

There seems little doubt that a large percentage of the antimachine vote in the primary can be directly attributed to Byrne's record while in office. Among the events that led to grievances listed by black political and community leaders, seven are especially glaring:

1. *Appointment of police superintendent.* Mayor Byrne had informed black Police Board member, Renault Robinson, that she wanted to bring in a new police chief from outside the department. Robinson supported the mayor in this move and did not insist that Sam Nolan, a black assistant

chief in the department, be considered. With Robinson's assurance of no backlash about Nolan, the mayor then turned 360° and appointed a white from inside the department, Richard J. Brzeczek (the only white on the list of recommendations from the Police Board).

2. *Transit strike.* The Reverend Jesse Jackson asserts that during the week-long strike of city transit workers that shut down the CTA and most of the city, the mayor tried to break the striking unions, both headed by black men. Her policy of refusing to negotiate with striking unions had a devastating impact on blacks who depend on public transportation.

3. *School board.* In 1979 Mayor Byrne bypassed the black deputy superintendent of public schools, Manfred Byrd, in consideration for superintendent; instead she appointed Dr. Byrd's subordinate, a white woman, Angeline Caruso. On top of this she planned to appoint a white board member as president of the board. (It is important to note here that the city schools are predominantly black.) A year later, after a major financial crisis that threatened to shut down the entire system, the mayor appointed a new school board more representative of the city's school population, but also attempted to install a white man, Thomas G. Ayers, as president. When the board chose a black, the Reverend Kenneth B. Smith, as its president, Mayor Byrne refused to swear the members in (although she did so at a later date).

4. *Teachers' strike.* As in the transit strike, minorities in the city suffered disproportionately during the teachers' strike. Especially hard hit were young children whose parents had to go to work and for whom there is a lack of alternative day care.

5. *Firefighters' strike.* The third major strike of 1979 also affected minorities more harshly than others, in part as a consequence of poor living conditions. The majority of deaths during the strike were among residents of the black community. This situation was not resolved until the Reverend Jesse Jackson stepped in and served as a mediator.

6. The mayor's support of Governor Thompson's transit package that resulted in a CTA fare increase.

7. Her failure to support state *legislation* that would have removed the state sales tax on food and medicine.[24]

In addition, Mayor Byrne had promised to strike down the patronage system dominated by 11th Ward jobholders in order to provide more and better jobs to the black community. Instead, after her election she began to dominate rather than dismantle the system. Moreover, there was no change in the quality or quantity of patronage jobs available to blacks. Probably the most serious blow to black voters was the realization that Byrne was neither antimachine nor a reformer, for after the election she embraced the very machine politicians whom she had criticized earlier.

The results of the primary election reflected their degree of dissatisfaction. A brief review of the 1980 races will illustrate the depths of black dissatisfaction with Byrne and her candidates.

U.S. HOUSE OF REPRESENTATIVES   In the First and Second Congressional Districts, black independents mounted strong challenges against black candidates endorsed by the regular organization. The widespread dissatisfaction felt among blacks toward the Democratic machine was translated into independent victories in both contests. In the First District, Harold Washington garnered almost 50 percent of the vote and easily won over machine-endorsed incumbent Bennett Stewart and Ralph Metcalfe, Jr. (an independent). In the Second District, Gus Savage took 45 percent of the vote in a four-person race, soundly defeating machine-endorsed Reginald Brown for the seat vacated by white machine congressman Morgan Murphy. The popularity of Washington and Savage may have a profound impact on the future of Chicago politics. It also means that Chicago and Los Angeles are the only cities with three black U.S. congressmen.

WARD COMMITTEEMEN   The most significant development of the 1980 primary, from the standpoint of black voters, came in the ward committeemen races. Five black regular Democratic organization committeemen lost their positions to independent challengers. Again, the anti-Byrne vote appears to have been a determining factor. All these wards supported Mayor Byrne in the 1979 primary. Three of the victories were registered in Southside black wards (9th, 17th, 21st), continuing the independent trend of Chicago's black community. In the 7th Ward, the first Latino ever was elected a committeeman, Raoul Castro.

Independent aldermen Shaw (9th), Sherman (21st), and McFolling (17th), who became aldermen in 1979, solidified their strength by capturing their respective ward committeemen positions. What is especially significant in these races was that, despite the drop in turnout, their electoral support actually increased. Traditionally the machine has counted on a low turnout with predictable results where a high proportion of voters "pay the machine back." According to Kemp and Lineberry,[25] machines "thrive on low-turnout elections." In this instance, however, the most active voters in the 9th, 17th, and 21st wards were apparently also the most independent. The party organization's use of benefits and incentives to control low-turnout elections simply failed.

It should also be noted that Alderman Robert Shaw (9th) and Niles Sherman (21st) had been thorns in the side of the mayor. In their campaigns for committeeman, they faced a serious organizational effort to defeat them. That effort failed. The election of these two increased the number of black committeemen to 15 of the 50-member body.

The results of the 1980 Illinois primary may prove to be a watershed in Chicago politics. The election results indicate the birth of an extremely sophisticated black voter, a voter who is beginning to reward political friends and punish political enemies. The loyalty of black voters was unquestioned in Daley's early years; in the late 1960s, protests were heard (voice), and in the 1970s, disenchantment set in and black voters began a slow but steady exit. In the 1980s the tide is so large that a floodgate may be needed to stop it.

In addition to the policy issues already mentioned, several others are likely to be important to the quality of life of blacks in Chicago. In each case, politics will have a critical role to play in the outcome.

Poverty, Politics, and Public Policy: A Synopsis

Several policy issues are and will continue to be of central concern to blacks in Chicago: poverty and employment, school politics, transportation, and redistricting. We briefly summarize each of these issues in this section.

Poverty and Employment

The socioeconomic condition of the black population in Chicago is poor and is likely to get worse. A mid-1970 report by the Chicago Urban League found that poverty in the south and west sides (which contain over 624,942 people) was near 36 percent.[26] A more recent report by the *Chicago Reporter* (February 1980), found that over 600,000 people are *permanently* trapped in what they call the "new poverty." Of these, more than 85 percent are nonwhite. The findings also suggest that 40 percent of black children are growing up in poverty.[27]

William J. Wilson, a University of Chicago sociologist, is quoted in this issue of the *Chicago Reporter* as arguing that this poverty is new, different, and more severe than that faced by any previous generation of low-income Americans. He estimates that, nationwide, one-third of blacks, together with a much smaller proportion of whites, comprise a "vast underclass," a massive population at the very bottom of the social-class ladder plagued by poor education and low-paying, unstable jobs. The members of this underclass, says Wilson, "are in a hopeless state of economic stagnation, falling further behind the rest of society."[28]

The most comprehensive estimate of the number of Chicagoans living in persistent poverty was provided by the Mayor's Office of Employment and Training for use in job training programs. They gave the following estimates on the black economic condition:

• 586,000 Chicago teenagers and adults qualify for CETA's job training program for the "economically disadvantaged." More than 66 percent are black, and 12 percent are Latino.
• In Cook County 350,000 children and close to 300,000 adults are public-aid recipients. They form the largest and most permanent section of this disadvantaged population.
• The poorest people are concentrated in the low-income communities of the west and near south sides. Virtually all children and about half the adults are receiving Aid to Families with Dependent Children. Also on welfare are 60,000 General Assistance recipients, poor teenagers, and adults with no children to support and 100,000 recipients of Aid to the Aged, Blind and Disabled.
• Like welfare recipients, most of Chicago's unemployed are black. Some merely suffer what is known as "frictional" unemployment, a brief jobless spell while changing employers. But recent research has shown that most people on the jobless rolls are persistently unemployed.
• More than 100,000 Chicagoans are officially counted as unemployed. But these figures exclude most persistently jobless: people who are so discouraged they don't even try to find jobs. The number of prime working-age black men who have stopped looking for jobs has grown considerably in recent decades. Among men between ages twenty-five and thirty-four, 9 percent of blacks as compared to 4 percent of whites are counted by the federal government as "not in the labor force." [29]

The decline of manufacturing jobs (71 percent of blacks are employed in this sector), shifts of jobs to the suburbs and sunbelt states, and continued discrimination by labor unions does not argue well for black Chicago. It should be noted, however, that there has been an increase in the number of blacks hired by the city and private sector in the last ten years.[30] But this increase does not come close to offsetting the high level of poverty in the city.

From a political standpoint, it is these (lower income) voters that are the most vulnerable; they tend to be supporters of Mayor Byrne and black politicians that are loyal to the machine. And it is these voters that Mayor Byrne will rely on, should she run for a second term. In brief, Mayor Byrne's ploy to move into Cabrini-Green was not just a media extravaganza; it was a calculated political move to build her support in these and other low-income black areas. Thus, her insensitivity to the needs of middle-class blacks is balanced with her sensitivity to low-income people—her likely supporters. Those who think Mayor Byrne a fool need to think twice. Whether black low-income voters will buy her latest dramatic move is open to serious question. Mayor Byrne has proved, however, that the politics of theater is alive and well and has been put back on center stage in Chicago and the nation.

School Politics

Milton Rakove is fond of saying that everything that takes place in Chicago has significant political overtones. He is correct. The recent controversy over the selection of a school superintendent and over the replacement of two black male school board members with two white females illustrates this point. In the first case, a black school official for over twenty-seven years, Manfred Byrd, was rejected for the job, and the vote was along racial lines. All five blacks approved, but three Hispanics and three whites opposed. The black-Hispanic coalition that some had hoped for did not materialize. It was clearly a defeat for the black middle class and may suggest that a coalition by white ethnics and Hispanics is a real possibility. In this case, Mayor Byrne's ability to weld this coalition together with poorer blacks may help her reelection chances. Her success may depend on what other politicians decide to do—mainly Richard M. Daley (the son of the late mayor) and independent black politicians.

In the second case, the appointment of two whites has significant overtones. The real question is, Why would Mayor Byrne alienate black voters by reducing their representation at a time when their proportion of the school population is going up? The answer, according to Vernon Jarrett, lies in the *state* political area.

> Recently, Jane Byrne has had to justify her decision to replace two blacks with two whites on Chicago's Board of Education by pointing her finger at the Democratic leaders of the Illinois Legislature. They supposedly advised her to add two "white ethnics" to the board in order to assure a sorely needed tax increase for Chicago schools. Of course, the Democratic boss of the state Senate, Philip J. Rock (18th Dist.) and the leader of the House, Michael J. Madigan (27th Dist.) both deny ever tendering such outrageous advice to the Mayor.
>
> Byrne is probably right in pointing the finger at these people but her immoral judgment in the way she handled the school board appointments was a desperate political move on her part.[31]

The implications were clear: Unless Mayor Byrne appointed more whites to the board, the state legislature would not vote money for Chicago's schools—that is, to support a predominantly black student population. Jarrett also suggests that white machine politicians were sending another message to the black community and to regular black politicians.

> . . . a white politician in Chicago can be a regular Democrat while exercising accountability to and respect for his or her white constituents. But you black regular Democrats are to be loyal and respect only the white leadership of the Democratic party. . . .

There doesn't seem to be any question about how the regular Democrats who are white will react when the wishes of their constituents are at
stake. But the salient question is why don't the black regular Democrats
insist on their right to constituencies too? How long can they go on being
silent?[32]

School politics in Chicago, then, centers on race, politics, and money.
And while it is clear that black politicians are involved in the process, it is
not clear how long they will continue in their supporting role before they
seek a more important role in the play of power.

Regional Transportation Authority

The fiscal problems of the Regional Transportation Authority (RTA) illustrate the shift of political power from Chicago to the state capital. They
also raise another set of problems: the fight between Chicago and the
suburbs and the antagonism of downstate voters to the big city up north.
In short, the problems are fiscal, but the solution is highly political.

The cost of saving RTA is high, but nobody has really ascertained the
true cost. At present, it is estimated that RTA has debts that include about
$70 million in outstanding loans from the state; it is projected to go in the
hole about $80 million more by the end of 1981. Over the next five years,
to keep current transportation programs going, the RTA will face a shor-
tage of some $1.1 billion; this is needed just to meet operating expenses.
Currently, the RTA spends $10 million more a month than it takes in. At
this writing, suburban bus services are being curtailed and state and local
politicians are no closer to a solution than they were in March of 1981.
Solutions proposed to date have been opposed by downstate, suburban,
or Chicago politicians. Table 7.3 gives the revenue and expenditures for
RTA for 1975–81.[33]

Part of the RTA's fiscal problems stem from the fact that its costs are 77
to 85 percent labor intensive. The Chicago Transit Authority has about
13,000 drivers making around $35,000 a year. RTA has 362 employees.
Compensating board members cost the authority (RTA, CTA) $430,000,
not including upkeep of the two chairmen at $72,500 and $75,000, respectively, a year.

Solutions: City, Federal, State

Farebox increases are one solution, but Chicagoan's single-ride fare is
already 80 cents. And a fare increase is not likely to solve the basic fiscal
problem. Fare increases take care of the short run but are outstripped by
hikes in labor and fuel costs. In addition, high fares decrease ridership.

Political Problems

The federal government is going out of the subsidy business for cities. The suburbs provide a large amount of the loop workforce, and some 80 percent use public transportation. Yet they feel that RTA has shortchanged them, and they don't want to pay for a mass transit system they don't want and don't need. They feel that if the RTA shut down, they could still get to work. It would just take longer.

The city is looking to Springfield for a solution. The legislature has one: On March 18, 1981, the Senate Transportation Committee approved a bill sponsored by Philip Rock to allow the RTA to sell almost $1 billion in bonds to the state (to pay new bills, not to cover the present $73 million debt). But the governor has another solution: Thompson wants to tax oil

TABLE 7.3   RTA REVENUES AND EXPENSES FOR FISCAL YEARS 1975–81

(in millions)

Revenues	1975	1976	1977	1978	1979	1980 [a]	1981 (estimated)
Public Transportation Fund	113.2	105.0	114.4	126.8	138.3	83.0	—
Cook County and Chicago	—	—	5.0	5.0	5.0	5.0	5.0
Federal subsidy	—	49.4	49.6	49.3	79.9	130.6	30.8
Gas tax	—	—	—	43.5	74.9	34.0	1.5
Sales tax	—	—	—	—	—	229.6	292.5
Other	1.7	1.1	.9	2.4	5.7	10.3	3.7
TOTAL	114.9	155.5	169.9	227.0	303.8	492.8	333.5

Expenses							
Trans. Loan Act Obligation	12.0	—	—	—	—	—	—
Trans. grants to carriers	93.7	134.4	168.2	207.0	264.5	455.4	454.8
Transportation support	—	—	—	.2	2.5	8.4	9.9
Admin. and operating costs	1.2	3.7	7.4	13.3	16.0	44.3	45.2
Debt service	—	—	—	.9	2.6	16.2	21.0
TOTAL	106.9	138.1	175.6	221.4	285.6	508.1	509.8
NET BALANCE	8.0	17.3	(5.6)	5.5	16.4	(15.3)	176.3

SOURCE: Illinois Issues 7, no. 4 (April 1981): 6. FY 1975–79 from RTA annual reports: FY 1980–81 from the Metropolitan Housing and Planning Council, December 1980 RTA study.
[a] FY 1980 was made up of five quarters due to a change in the fiscal year from July 1–June 31 to October 1–September 31.

companies and use the money for downstate roads and the rest for RTA. At present, the governor is not having much success in selling his proposal. Thompson is likely to be hurt politically no matter what solution is found. The shutdown of the RTA would have statewide economic impact and cost significant losses of sales and income tax revenue to the state.

Political Impact on Blacks

Public transportation is the primary means for a lot of city blacks to get to their jobs: One of every three wage earners in the Chicago area rides mass transit to work; that amounts to approximately 875,000 people.

Loss of public transportation could lead to severe economic consequences for this group. Unable to commute to jobs, they may lose them. Or, trying to purchase other means of transportation could cut deep into their incomes, decreasing their purchasing power. And loss of economic power could mean loss of political power.

In general, loss of the mass transportation system is detrimental to the quality of life for city blacks, but it also may cause political mobilization to occur for the group. In brief, economic immobilization may lead to political mobilization for the losers. And unless things change, blacks tend to be the losers. The solution to this problem may well be one of the most heatedly debated programs in state, city, and suburban areas in the years ahead.[34]

Redistricting in Illinois: Implications for Black Representation in Chicago

Illinois no longer has the population to sustain 24 congressional seats and is therefore likely to lose two seats. The question is: How will it be done? Who gains and who loses? The prediction is that one of these seats will certainly come out of Chicago. The other prediction is that black representation is likely to suffer.

Chicago has lost an estimated 400,000 people since 1970, while the Cook County suburbs have gained 150,000 people. This is enough for Cook County to hold its proportion of seats in the U.S. House of Representatives. Of the 400,000 persons lost in Chicago, an estimated 97,000-plus come out of one district: the heavily black South Side First Congressional District.[35]

Solutions

According to Mark Gruenberg, there are several ways to solve the redistricting problem, including breaking the natural boundaries. One method is to preserve or strengthen the historic city-suburban differentiation in Cook County (see Figure 7.1).

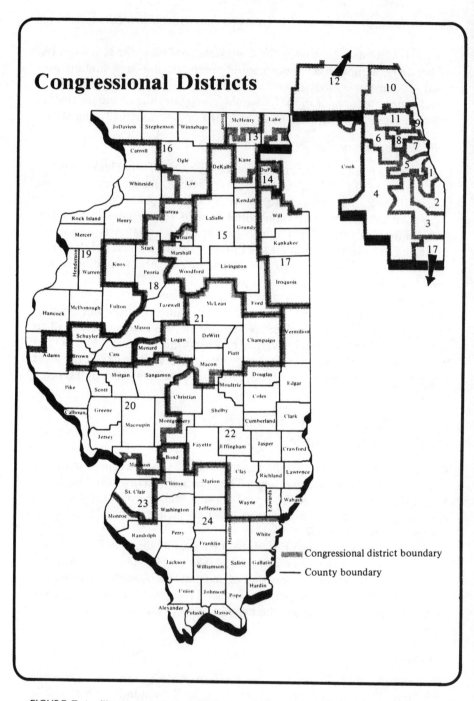

FIGURE 7.1 Illinois congressional districts (Peter W. Colby et al., **Illinois Elections:** [**Parties, Patterns, Reappointment, Consolidation.** Sangamon State University, Springfield, Ill., 1976. p. 43] p. 43).

Under this plan, the First District would be totally eliminated, with the bulk of it going to the Seventh and Second districts. The white-liberal Fifth Ward would be tacked on to the Fifth District, "effectively drowning its independent voters in a sea of pro-machine Bridgeport (and allied areas)—while keeping the Fifth a majority white area." The Second and Fourth wards, heavily black, would be tacked on to the black majority Seventh District.

The second method would break the city-suburban line, but only in the north. It would eliminate the North Shore Tenth District and split it between the Ninth and Eleventh districts; note that the object of this map is to *preserve* the First District's black majority and at the same time "rid the delegation of liberal Abner Mikva of the Tenth District" (Mikva is no longer a congressman).

The political problem with the first method is that by eliminating the First District, the legislature would be eliminating one of the two black representatives who now go to Washington. The problem with the second method is that the Eleventh and Third districts would become marginal districts for the Democrats, although this method would retain the two blacks.[36]

Robert Starks of Northeastern University in Chicago notes that there are three areas to concentrate on in congressional redistricting in Chicago: the First, Second, and Seventh districts. He says that all three have shown declines in population in spite of the fact that the overall black population has increased significantly. Stark says that not only are blacks underrepresented but that the black inner-city residents have a greater claim to the charge of underrepresentation than do the white suburbanites. His support: Blacks represent almost half of the city population, and if congressional representation reflects that reality, blacks should control half of the seats in the city congressional districts (4–6 seats).

A prime example of blacks getting robbed of representation is in the Fifth District. The Fifth District is a prime target for elimination or reconstruction in 1981; it falls more than 150,000 people short of "ideal" district size, according to the 1980 U.S. Census Bureau estimates. But, given the combination of political influence and tradeoffs that its powerful Eleventh Ward has at its disposal, it will try to maintain, and probably succeed in maintaining, its power by bargaining anything it can, including black interests.

Starks concluded that the districts with significant black populations, the First, Second, Fifth, Seventh, and Eighth, will show significant increases in black population in the new census.

It will be interesting to watch attempts to maneuver (i.e., gerrymander) 70 percent of the city's black population into two congressional districts, and spread the other 30 percent over the rest of the remaining districts, in an

attempt to dilute its power. Besides the numerical inequitability of the im-
pending decision, there is the issue of the quality of representation. The
ensuing battle implies that independent representation will be cut, and
machine representation will take another step towards reigning.
   It especially seems likely to happen since Byrne's handpicked James
Taylor is one of the legislators heading up the redistricting committee.[37]

Starks also says that James Taylor (26th) was "carefully chosen by the
Byrne factions to participate in the maintenance of the Democratic dominance of black politics in the city." [38]

New Development

This situation may in some way be a step forward for the black community. The redistricting debate has catalyzed a coalition of black legislators
into defensive action. According to L. Williams of the *Sun-Times,* a group
called the Black Elected Officials of Cook County, a coalition of more
than twenty of the state's top black politicians, have pledged "to resist
any effort to reduce the number of black Congressmen from Illinois."
Williams says they are "sincere"; they are working with computer experts and may hire a legal staff to devise proposed maps of congressional
districts.[39]
   Reapportionment in Chicago, then, may mean that blacks may lose not
only a congressional seat, but an independent seat. It seems that in addition to a political participation battle on one level, black independent
politicians now are battling the machine on another level: the politics of
reapportionment, drawing lines that could make or break a faction. The
historic part about the situation is that they are fighting back; the black
community is not accepting the inequitable as the inevitable.

Conclusion

Black politics in Chicago offers a direct challenge to some of the key
assumptions underlying the new black politics. For example, the assumption that black leaders share a community of interest and thus would
operate in a collective fashion in the interest of the black community is not
true in Chicago. Black regular Democrats vote their self-interest over the
needs and desires of their constituents. Independents, while more accountable than the regulars, do not have the numbers to change outcomes. It may be that we should not be surprised at the lack of unity. It is
as evident among major civil rights leaders as it is among black politicians
in Chicago.[40] In an ideal world, this would not be a major problem; but in
a situation where forces are aligned against a group, it is, to a large degree,
dysfunctional.

Another assumption challenged is the belief in the power of numbers. In Chicago, at least at present, the power of numbers has been limited. Black voters have helped elect officials, but most of these officials have not been responsive to black needs. It should be noted again that the machine aspect of Chicago politics might set these officials apart from other black elected officials, though I doubt it.

Black Chicago politics does seem to confirm one of the major assumptions of the new black politics—that black voters are beginning to use the vote to reward friends and punish enemies (both black and white). Since 1975, black voters have become antimachine; and it is important to acknowledge that they, rather than whites, are the leaders in the independent political movement in Chicago.

This chapter also illustrates how broader political issues raise potential challenges to electoral politics. For example, the redistricting process may determine to a large degree the amount of political influence that blacks are likely to gain or lose in the country in the 1980s. Black Chicago's representation, as elsewhere, will depend on the creativity of political artists (normally not a powerful force in American politics). It is also clear that even when they desire to do so, black politicians are limited in what they can do about poor economic conditions. And the poverty that exists in Chicago, as in other large urban areas, will severely constrain the effectiveness of black elected officials.

It may well be that we need to evaluate the new black politics in a different manner. The point here is that by focusing on the limitations, we may lose sight of the opportunities. Limitations may well define the objective conditions that exist today for black politicians, but they do not describe the future opportunities. It is the vision to see what is possible and how to achieve it that will give black political leaders their special significance in the future.

My argument here is that, given the demographic and political changes taking place in this country, strong black political leadership will be needed *more* rather than *less* in the years ahead. For example, the 1980 census showed that whites are continuing to leave most central cities in large numbers; this means that blacks will become majorities in these cities, if they are not already so. It is also clear that unorganized majorities are likely to be as powerless as unorganized minorities. It is here that black political leadership can play its most important role.

A strong black political leadership can provide organization, resources, and linkages to significant others in ways that benefit the black community. They can help educate and mobilize citizens to the realities of politics—what is possible and how to achieve it. To be successful in the future, these politicians must learn how to link politics with economics. There is ample evidence to suggest that a strong, well-organized political organization can encourage economic investment. Mayor Maynard Jackson of Atlanta came to this conclusion—and it seems to have been successful. Economic growth and development can also ensure a stable and strong political organization. Mayor Jackson, for example, insisted on minority participation in all jobs and building programs by companies doing business with the city. Boston has also developed a job set-aside program that will guarantee minority residents and other Boston citizens access to these new jobs. A black political leadership with vision can explore these as well as develop other options that will be beneficial to its constituents.

Finally, it should be clear that the needs of black citizens are not the sole responsibility of black elected officials. Politics has its limits. Nevertheless, when political leaders combine their efforts with other black leaders—in education, business, civil rights and protest organizations—plus an enlightened black community, politics can become a key instrument for social change for black Americans.

Notes

1. See, for example, Eddie N. Williams, "Black Political Progress in the 1970s: The Electoral Arena," Chapter 4 in this volume.
2. For a more detailed discussion of these assumptions and implications, see Michael B. Preston, "Limitations of Black Urban Power: The Case of Black Mayors," in *The New Urban Politics* (Cambridge, MA: Ballinger, 1976), pp. 111–30; also see Michael B. Preston, "Black Elected Officials and Public Policy: Symbolic or Substantive Representation?" *Policy Studies Journal* 7, no. 2 (December 1978): 196–200.
3. Basil Talbott, Jr., "Windy City Going Gustless," *Chicago Sun-Times*, December 24, 1979.
4. Michael B. Preston, "Black Politics in the Post-Daley Era," in *Chicago Politics After Daley*, ed. Louis Masotti and Samuel K. Gove (Urbana: University of Illinois Press, 1981). Some of the information in this section is drawn from that chapter. In other sections I draw on an earlier version, "Black Machine Politics in the Post-Daley Era," in *The Chicago Political Papers*, ed. Louis Masotti, Robert L. Lineberry, and Samuel K. Gove (Evanston, IL: Center for Urban Affairs, Northwestern University; and Urbana, IL: Institute of Government and Public Affairs, University of Illinois, 1979).
5. Preston, "Black Machine Politics in the Post-Daley Era," p. 2.
6. Robert L. Lineberry, *Government in America: People, Politics, and Policy* (Boston: Little, Brown, 1980), p. 8.
7. Ken Watson, "Minorities at Record Levels in General Assembly," *Globe Democrat*, March 11, 1981, p. 3.
8. Of the 16 black aldermen, 3 are independents. However, McFolling, elected as an Independent (17th), has resigned, and Mayor Byrne has appointed Allan Streeter to his position. Streeter is a Byrne loyalist.

9. "Ballot Power, Patronage Elude Black Ward Committeemen," *Chicago Reporter* 8, no. 6 (June 1979): 11.
10. Ibid., p. 2.
11. Paula Wilson, in *Chicago Reporter* 7, no. 1 (January 1978): 4–5.
12. "Ballot Power, Patronage Elude Black Ward Committeemen," p. 1.
13. Preston, "Black Machine Politics in the Post-Daley Era," pp. 6–8.
14. "New Poverty Traps 600,000 Chicagoans—Permanently," *Chicago Reporter* 9, no. 2 (February 1980): 1.
15. Preston, "Black Machine Politics in the Post-Daley Era," pp. 5–6.
16. Wilson, in *Chicago Reporter,* pp. 4–5.
17. Aldermen Shaw, Barnett, and Borden.
18. Vernon Jarrett, "Board Vote Tests Blacks' Loyalties," *Chicago Tribune,* March 22, 1981.
19. Robert Davis, "Panel OKs Two Whites For School Board," *Chicago Tribune,* March 25, 1981.
20. Much of the material in this section is drawn from Preston, "Black Machine Politics in the Post-Daley Era," pp. 28–38.
21. Ibid.
22. "Black Aldermen Search for New Power in Post-Daley Era," *Chicago Reporter* 7, no. 1 (January 1978): 1–6 and 7.
23. Ibid., p. 7.
24. Jacqueline Thomas, "Black Voters Send Message to the Machine: You Need Us," *Chicago Sun-Times,* March 24, 1981.
25. Kathleen A. Kemp and Robert L. Lineberry, "The Last of the Great Urban Machines and the Last of the Great Urban Mayors?" in Masotti, Lineberry, and Gove, *The Chicago Politics Papers,* p. 25.
26. Preston, "Black Machine Politics in the Post-Daley Era," p. 7.
27. "New Poverty Traps 600,000 Chicagoans—Permanently," pp. 1 and 4.
28. Ibid., p. 4.
29. Ibid., pp. 4–5.
30. Preston, "Black Machine Politics in the Post-Daley Era," pp. 7–9.
31. Vernon Jarrett, in *Chicago Tribune,* February 20, 1981.
32. Ibid.
33. Shelley Davis, "RTA Crisis: Not the First, but the Worst," *Illinois Issues* 7, no. 4 (April 1981): 5–6. The sales tax category, beginning in 1980, results from the Thompson/Byrne plan. The plan was to eliminate both the state subsidy (about $138 million in 1979) and the unpopular two-year-old 5 percent tax on gas (approximately $175 million in 1979). In their place was to be a new surtax on sales of 1 percent in Cook County and one-quarter percent in the five collar counties. The total revenue estimate under the Thompson/Byrne plan was $300 million annually. Actual sales tax revenues were $280 million.
34. An important blow to Chicago if the system shut down would be the impact on businessmen. "A shutdown is also bad for business, both at the state and metro levels. When the transit system in Boston stopped rolling for just one day in December, the losses were around $6 million. Predictions are that Chicago, and Illinois, would experience a worse blow" if RTA shut down in northeastern Illinois. Davis, "RTA Crisis," p. 7.

35. Population projections provided by the U.S. Department of Commerce, Bureau of the Census, 1980 Census of Population.
36. Mark Gruenberg, "Musical Chairs in Congressional Redistricting: Illinois May Lose One Seat," in *Illinois Elections,* ed. Peter W. Colby, David H. Everson, and Paul Michael Green (Springfield, IL: Sangamon State University, 1979), pp. 41–46. Also see Charles W. Wheeler III, "Reapportionment Begins Now," same source, pp. 46–53.
37. Robert Terry Starks, "Congressional and Legislative Redistricting in Illinois: Implications for Black Chicago" (speech given at a conference on redistricting in Illinois, sponsored by the Department of Journalism and Institute of Government and Public Affairs, University of Illinois, Urbana, February 7, 1981), p. 6.
38. Ibid., p. 4.
39. Lillian Williams, "Blacks Vow Fight for U.S. Seats," *Chicago Sun-Times,* March 3, 1981.
40. For an excellent review of this problem, see Charles V. Hamilton, "On Black Leadership," in *The State of Black America 1981* (New York: National Urban League, 1981), pp. 258–62.

EIGHT

Cleveland: The Rise and Fall of The New Black Politics[1]

William E. Nelson, Jr.

One of the more salient aspects of black life in the 1970s was the shift in the movement for black freedom from protest to electoral politics. This shift was manifested in the tapering off in frequency and intensity of protest activity and a concomitant increase in campaigns to elect black politicians to key public offices. By the mid-1970s the idea that electoral politics provided the best avenue for advancing black interests had gained broad acceptance in the black community.[2] Black attitudes regarding the efficiency of electoral politics were shaped, in part, by the significant gains registered by blacks in the electoral arena in the 1960s and '70s. Between 1964 and 1974 the number of blacks holding public office increased from 914 to 2,991. This increase reflected a growth in the number of black mayors from 29 in 1968 to 108 in 1974; it also reflected a dramatic increase from 1964 to 1974 in the number of blacks serving in the U.S. House of Representatives (from 5 to 17) and in state legislative bodies (from 94 to 239).[3] In fact, between 1965 and 1975, few areas of local, state, and national government were unaffected by the powerful upsurge in electoral activity occurring in the black community.

The emergence of the black community to a level of broad participation and unassailable influence represents an important dimension of what has been widely proclaimed as the new black politics. At bottom the new black politics is a politics of social and economic transformation based on the mobilization of community power. A central premise of this approach to black political life is the notion that genuine progress can be made only if the pursuit of community goals is placed ahead of individual goals as an organizing priority. Proponents of the new black politics believe very strongly that the most potent form of power available to black America is power that emanates from the collective action of the community. Those who would seek to represent the community in public life must have their roots planted in the cultural and institutional network of the community and must manifest an unabashed concern for the enlargement of the community's impact on the policy-making process.[4]

The new black politics represents an effort by black political leaders to capitalize on the increasing size of the black electorate; the strategic position of black voters in many cities, counties, and congressional districts; and the growing political consciousness of the black population. It constitutes an immensely serious effort to build bases of electoral strength in the black community and organize black political interests around the power of the vote.

Bayard Rustin, in an article published in 1965, first called attention to the need for the black community to develop its potential power in the electoral arena.[5] Pointing to the limited success of protest activity in changing the social and economic position of blacks in the American social order, Rustin called for the subordination of direct-action techniques to a strategy calculated to build community institutions capable of providing a base of power for the black community in the political process.

Since the publication of Rustin's article, the idea of institution building has been expanded to embrace the concept of political independence. In contrast to traditional machine politics, which facilitated the control of black political preferences from the outside, the new black politics hoped to place the resources of the black community totally under black control. The electoral power of the black community would be independent in the sense that it would be permanently wedded to neither of the major political parties. Rather, it would oscillate between the two parties, forging coalitions and striking bargains on terms calculated to maximize the impact of the black community in the policy-making process.[6] The idea of political independence was best expressed in the slogan of the Black Congressional Caucus: "We have no permanent friends, no permanent enemies, just permanent interests." Committed unswervingly to the goal of community advancement, independent organizations would emerge from the ashes of moribund political machines to undertake the critical tasks of political education, candidate recruitment, government lobbying, and the mass mobilization of black voters.

Significant movement toward the actual building of independent black power bases was stimulated by the development of black majorities in key jurisdictions and the decreasing capacity of the Democratic party to hold blacks in its electoral coalition. The rebellion of the Mississippi Freedom Democratic party, the formation of the Lowndes County Freedom Organization, and the realization of independence by nations on the African continent all served as powerful inducements to the formation of independent political movements by grass-roots, community-oriented black groups.

The new black politics looked inward to the reservoir of strength in the black community for the power required to move the struggle for black freedom to higher levels. By electing a "new breed" of politician to public office and by the unification of the black masses through community-based institutions, it was hoped that the social and economic position of the black community would be transformed. In places where they represented electoral majorities, blacks would take over local governments and reorient policy priorities toward a concern for the vital needs of the black community. Wherever blacks existed in significant numbers, the prevailing power structure would be compelled to address itself to the welfare of black citizens. In this sense, the new black politics would become an instrument of social change, permanently eradicating obstacles to the upward mobility and continuing progress of the entire black community.

Despite significant gains in the election of blacks to public office since 1965, the policy goals of the new black politics have not been realized. Social and economic conditions in the black community have not been dramatically transformed. Black politicians have encountered enormous difficulty in their efforts to use the authority of their public offices to deliver meaningful benefits to their black constituents.[7] In part, the problems they have encountered in transferring benefits reflect the failure of the black community to maintain viable institutional mechanisms for mobilizing black political interests. The experience of the black community with the new black politics reveals a significant gap between theory and practice. This chapter examines the difficulties inherent in the effort to build a new power base for the black community through the electoral process. The focus of the study is on transitions in the political status of the black community in Cleveland, Ohio, since the late 1960s.

The Emergence of a New Black Politics

Before the 1960s, Cleveland, Ohio, had the reputation of being a city blessed with extraordinarily good relations between blacks and whites. In many respects the reputation was undeserved. Many Cleveland citizens equated good race relations with an absence of racial conflict. But the relatively tranquil environment did not prevent the buildup of black grievances against widespread practices of racial discrimination.[8] During the 1940s and '50s black anger was held in check through the diplomatic maneuverings of the NAACP. In the 1960s, however, the NAACP's leadership role was overshadowed by the work of more militant civil rights organizations committed to the strategy of street-level confrontation.

Militant civil rights protests provided the basis for the emergence of a new form of black politics in Cleveland. Since the 1930s the black community had functioned as an integral part of the Democratic party coalition that dominated politics in Cleveland. Although heavily reliant on black votes, the Cuyahoga County Democratic party adamantly refused to share power with the black community. Blacks were never elected or appointed to major party positions, were deprived of substantial patronage benefits, and were sponsored for elective office only for councilman's positions in wards that were overwhelmingly black.

The civil rights movement in Cleveland created a corps of new black politicians committed to establishing a power base for the black community in Cleveland politics. They were convinced that this could best be done by unifying the electoral strength of the black community behind the candidacy of a prominent black politician for mayor. In 1965 Carl Stokes was tapped for this role. Stokes was a native of Cleveland, a lawyer, and a veteran in the civil rights movement. He had run unsuccessfully for the Ohio House of Representatives in 1960; two years later he tossed his hat in the ring for this position again and won, becoming the first black Democrat to serve in the Ohio legislature.

The Stokes candidacy in 1965 took on the character of a community crusade. Stokes and his supporters made a strategic decision to bypass the Democratic primary when it became clear that three white candidates would be in the race—the Democratic and Republican nominees and a white independent. Blacks constituted approximately 40 percent of the registered voters in Cleveland in 1965. With the white vote split three ways, it was clear to Stokes that he would have an excellent chance for victory if he could mobilize a large black vote in his behalf. To achieve this, Stokes established a grassroots campaign organization composed mainly of political amateurs. This campaign structure was successful in overriding the traditional mechanisms of party control in the black community and forging political ties between Stokes and rank-and-file black voters. Enthusiasm for Stokes reached such a high pitch that a number of black citizens who had never before participated in an election were motivated to register and cast a vote for Stokes in the 1965 general election.

Stokes' campaign for mayor in 1965 was unsuccessful. He was defeated by the incumbent Democrat, Ralph Locher, by a margin of 2,142 votes. In many respects, however, Stokes was a victor in defeat.[9] Stokes was able to turn out an unprecedented 72 percent of the black vote and to persuade 85 percent of the blacks who turned out to vote for him. Stokes'

1965 campaign destroyed the myths that blacks are politically apathetic and that a black candidate does not have a chance of being elected.

The 1965 campaign established the foundation for Stokes' eventual election in 1967. In the 1967 Democratic primary, Stokes established a sophisticated campaign organization that successfully reunited thousands of Cleveland citizens and college students to work as street-level volunteers. The Stokes campaign created a bandwagon effect that united most of the black community around his candidacy. Although the demographic character of the electorate required Stokes to wage a vigorous campaign for white votes, the key to his victory in both the primary and general elections was the extremely strong support he was able to generate in the black community.[10]

The outcome of the 1967 mayoral contest represented not only a personal triumph for Stokes but the ascendancy of the black community to a position of commanding influence and power in the Cleveland political system.[11] By and large, Stokes' victory represented a massive uprising by the black community against the system of domestic colonialism with which they were confronted. In the summer of 1966, black rebellion in Cleveland had taken the form of several days of rioting in the depressed Hough area. Cleveland officials dismissed the rebellion as acts of wanton violence by hoodlums and communists. The anger of black citizens was still smoldering during the fall of 1967 when Carl Stokes was running for mayor; this time their response took the form of a driving determination to elevate a member of their community to the highest public office in the city.

Stokes interpreted his election victory as a mandate for change. Adopting an activist-entrepreneur style of leadership, he sought to realize the goals of the new black politics by bringing the administrative apparatus of city government to bear on pressing black problems. Almost immediately on taking public office, Stokes launched a vigorous search for funds to begin the construction of new low- and moderate-income housing for the black poor. By the end of his second term he had succeeded in actually building 5,496 units of such housing at a cost of more than $102 million.[12] Stokes attempted to improve the financial position of the black community by employing more than 270 minority individuals in professional positions in city government at an annual aggregate income of more than $3 million.[13] In addition, he assisted black businesses by initiating a policy that encouraged competitive bidding by black firms for city contracts. This policy was accompanied by threats from the mayor to deny city contracts to white-dominated companies and unions that engaged in practices of employment discrimination.

Stokes' most ambitious community development effort was a fund-raising venture called Cleveland Now, which sought to raise $177 million over a period of eighteen months. Its purpose was to attack problems in such areas as employment, health and welfare, and neighborhood rehabilitation. The bulk of these funds was to be targeted for depressed sectors of the black community.[14] During the first phase of the campaign more than $5,678,000 was raised. These funds in turn earned over $188,000 in interest.

A Declaration of Political Independence

Stokes' commitment to change compelled him to take steps to build a strong enduring base of power for the black community in the city's political system. This required, first and foremost, the unification of black councilmen under one political banner. Cleveland's ward system for the election of city councilmen had established over the years a highly fragmented political power structure in the black community. Black councilmen tended to focus their attention on the problems of their individual wards rather than on issues affecting the black community as a whole. This tendency toward parochialism fostered conflict and competition among black councilmen representing different constituencies and a myriad of social, economic, and political interests. Stokes attempted to dilute the tension in these relationships by persuading black councilmen to work together in his campaign. After the election he sought to mold them into a political bloc that would lobby in support of his policies in the city council.

During his first term in office, Stokes recognized that he would not be successful in his efforts to reform Cleveland city government without a political organization that sought to unify all black Democratic politicians—including Democratic ward committeemen—under the banner of a separate black caucus. The need for such an organization became clear in the wake of efforts by white Democrats to sabotage many of his most important legislative initiatives.

Democratic party attacks against Stokes were led by City Council President James Stanton, who fought Stokes on every issue. Stanton's opposition to Stokes' legislative program was so devastating that Stokes accused him of stopping the wheels of government single-handedly.[15] By the end of his first term, Stokes' relations with the party were so poor that a serious effort was mounted by forces inside the party to deny him the nomination for a second term. When it became clear that Stokes would get the party's endorsement, Stanton and his supporters were so angered that they boycotted the executive committee session at which official action on this issue was to be taken.[16]

Shortly after his reelection in 1969, Stokes took the lead in forming the Twenty-first District Democratic Caucus. The name of the organization reflected the geographic concentration of blacks in the Twenty-first Congressional District; it also signaled the intention of the organization to operate within the framework of the Democratic party.

The key consideration underlying the formation of the caucus was the need to make the Democratic party in Cuyahoga County responsive to the needs and interests of the black community. Members of the caucus noted the failure of the party over the years to support blacks for key positions either within the party or in the broader public sector. They reasoned that this situation would change only if black politicians joined together to pressure the party leadership for representation, patronage, and other concrete benefits.

The caucus mounted its first challenge to the party in May 1970. It forcefully objected when the Party Policy Committee did not consult caucus representatives about the selection of candidates for party positions. Arnold Pinckney, vice-chairman of the caucus, threatened a massive withdrawal of black Democrats from the party if the caucus was not allowed significant input into the party's decision-making process: "If we cannot have a voice in the Democratic party, maybe it is time the black people determined they do not belong to either party. Maybe it is time we traded off with both parties." [17] When final party selections were made, Stokes denounced them as unrepresentative of the interests of black people and declared that because of the party's action, he would no longer associate with the county Democratic party organization:

> So far as I am concerned, nobody asked me and I was not included in the original talks that were held to make up the structure that was adopted by the convention. I consider this a serious affront to the mayor. At this point I know that what they subsequently did (at the convention) is not binding on me. They can't exclude the mayor of the eighth largest city from their talks in the development of the party, then expect him to ratify their talks and actions. [18]

The decision by Stokes to disavow the party was a prelude to the eventual withdrawal of the caucus as a whole from the party organization. At its first regular meeting after the county convention, the caucus passed a resolution prohibiting all elected officials, ward leaders, or precinct committeemen associated with the caucus from holding office in the Democratic party organization or accepting membership on the executive committee. The caucus also decided to put forth its own slate of candidates for the November election. Translating the meaning of the caucus actions, Arnold Pinckney told newsmen, "We are not out of the Democratic party, we are temporarily out of the Cuyahoga Democratic party." [19]

The final break with the county party organization came in the wake of the caucus announcement that it was endorsing ten Republicans as well as Democrats in the November election. Congressman Charles A. Vanik retaliated by announcing that he would not nominate Representative

Louis Stokes to the House Appropriation Committee since, as a member of the caucus, he was no longer a loyal Democrat. When Mayor Stokes received word of Vanik's position, he observed that this sealed off any possibility of a reconciliation between the caucus and the county party organization. Rejecting Vanik's offer to nominate Congressman Stokes if the caucus moved back into the party, 400 members of the caucus unanimously adopted a resolution to withdraw permanently from the party by dropping the word "Democratic" from the caucus's title in papers of incorporation filed with the secretary of state of Ohio.

Ascendancy of the Stokes Machine

Under the leadership of Carl Stokes, the Twenty-first Congressional District Caucus emerged as one of the most powerful political organizations in Cuyahoga County. Maintaining an open membership to maximize participation by rank-and-file citizens, the caucus boasted a paid membership of 700 to 1,000 individuals. General meetings of the organization drew an average attendance of 500. With a candidate screening process in place, the caucus began making political endorsements across party lines. Establishing organizational networks that paralleled the regular party ward structure, the caucus was able to establish firm control over the black vote in Cuyahoga County. In doing so, it began to take on the characteristics of a powerful urban machine.

Evidence of the political clout of the caucus began to surface in the 1970 party primaries. For example, the caucus gave a powerful boost to the candidacy of Howard Metzenbaum, who was running for the U.S. Senate against a well-known black physician, Kenneth Clement. Dr. Clement had aroused the anger of some caucus members by resigning a position in the Stokes administration and joining forces with the Stanton camp. The caucus not only endorsed Metzenbaum but worked energetically in his behalf; as a consequence, Metzenbaum ran exceptionally well in the black community. Blacks gave Metzenbaum the margin of difference he needed to win the primary. Caucus members also took credit in the 1970 primaries for the defeat of incumbent state legislators Thomas Hill and Philip DeLaine.[20]

The most important test of the caucus's political influence came in the general election when the caucus endorsed Seth Taft for county commissioner. Taft was a long-time Republican who had come extremely close to defeating Carl Stokes for mayor in 1967. In 1970 Taft was running for county commissioner against Frank M. Gorman, who had won the Democratic primary over black Cleveland councilman Leo Jackson. In the general election a calculated decision was made by caucus leaders to make the race between Taft and Gorman the criticalest of its power, demonstrating once and for all that the caucus was a force to be reckoned with in Cuyahoga County politics. In the words of one Cleveland citizen, "It was a matter of Stokes and the caucus telling the Democratic party—man, we're for real, and if you don't do business with us, we'll elect your opponent." [21]

An all-out effort was mounted by caucus members to elect Taft to the county commission. The mobilization activities in the black community were a smashing success. Taft calculated he needed 20 percent of the black vote to win. A poll conducted by his organization before the caucus endorsement indicated that he could expect a maximum of 18 percent of the black vote. Running with the backing of the caucus, Taft received an unprecedented 48 percent of the black vote, easily defeating Gorman for the county commissioner position. [22]

This display of political clout continued to manifest itself in the 1971 primary elections. Due primarily to the work of the caucus and the personal endorsement of Carl Stokes, James Carney upset Anthony J. Garafoli, council president, in the Democratic primary for mayor. Perhaps even more impressive was the fact that the caucus won every council and state representative race in which it was involved. Demonstrating its political clout, the caucus severely punished three black politicians who had refused to support Stokes' legislative program in the council. All three went down to defeat. One assessment of the election estimated that Stokes would control 40 percent of the council vote when the new council was installed, making the Twenty-first District Caucus the only real opposition party in the council. [23] A ward-by-ward analysis of the vote revealed that candidates supported by the caucus had chalked up decisive majorities. After this election, Stokes was being touted as the boss of the most powerful urban machine in the country. This fact led to a nearly universal conclusion that black political power had become an institutionalized and unalterable reality in the Cleveland political system. Blacks were said to be in a position to make demands for social and economic changes that the white power structure could no longer ignore.

Conflict and Political Decline

In retrospect, descriptions of the caucus as a stable and invincible force in the Cleveland political system overestimated the extent to which a new black politics had taken root in Cleveland's black community. Much of the success of the caucus turned on the personal popularity, charisma, and political sagacity of Carl Stokes. It was therefore inevitable that political momentum would be lost and organizational prowess diminished in the wake of Stokes' dramatic announcement in April 1971 that he would not seek a third term as mayor of Cleveland.

Decline in the caucus's power was not immediate. Stokes attempted to avert such a decline by passing the mantle of executive power to one of his chief lieutenants, Arnold Pinkney. In doing so, Stokes suffered one of the worst defeats in his political career. Following the strategy adopted in 1965, Pinkney decided to bypass the Democratic primary and run as an independent in the general election. In the absence of a black candidate in the primary, Stokes decided to endorse James Carney, a millionaire real estate broker, over Anthony Garafoli, who was running with the strong backing of the county organization. At the same time he was asking the black community to support Carney in the primary, Stokes was composing a letter urging blacks to support Pinkney in the general election. Both Pinkney and Councilman George Forbes were strongly opposed to the strategy because they believed it would create confusion and anxiety in the minds of the black voters. In an interview, Pinkney said:

> The letter stated clearly that he [Stokes] supported my candidacy but since I was not in the primary he was asking black people to support Jim Carney and support Arnold Pinkney in the general election. He wanted to go out to the radio station and come out publicly for Carney. Forbes and I opposed it. Of course, we could not afford to get into an argument with Stokes. Because of his popularity and base I needed him to win. Reluctantly, we went along with it.[24]

As Pinkney had predicted, Stokes' strategy of endorsing two candidates backfired. In Cleveland the general election is held within weeks of the primary election. Many blacks were unable to make the political transition from Carney to Pinkney in such a short period of time. The upshot was that Carney and Pinkney split the black vote, allowing Ralph Perk, the Republican candidate, to ride into city hall on the back of solid support from Cleveland's west side ethnic communities.

In the face of the loss of the mayoralty to the Republicans and Stokes' departure to New York to work as a television journalist, the black power base that Stokes had so carefully crafted began to crumble.[25] With the Republicans now in charge of city patronage, both the caucus and the county organization began to reassess the wisdom of their continuing conflict. In this regard black City Councilman George Forbes observed, "One of the lessons we learned from the election is that blacks cannot elect a mayor without whites and the Democratic party cannot elect a mayor without blacks."[26]

Pressure on black elected officials associated with the caucus to return to the party was immense. Cut off from patronage at the city level, many of them began to express grave concern that their ward organizations would dry up if they were not given access to patronage controlled by the Democrats at the county and state levels.

The base of politics is the patronage system . . . once we lost the mayor's chair we no longer had the patronage of the mayor's office and without the Democratic party's patronage we had nothing. We couldn't get jobs for people who were working for us. As Perk put them out of jobs—which he did—we had nowhere else for them to turn. The lack of patronage by the caucus was the fallacy in it. You must be able to back up the protest with delivery. Everything we went after we won but we still had to feed our people.[27]

In response to strong urgings from black elected officials, the leaders of the caucus began negotiating with county party officials over terms for the return of the caucus into the county party organization. The chief conditions agreed to by the leaders for both sides were that blacks would get one-third of county jobs under the party's control, a caucus representative would be named a cochairman of the county party organization, black councilmen would support a party regular for president of the Cleveland City Council, black councilmen would be appointed chairpersons and members of major councilmanic committees, and the control of patronage in black council wards would be placed in the hands of city councilmen.

The decision to return to the party fold was not universally applauded. W. O. Walker, editor of the *Call and Post* and the most powerful black Republican in Ohio, strongly criticized the caucus for abandoning its independent posture. Walker noted that it would be impossible for many black Republicans to continue to affiliate with an organization that was, in effect, a satellite of the Democratic party.

Eventually, unresolved issues relating to the return of the caucus to the party sparked an intense struggle for power among the top leadership of the caucus. Chief participants in this power struggle were Arnold Pinkney, George Forbes, and Congressman Louis Stokes. Forbes and Stokes clashed over the appointment of a member of the caucus to the cochairmanship of the county party organization. Although Forbes claimed a right to the position because he had helped create it, Stokes stepped forward and virtually demanded that he be given the position.[28] Stokes' position prevailed, leaving Forbes and his supporters extremely disgruntled. Labeling Stokes' action a blatant power grab, several black councilmen and state legislators threatened to bolt the caucus.

Stokes, Pinkney, and Forbes made a valiant attempt to patch up their differences. To avert open warfare, they agreed that leadership responsibilities would be divided among them. Under this arrangement, Stokes agreed to resign the party cochairmanship in favor of Forbes; Arnold Pinkney would take over the leadership of the caucus as its executive director; and Stokes would retain his seat in Congress without fear of opposition from Forbes and Pinkney.

This marriage of convenience enjoyed a brief honeymoon and then fell apart. An enormous split between Stokes, on the one side, and Pinkney and Forbes, on the other, was provoked by a caucus decision to endorse Albert Porter over Ralph Tyler, a black Republican, for the position of county engineer.[29] Stokes was bitterly opposed to the Porter endorsement because of Porter's treatment of Stokes' brother Carl in earlier elections, and because he considered Porter a racist. He accused Pinkney of illegally manipulating caucus procedures in favor of the Porter endorsement by refusing to read a letter he wrote in opposition to the endorsement to the general membership of the caucus. Pinkney responded that he was opposed to the Tyler endorsement on the grounds that the caucus, in returning to the Democratic party, had pledged to support all Democrats. He viewed Stokes' position as a violation of that pledge.

Taking advantage of his authority as chairman of the caucus, Louis Stokes called a special meeting of the caucus to reconsider the Porter endorsement. Acting decisively, Stokes rammed through an amendment to the constitution abolishing the position of executive director held by Pinkney and placing all administrative authority in his own hands. The amendment was approved by voice vote in an atmosphere so tense and chaotic that many persons questioned the validity of Stokes' decision that the yeas were greater than the nays. Action taken by the caucus on this issue had the effect of reducing Pinkney's status to that of a sixth vice-chairman. Given an opportunity to respond, Pinkney denounced the action of the caucus and indicated he would no longer be part of an organization characterized by one-man rule. Pinkney was followed to the rostrum by George Forbes, who sharply rebuked the caucus for removing Pinkney from his administrative position and reducing his own status to fifth vice-chairman. Because of Stokes' actions, Forbes also indicated that he would no longer be affiliated with the caucus.

The bitter dispute leading to the departure of Pinkney and Forbes effectively marked the death of the Twenty-first District Caucus as a viable political organization. Within weeks of the meeting in which Stokes took command of the caucus, all but a few black elected officials had permanently dropped their membership in the caucus. With the mass exodus of black elected officials, the caucus changed its political orientation. Decisively defeated in the 1973 elections by a rival slate headed by George Forbes, the caucus ceased its policy of endorsing candidates, except for Congressman Stokes, and concentrated its attention on civic, social, and religious affairs.

The death of the Twenty-first District Caucus has had a catastrophic effect on the political influence of the black community in Cleveland politics. Since the demise of the caucus, no effective organization has emerged to undertake the critical tasks of voter education, candidate recruitment, voter registration, and electoral political mobilization. Reminiscent of the pre-Carl Stokes years, black politics in Cleveland has reverted to a predominantly ward-based concentration. Few black politicians aspire to positions whose constituencies are broader than the black community.[30] Currently, no institutional mechanism exists for organizing black political resources, mapping out long-range strategies, and maximizing the impact of the black vote on the electoral process.

Initiative for the formation of such an organization would logically spring from the ranks of council ward organizations under the direction of Council President George Forbes. At the moment, Forbes appears disinclined to encourage the building of a citywide organization to coordinate the mobilization of black influence in the electoral process. Unquestionably, Forbes is the most powerful active black politician in Cleveland. As council president, he has accumulated enormous personal power; his control over council Democrats has been nearly absolute. During the Kucinich administration, he orchestrated the city's economic recovery program, consistently blocking the mayor's efforts to enact an increase in the city's income tax without first selling the city's interest in the Municipal Light Company. Forbes has not sought to utilize his personal power to build a base of effective political influence in the black community. Instead, he has concentrated on cultivating ties with the business community and serving as an effective bridge between the black community and the leadership structure of the Cuyahoga County Democratic party. On this score he has sometimes been strongly criticized by grass-roots blacks for being too establishment oriented and too aloof from the basic issues affecting the welfare of the black underclass. Persons holding this view claim that Forbes is politically vulnerable because he is out of touch with his constituents.

> The clout that Forbes wields today does not come from the community but from the business structure. If he were seriously challenged, he would have a difficult time being reelected. In the last election, out of 4,000 potential voters in his ward, he received only 1,800 votes to 300 for his opponent. A serious candidate willing to put together a solid grass-roots organization could steal that ward right from under his nose.[31]

Whatever the community's view of Forbes, the fact remains that he is, at the moment, the only black leader possessing the stature and resource base required to organize the black community for effective political action on a citywide basis. A number of black citizens in Cleveland lament the absence of a strong, diverse, and effective leadership structure in the black community.

> Since the days of Carl Stokes, the quality of leadership in our community
> has declined significantly. George Forbes is the only leader we have with
> real clout, and he has been neutralized by the carnival affair.[32] Other black
> leaders have not challenged him because he's black. When he comes under
> attack, the community will say let's support him because he's one of us. We
> are in bad shape. Our schools are going to hell. The enrollment is dropping;
> schools are closing; integration has backfired. We have no leader on the
> scene with the power and guts to protect our children from the abominations
> of the Cleveland school system.[33]

The most telling indication of organizational and leadership decline in
the black community is the decline in black participation in elections over
the past decade. Table 8.1 summarizes black voting patterns in Cleveland
since 1961. This table clearly shows the declining ability on the part of
black politicians to deliver the black vote. Black registration was 99,885 in
1967 when Carl Stokes was elected mayor. By 1971 it had climbed to
126,643. Between 1971 and 1979 black registration declined, falling to a
low of 102,380 in 1975 and rising again to 122,811 in 1979. Significantly,
the presence of a black mayoral candidate on the ballot in 1975 did not
serve as a stimulus to black registration. The general pattern of black
turnout has also been downward. Reaching an all-time high of 81.7 percent in 1967, black turnout had plummeted to 47.69 percent by 1979,
compared with a 48.5 percent turnout rate for white voters. It appears that
the 1978 recall election captured the imagination of the nation but did not
excite black voters in Cleveland. In this highly controversial election,
with black leaders almost unanimously supporting the recall petition, the
turnout among black voters was less than 31 percent of the total number
of registered black voters. Data in Table 8.2 suggest that the incidence of
nonparticipation by blacks is higher in council races than it is in citywide
races. These data suggest unequivocally a broad-scale withdrawal by
blacks in Cleveland from active involvement in electoral politics.

In addition to leadership and organizational decline, black political
influence in Cleveland has been undermined by the increasing suburbanization of key sectors of the black population. Data bearing on this phenomenon are reported in Table 8.3. These data suggest that the exodus of
blacks from the central city to surrounding suburbs has been fairly dramatic. It is significant that the exodus has focused on a few select suburbs,
creating a clustering effect. The strongest movement has been the settlement of lower-middle-class blacks into East Cleveland where blacks now
make up 86.7 percent of the population and are rapidly taking over the
instruments of local government. Not to be discounted, however, is the
movement of the black middle class to former white enclaves such as
Shaker Heights, Warrensville Heights, Oakwood, and Woodmere. The
exodus of the black middle class has special political significance because

TABLE 8.1 SUMMARY OF CLEVELAND'S MAYORAL GENERAL ELECTIONS IN BLACK WARDS, 1961–79

	1961	1963	1965	1967	1969	1971	1973	1975	1977	1978	1979
Registered voters	85,535	71,847	103,123	99,885	90,819	126,643	116,501	102,380	107,919		107,919
Turnout (N)	46,543	39,466	76,377	81,646	73,093	95,681	64,676	75,253	65,317	33,205	58,570
Turnout (%)	54.4	54.9	74.1	81.7	80.4	75.6	55.5	73.5	59.6	30.76	47.69

SOURCE: Joseph P. McCormick, "The Continuing Significance of Race: Racial Change and Electoral Politics in Cleveland, Ohio, 1961–1977" (paper presented at the Annual Meeting of the American Political Science Association, August 31–September 3, 1979, Washington, DC); and the Cuyahoga County Board of Elections.

201

TABLE 8.2   SUMMARY OF COUNCIL ELECTIONS IN CLEVELAND'S
BLACK WARDS, 1979

Ward	Registered Voters	Votes Cast	Votes for Winner
10	11,647	5,780	3,382
11	6,720	2,534	1,295
12	8,622	2,005	2,005
13	12,417	7,307	4,280
16	11,885	3,940	2,983
17	9,076	3,507	1,842
18	8,342	3,251	2,553
20	8,614	3,818	2,899
24	8,456	2,898	2,898
25	9,774	3,885	2,050
27	8,571	3,836	2,067
28	10,311	4,636	2,836
29	9,285	4,450	3,520
30	10,953	5,645	2,864

SOURCE: *Cuyahoga County Board of Elections.*

it represents a permanent loss in terms of organizing skills, leadership potential, money, political experience, and political consciousness. A number of black political leaders from the late 1960s and early '70s—including Arnold Pinkney and Carl Stokes—have moved to surrounding suburbs. Most importantly, many of the middle-class citizens who served as a solid base of support for Carl Stokes during his campaigns for mayor are no longer Cleveland residents. The members of the black lower class that are left are far more difficult to mobilize for political purposes than those who have moved to the suburbs over the past ten years.

> Most of your black middle class has moved away. Now you find that even blacks lower down on the totem pole no longer consider the inner city a desirable place to live. It is obvious that the abandonment of the city by the middle class has hurt us politically. Look around you. Look at the way our people are forced to live—poor housing, no job, and no hope of getting a job. Politics is way down the list of priorities. It is next to impossible to get poor people in Hough out to vote. They are worried about where the next meal is coming from. They are not interested in the kind of rhetoric our modern day politicians are laying down.[34]

The shifting demographic character of the black population has greatly accentuated the problem of political development and effectiveness in Cleveland. Prospects are not very great that the pattern of political decline can be halted or that the black community can be returned to a position of significant political strength.

TABLE 8.3 BLACK RESIDENTIAL SETTLEMENT IN SELECTED SUBURBAN COMMUNITIES IN CUYAHOGA COUNTY, OHIO, 1970–80

Community	Population 1970	Population 1980	% White 1970	% Black 1970	% White 1980	% Black 1980	% Increase in Black Population 1970–80
Beachwood	9,631	9,983	97.6	2.1[a]	93.1	5.9	180
Bedford Hts.	13,063	13,214	99.6	0.1	71.2	26.7	2866.6
Cleveland Hts.	60,767	56,438	96.7	2.4	73.0	24.9	937.5
E. Cleveland	39,600	36,957	40.2	58.6	12.2	86.7	47.9
Garfield Hts.	41,417	33,380	95.4	4.3	85.0	15.0	248
North Randall	1,212	1,054	99.7	.2	19.4	19.2	9,500
Oakwood	3,127	3,786	70.5	29	55.7	43.1	48.6
Orange	2,112	2,376	99.0	2	90.4	8.5	325
Shaker Hts.	36,306	32,587	85	14.5	74.7	24.4	68.2
University Hts.	11,055	15,401	99.2	.5	89.3	9.6	1,800
Warrensville Twsp.	2,160	1,640	67.5	29.4	51.0	45.2	113.2
Warrensville Hts.	18,925	16,565	77.6	21.2	23.4	75.0	155.1
Woodmere	976	772	69.0	28.4	55.7	42.0	47.8

SOURCE: U.S. Population Census, 1970 and 1980.
[a] Blacks and whites do not make up 100% of the population in most Cuyahoga County communities.

The New Black Politics: A Reassessment

The experience of black communities moving from protest to politics requires that we raise serious questions concerning the basic assumptions of the new black politics. One key assumption is that the movement for black social and economic freedom is always progressive—that once black political power reaches a certain plateau it can build on its accomplishments and move to higher ground. Professor Hanes Walton has called our attention to the fact that the political development of the black community has been characterized by reversal as well as forward movement. Cleveland provides one concrete example of black politics moving in reverse. After achieving the pinnacle of power with the election of Carl Stokes to the mayor's office in 1967 and 1969, black political influence in Cleveland has declined to a position of relative insignificance. The chances of blacks electing a black mayor of Cleveland today are far more remote than they were when Stokes first tossed his hat in the ring in 1965. Black politicians in Cleveland no longer embrace the concept of political independence even in a symbolic sense. Patronage and economic gain, rather than community service, have become the main factors shaping their political alliances and policy preferences. Few of them could be persuaded to join a rejuvenated version of the caucus founded by Carl Stokes. Collective struggle and unity of purpose are relics of the past. The Cleveland example could be multiplied several fold. A recent report in the *New York Times* documents in painful detail the phenomenal decline of black political power in New York City in recent years.[35]

Another key assumption of the new black politics is that black leaders share a community of interest that will provide the basis for unity and cohesion over an extended period of time. In reality, the issues and emotional circumstances that create unity among black leaders are transitory. The more normal condition is one in which powerful centrifugal forces create tension and conflict among black leaders that renders impossible the maintenance of unity and the promotion of collective activity.[36] On this score, Professor Mack Jones has noted that the area of agreement is frequently greater between black leaders and white leaders than it is between two sets of black leaders.[37] If black leaders do not naturally share a community of interests, strong pressure must be applied from an outside source. In Cleveland, Carl Stokes served as a catalyst for black political leaders, welding them together into a powerful political force. Once Stokes was gone, the pressure was released, and black politicians began to focus the bulk of their attention on the problems in their own wards rather than the problems of the wider community.

The assumption of the new black politics that numbers will continue to be a key political resource for the black community also demands reexamination. Erosion of the black power base in Cleveland in the wake of the suburbanization of the middle class is a poignant reminder that the demographic character of central cities is not static. In some cities deliberate efforts are being made to break up black communities in order to dilute black influence. In other cities natural changes in living patterns have stripped blacks of their numerical advantage. Black movement to the suburbs, such as that occurring in Cleveland, has often been accompanied by increased white settlement in inner-city neighborhoods. The political consequence has been a decline in the strategic position of the black community vis-à-vis election outcomes.

Finally, the tremendous emphasis on electoral politics by the advocates of the new black politics obscures the fact that much of the political power in America is nonelectoral in nature. Pressure politics, protest politics, and political communication are all vital tools in the exercise of influence over policymaking in America.[38] A single-minded concentration on electoral politics runs the risk of placing such narrow limits on the resource base of the black community that it will be incapable of coping with challenges from other groups utilizing a medley of strategies in their quest for enhanced political power. The argument can be persuasively made that during its heyday, the Twenty-first District Caucus was successful, not because of its electoral activities, but because of its ability to command the attention of the public, communicate with the masses, raise largs sums of money rapidly, and inspire its members to commit themselves to the goal of community uplift. These latter activities transcend electoral politics and provide the crucial underpinnings for a wide variety of political programs.

The concentration on electoral politics also exaggerates the importance of the vote as an instrument of black liberation. Voting is rarely a revolutionary act. A number of studies have pointed out that black elected officials are severely limited in what they can accomplish for the black community through their offices.[39] To the extent that a new politics for the black community genuinely seeks a social transformation of American society, a search for strategies, beyond the act of voting or electoral mobilization, is required. Again the experience of Cleveland is instructive. Despite his talent, his energy, and his abiding commitment to the welfare of his people, Carl Stokes, as mayor of Cleveland, could make little headway in removing the barriers to upward mobility for the great majority of Cleveland's black population.

Notes

1. I wish to thank Professor James Kweder and Walter Moody for supplying a portion of the data used in this paper. I would also like to thank Professor

James Upton and Martha Dillard for assistance in the preparation of statistical summaries.

2. Congressman Mervyn Dymally of California, for example, has described politics as "the cutting edge of the civil rights movement." Similar statements regarding the critical importance of electoral politics to the struggle for black freedom have been made by Chuck Stone, Harry Bailey, and other black scholars and social activists. See Michael Preston, "Limitations of Black Urban Power: The Case of Black Mayors," in *The New Urban Politics,* ed. Louis H. Masotti and Robert L. Lineberry (Cambridge, MA: Ballinger, 1976), p. 111. See also Hanes Walton, Jr., *Black Politics: A Theoretical and Structural Analysis* (Philadelphia: Lippincott, 1972), p. 3.

3. Milton D. Morris, *The Politics of Black America* (New York: Harper & Row, 1975), p. 153; Joint Center for Political Studies, *Roster of Black Elected Officials,* vol. 4 (April 1974).

4. Stokely Carmichael and Charles V. Hamilton, *Black Power: The Politics of Liberation in America* (New York: Vintage, 1967), pp. 24–25.

5. Bayard Rustin, "From Protest to Politics: The Future of the Civil Rights Movement," *Commentary,* February 1965, pp. 25–31. This article is reprinted in Edward Greer, *Black Liberation Politics: A Reader* (Boston: Allyn and Bacon, 1971), pp. 241–53.

6. The strategy of black political oscillation has been analyzed most thoroughly by Chuck Stone. See his *Black Political Power in America* (New York: Dell, 1970), esp. chap. 4. Bayard Rustin was opposed to the notion of oscillation; he believed instead that the black community should forge permanent coalitions with liberal-labor groups inside the Democratic party. Rustin was sharply critical of black power advocates who preached a doctrine of political independence. He believed the political isolation of blacks from the liberal-labor coalition inside the Democratic party represented a "no win" strategy that was self-defeating. See Bayard Rustin, "From Protest to Politics: The Future of the Civil Rights Movement," *Commentary,* February 1965, pp. 25–31; also see Rustin's "Black Power and Coalition Politics," *Commentary,* September 1966, pp. 35–40.

7. William E. Nelson, Jr., and Winston Van Horne, "Black Elected Administrators: The Trials of Office," *Public Administration Review,* November-December 1974, pp. 526–33.

8. For a description of these practices, see William E. Nelson, Jr., and Philip Meranto, *Electing Black Mayors: Political Action in the Black Community* (Columbus: Ohio State University Press, 1977), pp. 78–84.

9. Nelson and Meranto, *Electing Black Mayors,* p. 103.

10. Ibid., chaps. 4 and 5.

11. Penn Kimball has noted, however, that the prospect of electing a black man as mayor of Cleveland failed to excite the interest of two in ten black voters in 1967. See Penn Kimball, *The Disconnected* (New York: Columbia University Press, 1972), p. 147.

12. Carl B. Stokes, *Promises of Power: A Political Autobiography* (New York: Simon and Schuster, 1973), p. 124.

13. Office of the Mayor, Cleveland, Ohio, *Meaningful Minority Employment* (1971).

14. Charles Levine, *Racial Conflict and the American Mayor* (Lexington, MA: Lexington Books, 1974), p.60.

15. Nelson and Meranto, *Electing Black Mayors*, p. 358.

16. "Democrats Ask Porter to Stay Until May 17," *Cleveland Press*, August 1, 1969.

17. "Party-Slate Defections Threatened," *Plain Dealer*, May 17, 1970.

18. "Stokes Deepens Dem Split, Call Convention an Affront," *Cleveland Press*, May 18, 1970.

19. "Rebel Democrats Cut County Ties," *Plain Dealer*, May 23, 1970.

20. "Democratic Caucus Only an Infant, Already Shows Political Clout," *Cleveland Press*, May 21, 1970.

21. This quote it taken from a series of interviews conducted by the author in Cleveland on black community politics in the summer of 1975.

22. Seth Taft readily acknowledged the contribution of the caucus to his election victory. He contended that the caucus exercised tremendous influence in the black community because "Carl was the man on high. If he said let's do something an awful lot of people said if he says do it I am going to do it." Interview by the author with Seth Taft, June 1975.

23. Editorial, *Plain Dealer*, December 30, 1971.

24. Interview with Arnold Pinkney, June 1975.

25. Some evidence of the deterioration of the black power base was revealed in the 1971 general election. Pinkney ran 20 percentage points behind Stokes in black east side wards, and the fall-off in voter turnout from 1969 was twice as high in black wards as it was in white wards. See Kimball, *The Disconnected*, pp. 156–57.

26. "Will Perk Election Unify Caucus, Democrats?" *Plain Dealer*, November 4, 1971.

27. Cleveland interview, Summer 1975. See note 21.

28. Stokes defended his actions on the grounds that since he had been involved in the negotiations and was the chairman of the Twenty-first District Caucus, he felt a "responsibility to acept the initial cochairmanship." Interview with Louis Stokes, August 1975.

29. Porter was a former chairman of the Cuyahoga Democratic party and political adversary of the Stokes brothers.

30. The only black politician in Cleveland since Carl Stokes that has been able to overcome the handicap of race and win an office with political jurisdiction beyond the black community is Virgil Brown, a black Republican, elected to the Cuyahoga County Commission in November 1980.

31. This quote is taken from a series of interviews conducted by the author in Cleveland on black community politics in the summer and fall of 1980 and winter of 1981.

32. A scandal in which Forbes and 17 other public officials were charged with accepting kickbacks from community carnival operators. The specific charges against Forbes were extortion, bribery, theft in office, and intimidating an officer. Forbes was found not guilty of all charges by Common Pleas Judge George A. Tyack.

33. Cleveland interview, winter 1981. See note 31.

34. Cleveland interview, fall 1980. See note 31.

35. See *New York Times*, March 29, 1981.
36. Matthew Holden, Jr., *The Politics of the Black "Nation"* (New York: Chandler, 1973), p. 3.
37. Mack H. Jones, "A Frame of Reference for Black Politics," in *Black Political Life in the United States*, ed. Lenneal Henderson, Jr., (San Francisco: Chandler, 1972), pp. 17–18.
38. Walton, *Black Politics*, pp. 8–9.
39. See Preston, "Limitations of Black Urban Power"; William E. Nelson, Jr., "Black Mayors as Urban Managers," in *Urban Black Politics: The Annals of the Academy of Political and Social Science*, ed. John R. Howard and Robert C. Smith, vol. 439 (September 1978): 53–67.

NINE

The Impact of Public Authorities on Urban Politics: Challenges for Black Politicians and Interest Groups

Wilbur C. Rich

At the beginning of the twentieth century, no political idea seemed more venerated than that of municipal home rule. Many reformers, politicians, and academics regarded home rule as essential for effective government. At the mid-point of this century, faith in home rule remained strong. Since then, the nation has had urban race riots in the 1960s and population shifts in the 1970s. As we enter the 1980s our nation faces enormous economic strains. Municipal home rule boosters are beginning to hedge, and heretics are openly questioning the independence of some city functions. Reformers have shifted their attention to municipal financial stability and administrative efficiency.

Many state legislatures have taken advantage of this situation to bypass long-standing municipal governments and create new special districts and authorities. These new forms of government have the advantage of managerial flexibility, revenue-producing capacities, and catchment growth (i.e., expansion beyond political boundaries). Designed to be self-supporting, these state-chartered organizations can operate as a single or multipurpose agency. They can exist within a single city boundary or encompass many cities. Originally conceived as a scheme to circumvent the state-imposed debt limits on municipalities, these authorities now enjoy the dubious distinction of achieving relative financial stability while some municipalities (e.g., Detroit, 1981) struggle to meet the next payday.[1]

The need to achieve fiscal and managerial efficiency has caused these new forms of government to proliferate. Meanwhile, municipal governments lose both population and industries. One of the critical questions for the 1980s is determining the long-range effect of having parallel forms of local government service delivery systems. Has the growth of these entities eroded or accelerated the rate of fiscal decline of cities? Do they pose administrative problems (e.g., coordination) for cities? Will cities continue to lose their housekeeping functions? What will be the impact on the political situations in cities? What special problem do authorities pose for minorities? These are but a few of the issues these new political subdivisions raise.

This chapter examines the rise of these new political subdivisions and their relationship to administrative and political problems faced by urban minorities. It should be made clear at the outset that special districts and public authorities are of equal status to other local governments before the law. They are not subordinate to municipalities but have equality in many matters of policy. Moreover, special districts are frequently required to coordinate their policies with other local governments. In other words, they are not only alternatives for providing services but are also alternative governments. They exist in a universe parallel to that of traditional local governments.

The rise of these alternative governments comes at a time when minority groups, especially blacks, are consolidating their political gains in cities. Blacks have a special problem with authorities and special districts. They control few, if any, of these governmental entities. Blacks are also unprepared to barter with the professionals who administer these organizations. Their suburban white neighbors can outvote and outmaneuver them on policy issues affecting the region. Consequently, the proliferation of authorities threatens to undermine the newly won black political turf and subvert attempts to restore the general urban economy. To understand political displacements and consequences, it is necessary to review the concept of public authorities.

Varieties of Special Governments

Gerwig defines a public authority as "a limited legislative agency or instrumentality of corporate form intended to accomplish special purposes involving long-range finances of certain public facilities without legally or directly impinging upon the credit of the state." [2] In other words, Gerwig applies a financial definition to these political entities. In this definition, the stress is on self-management, financial autonomy, and long-term goals. The term "authority" is used loosely. Any government division can designate a subordinate department or agency as an authority. The confusion over titles is compounded by the fact that the U.S. Bureau of the Census lumps all special governments under the heading "special district." Authorities are also called special districts, municipal corporations, or commissions. They include a wide variety of organizational units, all the way from a giant tax-supported sanitation system to a tiny water commission that generates revenue from selling municipal bonds. The title "authority" simply indicates its status as a single and exclusive governing mechanism. Authorities can consist of a county or city agency whose power ends at the political boundary (e.g., New York City's Battery Park City Authority) or a multicounty jurisdiction (e.g., the Metropolitan Transit Authority that provides services to New York City and Westchester County).

The multicounty public authority has become a growth commodity in local governments. In the field of transportation, many large cities have joined forces with the surrounding suburbs to form transportation or transit authorities. The Bay Area Rapid transit District (BART) in San Francisco, the Massachusetts Bay Transportation Authority (MBTA) in the Boston area, the Metropolitan Transit Authority (MTA) in the New York City area, the Metropolitan Atlanta Rapid Transit Authority (MARTA), and so forth are examples of such authorities. Other multicounty authorities administer health, fire, and sewage systems. These service systems have become a common part of urban life. Authorities join communities that share common needs for service.

The single "special district" is perhaps the most common form of special government. In 1977 the Census Bureau counted 25,962 special districts in the United States. This is an increase of 2,077 units, or 8.7 percent, since the 1972 count. There are several states with more than 800 special districts (e.g., California, 2,227, Illinois 2,745, Pennsylvania 2,035). Most of the state of New York's 964 special districts are fire (874), and health (83) (see Table 9.1). Since the U.S. Bureau of the Census counts all special governments as special districts, it is difficult at times to distinguish one type of unit from another.

The increases in special districts (see Table 9.1), especially in housing and urban renewal, suggest that the shift to authorities is increasing, and consequently elected officials in municipalities will play a lesser role in decision making in these areas. Losing control of urban housing policy could have serious implications for minorities and their supporters. The

TABLE 9.1   FUNCTIONAL CLASSES OF SELECTED SPECIAL DISTRICTS

| | Number | | Increase | |
Function	1972	1977	Number	Percent
Fire protection	3,872	4,187	315	8.1
Housing and				
urban renewal	2,271	2,408	137	6.0
Sewerage	1,411	1,610	199	14.1
Urban water				
supply	2,333	2,480	147	6.3

SOURCE: U.S. Bureau of the Census, 1977 U.S. Census of Governments, Government Organization, vol. I, no. 1, pp. 4–5; Table XII, p. 70.

decision to build more public housing can change the location of community groups as well as the nature of the community.[3]

New York is a leader in creating the special-purpose municipal corporation. Public-benefit corporations have been created to manage anything from pari-mutuel betting (Off Track Betting Corporation, or OTB) to the Urban Development Corporation that constructed low- and middle-income housing units.[4] Municipal corporations are used to operate a multipurpose health delivery system (e.g., Health and Hospitals Corporation) and multi-income housing units (e.g., New York City Housing Authority).

The most famous and powerful authority structures are the interstate compacts. These units span states and require congressional approval. The Port Authority of New York and New Jersey, established in 1921, is one of the most powerful governmental entities in the United States. It operates bus terminals, railroads, ports, and office buildings in the bi-state area.

Public Authorities and the Politics of Governance: Appointed Versus Elected Officials

Students of public administration have long advocated an autonomous bureaucracy with a nonpartisan staff. In fact, most authorities recruit their staff and board members from the business community. However, the deliberate exclusion of politicos, labor leaders, and consumers from the governing boards creates a bias in favor of the business community who may be vendors for that authority. The narrow base of the governing board membership is a continuous source of controversy among elected officials and minority groups.

The U.S. Supreme Court has ruled that governing bodies of administrative agencies do not have to be representative. Indeed, in *Sailor* v. *Board of Education*, the Court held that the principle of one man one vote is not applicable to appointed boards.[5] Authority officials have used this case to block any attempt at placing minority members on the governing boards.

The federal courts have argued that appointed boards are not engaged in legislative activities. Any large-city mayor knows that these agencies do indeed make public policy. A decision to build a road can radically change a neighborhood's property values and offset zoning laws. By increasing the number of vehicles in the area, air and noise pollution will be increased. A transit authority can change its schedules, routes, or fares and literally alter the lives of many city passengers. Nevertheless, many authority officials think they are simply carrying out their service mandate.

Federal and state courts have been very solicitous of the political independence of these authorities. The U.S. Supreme Court recently held that New Jersey cannot force the Port Authority of New York and New Jersey to subsidize a mass transit system.[6] This ruling protects authorities from attempts to force them to invest in auxiliary and risky enterprises. The Port Authority claimed that such investments would impair contract obligations. In financial matters the Port Authority's first responsibility is to its bond holders and not to the general public. New York City is virtually powerless against the Port Authority. There are few linkages between the city's elected officials and the Port Authority. Consequently, the agency's decisions and nondecisions are made without consultation or deference to city planners.

Some states have attempted to solve the consultation problem by appointing local politicians to the governing boards of local transit authorities. For example, the Bay Area Rapid Transit District (BART) has significant linkages with local city halls in the San Francisco–Oakland area. Since the people-moving system is partly financed by local property taxes, the state also requires that each new construction project be approved by a public referendum. The governing board of BART is selected by a joint committee of mayors and county supervisors. BART is also required to open all board meetings to the public and provide local governments with annual reports.

The Massachusetts Bay Transportation Authority (MBTA) has a similar mechanism. MBTA covers seventy-eight communities and has an advisory board that includes mayors and city managers. Each city has one vote plus an assessment vote. The advisory board decides areas and budgets. The board of directors makes the day-to-day technical decisions.

Although not models of democracy, the governing boards of BART and MBTA are unique among special governments in that local elected officials are represented. Most state legislatures have insisted on appointed boards for these special districts. The argument made against elected boards is that they tend to politicize financial transactions. Elected officials might make policy judgments with the next election in mind. Poor financial judgment can jeopardize the investments of bond holders. For this reason, politicians, reformers, and businessmen prefer appointed boards. Politicians also see such appointments as an opportunity to get leading citizens involved in city government. Authority board membership, like a judgeship, is a sought-after upper-middle-class patronage plum. It allows these individuals to make a civic contribution with status. Reformers believe that appointed boards are more competent and reliable than elected boards. They claim that choices should be made on a merit and nonpartisan basis. Reformers argue that if such boards were elected, there would be a low turnout for the elections. Low voter turnout for school board elections, poverty boards, and referenda are merely a few political examples of voter apathy toward noncoordinate elections. Reformers also argue that zealots and ambitious politicians might use these elections to further other causes. Businessmen prefer appointed boards because they are less independent and more likely to select only successful and safe people. The preference for an appointed board does raise questions about an authority's commitment to the public interest. Herman Schwartz and James Riedel question the effectiveness of government- or agency-appointed boards. Schwartz doubts whether such bodies will be imaginative or efficacious.[7] Their basic argument suggests that local politicians and judges should not acquiesce to these appointed boards if there is evidence to suggest that they have been coopted by sponsoring agencies.[8] The lack of representation is only one of the problems associated with the growth of public authorities. Another problem is economic and political gerrymandering of the poor in the central cities.

Public Authorities as Economic and Political Gerrymanders

Political scientists have traditionally thought of gerrymandering in terms of voters, not taxpayers. The poor, however, can be robbed of their taxes as well as their votes. The poor are often the unwitting victims of regressive tax structures that maintain suburban growth (e.g., freeway transportation). Most public transportation authorities charge regressive fares regardless of the income or the place of residence of consumers. Many suburban residents travel to the city to use its facilities instead of creating similar ones in their communities. Consequently, ghetto residents are subsidizing the development of regional economic centers at the expense of the central-city service delivery system.

Since regional authorities overlap and transcend political jurisdictions, they contribute to dispersion of the urban population. For example, many working-class white suburban communities were created by the extension of the metro-bus and train system. Living in the suburbs has now become affordable, accessible, and preferable. The working class can enjoy the benefits of the city without living there. As transportation systems improved, many taxpayers left the city, some businesses followed, and the political economy was undermined. The cities were left with human-welfare delivery systems that are not only costly but are also unproductive in terms of revenue.

From a political standpoint, the move to regional systems may also be a means of denying to the new electoral majority in cities their proportional share in interlocal politics. Metropolitanism has always been viewed as a threat by ambitious black politicians.[9] In contrast, Hawley advises blacks to trust metropolitanism and enjoy its benefits. He claims that they have little to lose and much to gain:

> The role of metropolitan decision-making in urban America has yet to be fully defined, but structures are being evolved now. Presumably, Blacks will wish a say in developing that role, and in helping to modify the structures. Such influences can best be exercised if Black leaders enter the metropolitan decision-making arena now.[10]

This chapter is less sanguine about the political gains for blacks in a metropolitan government. Hawley believes that blacks should work for more representation in metro-governments to assure an equitable distribution of the cost of service systems. Though this goal is important, the real problem for black politicians is governing with a mutilated urban economy. Investors, usually suburban residents, have little interest in coopting money-losing enterprises such as education, welfare, and health.[11] They want to invest in urban services where the risk has been eliminated either by the state legislature or by an ironclad transaction between bureaucrats and investors. Thus the impact of public authorities on black urban residents may mean that the poor may end up subsidizing the rich, and at the same time have their potential political power eroded by regional government.

In contrast to suburban interests, a primary resource of the central city is its people.[12] The political and economic influence of blacks rests with their population advantage. Regional government would dilute this advantage, however. Table 9.2 shows the percentage of population loss by blacks when merged into the Standard Metropolitan Statistical Area.

It suggests that blacks lost their numerical advantage in every SMSA with the exception of Houston. Preliminary data from the 1980 census indicate that this trend is more pronounced. If public authority expansion were put to a vote, the suburbanites would simply outvote the core city. The Hawley position argued that blacks should welcome more white taxpayers into their revenue catchment area. Unfortunately, income generated from public authorities is not subject to municipal taxation. In effect, core-city residents are charged an extra fee for authority services because they lose tax revenues from having the authority headquarters located in the city. The facilities are tax exempt but use the city's fire, police, and sewerage services. Since many authorities have the power of eminent

TABLE 9.2   PERCENTAGE OF BLACKS IN SELECTED CENTRAL CITY
AND THE SMSA

	Percent Blacks in City	Percent Blacks in SMSA
New York City	21.1	19.7
Chicago	32.6	19.7
Detroit	43.6	19.2
Los Angeles	17.9	12.6
Houston	25.3	26.7
Philadelphia	33.5	17.5
Kansas City	22.1	13.6
Boston	16.3	4.7
Atlanta	51.3	18.3
San Francisco–Oakland	20.5	10.9

SOURCE: U.S. Bureau of the Census, Negro Population, 1970.

domain, they can select some of the city's best properties to build more untaxable facilities.

Authority, Bureaucrats, and the New Patronage

Bureaucrats usually live in fear that they will generate surpluses and have their budgets cut. Because fiscal authorities receive no appropriations from state legislatures, they can afford to generate a surplus. Indeed it is not unusual for authority bureaucrats to generate surpluses or at least break even to impress investors. These "profits" are usually reinvested in various enterprises that may or may not be related to the original mandate of the authority. New enterprises are usually of the "hard service" variety. Office buildings, roads, terminals, bridges, sewerage plants, and other constructions dominate their purchases. These projects create an enormous political constituency—civil engineering firms, general construction contractors, big labor, architects, management and university consultants. This vendor community uses its political clout to protect and promote authorities.

The protection afforded authorities allows them to create elaborate patronage systems. Among the patronage plums proffered are investment preferments, legal accounts, consultant contracts, construction contracts, and opportunities for status recognition.

The financial structure of authorities requires that they raise revenue through the bond markets. For this reason, the largest and most prestigious law firms, banks, and investment houses are recruited to promote the authority's interest. Many financial advisers will not represent public authorities that are open to politicization. They demand and receive assurances that management will adhere to accepted principles of business management.

The new patronage is a spoils system for the middle and upper classes. The benefits of the new system are not available to the working class. The classic big-city political machine never enjoyed the legal protections of the new system. The new spoils are legitimized by the use of legal and professional jargon. The legal contract gives legitimacy to the new patronage system and binds the public to obligations made by bureaucrats and businessmen. Rarely is the public fully informed about questionable transactions, self-serving financial recommendations, generality-oriented consultant reports, overlapping banking and authority board memberships, and sweetheart deals. These are legally sound but morally questionable. Robert Caro's description of the late Robert Moses' activities in New York City shows how authorities can be used to create a new form of political machine.

> For Moses was a political boss with a difference. He was not the stereotype with which Americans were familiar. His constituency was not the public but some of the most powerful men in the city and the state, and he kept these men in line by doling out to them, as Tammany Ward bosses once handed out turkeys to the poor at Thanksgiving, the goodies in which such men were interested, the sugar plums of public relations retainers, insurance commissions, and legal fees . . . Robert Moses made himself the Ward boss of the inner circle, the bankroller of the Four Hundred of politics. Far from being above the seamier aspects of politics, he was—for decades—the central figure about whom revolved much of the back-stage maneuvering of New York City politics. . . . Beyond graft and patronage, moreover, Moses displayed a genius for using the wealth of the public authorities to unite behind his aims—banks, labor unions, contractors, bond underwriters, insurance firms, the great retail stores, real estate manipulators—all the forces which enjoy immense political influence in New York. . . . *What Moses succeeded in doing really, was to replace graft with benefits from a public works project.* He had succeeded in centralizing his projects—all those forces which are not in theory supposed to, but which in practice do, play a decisive role in political decisions.[13]

Moses became the boss of a political machine with no significant relationship with the black community. The legacy of Moses will continue to shape policy as long as there are few if any black bridge and tunnel designers, construction companies, or black civil engineering firms large enough to bid for contracts. There are small black architectural firms, advertising agencies, subcontractors, and the like, but these cannot bid with or lobby with the larger firms. It would be difficult to prove discrimination since authorities rarely deal with smaller firms. Without the support of groups that do business with authorities, black elected officials are much more vulnerable than their white counterparts to manipulation by these power brokers.

Conclusions

This chapter has attempted to describe and analyze some of the challenges and opportunities that public authorities pose for minority politicians in the central cities. These are new challenges that cannot easily be characterized as power grabs by white politicians and business leaders. Predating the emergence of black political power, these special governments enjoy the support of the same reform coalitions that have long supported black causes. Some journalists see such governments as a way out of the "fiscal mess" of cities. These entities have attracted very powerful allies. Many politicians stand in awe of them and do not seek confrontations with them. In view of the observations and comments in this chapter, a prudent black politician cannot and should not attack these reform units simply as political institutions seeking to deny power and decision making to the new majority. A better strategy might be to attack the economic gerrymandering of cities. Unless this is done, public authorities will grow like dandelions across the regional terrain. Aside from the administrative and economic problems caused by these governments, they are also blatantly antidemocratic and unrepresentative.

The prescription for this situation may not be elected boards but the creation of more public leverage or access points in the decision-making process. If the investment industry wishes to make a profit from public resources, it must accept some of the uncertainty and risk of public transactions. Government for the financial interest of investors is not in the public interest.[14] We live in a period of expanding state governments. Encroachment on home rule prerogatives has become the norm. This expansion may be a natural condition of the postindustrialized urban experience, but urban politicians should not allow state legislatures to stampede them into agreeing to create "Leviathan" public organizations within their jurisdiction. Indeed, the miracle drug "authoritycin" is not a cure for the ills of the urban community. McLean asserts that "an overdose of authoritycin may produce not only confusion but serves as an embalming fluid in the body politic."[15] Gerwig also warns against using authorities as a panacea.

> In the hands of impetuous lawmakers, impelled by a normal anxiety "to get things done," the wholesale creation of authorities to accomplish customary governmental activities—or even worse, activities far removed from recognized public services—could result in the unleashing of overlapping gov-

ernmental monstrosities whose combined debt obligations could well-nigh paralyze future legislatures.[16]

The 1975 financial crisis of the New York State Urban Development Corporation (UDC) confirmed the McLean prognosis.[17] It is a classic case of inadequate financial planning. Yet paralysis has not struck the New York state legislature, which continues to create authorities.

Blacks must adopt strategies that allow them to cope with these expanding organizations. They must develop networks for the new patronage. This requires promoting black vendors, insisting on black authority board members, and seeking legislation that requires disclosure of the authority planning process. The black public must also be encouraged to attend public sessions of authority meetings. In other words, the black public must try to infuse authorities with a sense of public regardingness.

Finally, the literature and evidence suggest that interactions with authorities require of minority politicians something more than temper-tantrum politics. They must be much more calculating and persistent in their interactions with the state and metro systems. Survival in a postpartisan urban era will depend less upon professional politicians and more on professionals who are also politicians.

Notes

1. Joseph F. Zimmerman has called the advocates of authorities "statists"; see "Metropolitan Reform in the United States: An Overview," *Public Administration Review* 30, no. 5 (September/October 1970): 531–43.
2. Robert Gerwig, "Public Authorities in the Unites States," *Law and Contemporary Problems* 26, no. 4 (Autumn 1961): 591.
3. See Wilbur C. Rich, "Political Power and the Role of Housing Authority," in *Housing Form and Public Policy,* ed. Richard Plunz (New York: Praeger, 1980).
4. For a discussion of UDC, see Eleanor Brillant, *The Urban Development Corporation* (Lexington, KY: Lexington Books, 1975).
5. See *Sailor* v. *Board of Education,* 387 U.S. 105 (1967).
6. This case has serious implications for states that wish to use the revenues or expertise of authorities for urban purposes; see *U.S. Trust Co. of New York* v. *States of New York and New Jersey,* 45 U.S. L.W. 4418 (April 27, 1977).
7. Herman Schwartz, "A Dilemma for Government-Appointed Directors," *Harvard Law Review* 79, no. 2 (December 1965): 350–64.
8. James Riedel, "Citizen Participation: Myths and Realities," *Public Administration Review* 33 (May/June 1972): 211–19.
9. See Tobe Johnson, *Metropolitan Government: A Black Analytical Perspective* (Washington, DC: Joint Center for Political Studies, 1972), p. 21.
10. Willis D. Hawley, *Blacks and Metropolitan Governance: The Stakes of Reform* (Berkeley, CA: Institute of Governmental Studies, 1972), p. 21.

11. For discussion of the problems of interlocal cooperation, see Vincent Marando, "Interlocal Cooperation in Metropolitan Areas," *Urban Affairs Quarterly* 4 (December 1968): 185–200.
12. See Wilbur C. Rich, "Civil Servants, Unionism and the State of Cities," in *Urban Governance and Minorities*, ed. Harrington Bryce (New York: Praeger, 1976).
13. Robert A. Caro, *The Power Broker: Robert Moses and the Fall of New York* (New York: Knopf, 1974), pp. 17–18. Emphasis added.
14. For example, see *MTA* v. *County of Nassau*, 28 N.Y. 2d 385, 271 N.E. 2d.
15. Joseph E. McLean, "Uses and Abuses of Authorities," *National Municipal Review* 42, no. 9 (October 1953): 439.
16. Robert Gerwig, "Public Authorities: Legislatures Panacea," *Journal of Public Law* 5 (Fall 1956)): 385–407.
17. John E. Osborn, "Urban Development Corporations: A Study in Unchecked Power of a Public Authority," *Brooklyn Law Review* 43 (Winter 1977): 237–82.

TEN

Political Mobilization in the South: The Election of a Black Mayor in New Orleans

Alvin J. Schexnider

I advise anyone who thinks he knows
something about politics to go down in
Louisiana and take a postgraduate course.
SENATOR TOM CONNALLY

Nearly a decade ago, a handful of political analysts looked at the factors that would adversely affect black control of central cities. They concluded that (1) given the plethora of problems created by municipal dependence, black mayors will have to contend with white-dominated state legislatures that are unlikely to be responsive; (2) decreasing fiscal resources of black-dominated cities will increase their dependence on state and federal funds; and (3) the strategic locational value of the city will continue to decline as a result of various technological advances.[1] Under these circumstances, the election of black mayors was like winning a "hollow prize."

Since then, the number of black urban mayors in the United States has increased to over 150. The extent of severe economic and population decline in these cities is highly variable. Several of the larger ones manifest the worst signs of urban blight. Among them is New Orleans, Louisiana, the most recent addition to the ranks of large American cities with a black mayor.

New Orleans is the major metropolitan area of Louisiana. Both the city and the state are politically interesting; however, the city, with its admixture of French, Spanish, and southern cultures, provides the more fascinating laboratory for political research. New Orleans is, for many, a fabled city. For the cosmopolitans, it is a charming wonderland catering to its castelike aristocracy. For the locals, it is "Big Easy," a label that characterizes a city well known for its cavalier life style and tolerance for decadence, insouciance, and the grotesque. On the political economy side of the coin, New Orleans has been described by urbanologist Dr. Ralph E. Thayer as a "Northern mistake in a southern setting," owing to the severity of its urban ills. Perhaps most critically, it is a city that desperately needs to reverse an economic downturn that has persisted since the mid-1950s.

This chapter examines the politics of New Orleans and traces the factors that led to the election of its first black mayor in November 1977. At the same time, it is a study of the political economy of a major metropolitan area in the Sunbelt, one whose political culture is highly threatening to the social, political, and economic life of the city.

New Orleans' Political Culture

Located roughly in the southeast corner of the state, New Orleans is surrounded on three sides by swamps and on the fourth side by the Mississippi River. The city population stands at 564,000 and is approximately 50 percent black and 50 percent white. Whites hold the edge in the proportion of registered voters with 58 percent, while 42 percent of the registered voters are black. New Orleans has a strong-mayor form of government. It has a seven-member city council with two seats elected at-large and two seats currently held by blacks. The first black to sit on the council was chosen in 1976 by fellow council members to serve an unexpired four-year term. At that time, eight blacks already represented the city in the Louisiana legislature.

With its favorable location on the Mississippi River, New Orleans has for decades been a powerful mercantile, shipping, and financial center. Indeed, the New Orleans machine was well established and exerted much influence in state politics many years before Huey Long, one of the state's most famous citizens, ran for governor in 1928. While it remains a force to be reckoned with in statewide elections, there is no monolithic machine in New Orleans. Rather, power is brokered among influential economic interests and splintered political organizations mobilized along racial lines.

Its former mayor, Moon Landrieu, whose term expired in April 1978, was president of the U.S. Conference of Mayors and a highly vocal advocate of increased federal aid to cities. Yet, despite all the posturing and intensive lobbying, New Orleans is a city beset by grave economic problems. Fifty-seven percent of the city budget is provided by state and federal aid; white flight to the suburbs continues, as does the deterioration in housing stock; and the poor, the elderly, and the black are concentrated in the central-city core. Urban blight is as dramatic here as in any major metropolis in the country.

In an extensive analysis of the New Orleans economy, Dr. James R. Bobo, an economist at the University of New Orleans, concluded that the city's most intractable problem was economic:

> The local economy has experienced economic stagnation tendencies since the mid and late 1950s, with chronic and severe stagnation since 1966, not because there was an absence of economic growth, but because economic development did not provide adequate employment opportunities for an expanding labor force. . . . Employment opportunities have been inadequate since 1966 . . . consequently, unemployment has increased both absolutely and as a percentage of the labor force since 1966, reaching 9.0 percent in 1975.[2]

Thus, despite its long-standing internal strengths and its location in an oil-rich state and in a fast-growing region of the Sunbelt, New Orleans is experiencing serious economic difficulties. In many respects, its economic problems are inextricably linked and nearly unidimensional: low income and poverty, maldistribution of income, unemployment and subemployment, and low educational attainment. These immediate problems compound a situation of chronic economic stagnation from which the city cannot hope to recover except through an aggressive, broad-scale program involving both the public and private sectors. This derives from the fact that to a very large extent, wealth and power in New Orleans are concentrated in a small but powerful oligarchy that unduly influences the direction of economic development and public policy. This disturbing pattern of income distribution and resultant political impotence was borne out by data from the Bobo study.

> Income was highly concentrated among the upper 20 percent of the families in Metroplitan New Orleans, with the upper 20 percent of the families receiving 44 percent, the upper 40 percent of the families 68 percent, and the lower 60 percent of the families only 32 percent of total money income. The answer in large part is to be found in the concentration of economic power, economic discrimination, the refusal by New Orleans to participate in many of the federal programs of the 1960s, excessive subemployment, and a stagnating economy for about two decades. Significantly, there is a small but powerful, highly structured upper class and the middle income class is much smaller in metropolitan New Orleans, compared to all SMSA's, Atlanta, Dallas, and Houston. In few, if any, major metropolitan areas is income so inequitably distributed. And an inequitable income distribution is in part self-perpetuating.[3]

To a large extent, then, the upper-income groups also controlled the political arena.

In recent years blacks have begun to play a more visible role in local politics, due at least in part to demographic shifts that have been taking place since 1960. In fact, it is probable that the 1980 census will reveal a black population majority in New Orleans. A disproportionate number of these people, however, constitute an economic underclass, which may be unconvinced of the merits of political participation. Moreover, the economic and leadership problems continue unabated. Nonetheless, from the black citizen's perspective, something significant has taken place. The city has a black mayor.

Ernest N. Morial, a former state legislator and appellate court judge, took over the reins of New Orleans' city government on May 1, 1978. That he was able to gain control of both a political system that is highly fragmented, as well as a social structure that is possibly the most stratified of any city its size in the country, is nothing short of remarkable.

The Emergent Black Electorate

While it may be important to tease out distinguishing characteristics between blacks and whites, this can be misleading in some respects since all may share a common environmental setting. Such is the case of New Orleans blacks; in many respects they share a culture, a life style, and a world view shared by nearly all her citizens.

Professor Charles Y. W. Chai, who conducted a series of interviews to determine the community power structure in New Orleans, offers the following analysis of the "Mardi Gras syndrome" and its effect on the recruitment of political leadership:

> Most respondents expressed the opinion that the social system in the community tends to stifle new leadership. They observed that New Orleans is a city of tradition and that this tradition is reinforced and emphasized each year with the "greatest free show on earth." More than any other thing, the annual Carnival season is seen to exemplify the social attitude that pervades this community.
>
> Our respondents pointed out that the Mardi Gras balls help to perpetuate an archaic social system based on secrecy and tradition. The most prestigious balls are closed not only to the general public, but also to everyone except those whose families have been here since the turn of the century. . . . Thus, a young executive who moves to New Orleans with his family may soon become frustrated by a system which prevents him from enjoying many of the luxuries he feels he deserves. As a result, he may refuse to participate in community affairs. . . . They see no reason to work with the "locals" on community problems, since the "locals" refuse to socialize with outsiders.[4]

In sum, the Mardi Gras syndrome is endemic to the political culture of New Orleans. It is clearly dysfunctional to the political system in general, though its adverse impact on the life fortunes of black citizens is probably more pronounced. It was not until 1967 that the city sent its first black (Ernest Morial, the recently elected mayor) to the Louisiana House of Representatives. Nonetheless, it was easier to send a black to the state legislature than to the New Orleans City Council, which was finally integrated in the mid-1970s.

Race has been omnipresent in American politics. In addition, *color* among blacks is a key factor in New Orleans city politics. The sad and despicable role played by color—mulatto, octaroon, and quadroon is evident in nearly all aspects of the city's black life today. It goes without saying that this condition has been politically damaging.

A "black society" has existed in New Orleans as far back as 1718 when the city was founded. Originally, the black upper crust was chiefly composed of Creoles (historically, free men of color, but essentially blacks of French, Spanish, and American Indian heritage). Until the post-civil rights era, black leadership in New Orleans comprised Creoles and elements of the black middle class that included teachers, post office workers, Pullman car porters, "insurance men," undertakers, and an assortment of black businessmen. It has probably changed somewhat in the last fifteen years or so, but not much.

While about 25 percent of the black population in New Orleans can be classified as middle class in terms of jobs, education, and income, in large measure this rising black middle class is an extension of the Creole class whose Spanish-French ancestry set them apart from slaves. Thus distinctions of color continue to be translated into social status, thereby creating divisive tensions among New Orleans blacks.

> The legacy of this was generations of intra-racial conflict, based on color. The conventional wisdom, for many years, was that light-skinned people got the best of everything offered to the black community—that they became the black firsts in any racial progress.
>
> Andrew Young is a descendant of that heritage. . . . So is Mayor-elect "Dutch" Morial. . . . During his election campaign, Morial had to straddle skillfully these different worlds. One of his campaign organizations issued a fervent defense of his "blackness": "Believe us Brothers and Sisters, 'Dutch' may look white, but he lives and breathes BLACK." [5]

In short, black political progress in New Orleans has been retarded by tensions between an expanding class of affluent black professionals and a growing black underclass who are making increasingly strident demands of local leaders. Poverty has also played a role. Income remains a powerful predictor of political participation, and with an unusually large number of New Orleans blacks occupying the lower income strata, it is little wonder that they have fared so poorly in local elections. At least 57 percent of all black unrelated individuals are living below the poverty level, as indicated in Table 10.1, which shows black poverty in Orleans Parish (i.e., New Orleans) and neighboring parishes in the metropolitan area.

The black community in New Orleans underwent some quiet but ultimately significant changes in the 1960s. Between 1961 and 1969 black voter registration nearly doubled, from 36,000 to 66,000. This proved crucial to the election of its most liberal mayor to date, Moon Landrieu. Landrieu actively sought black support and during his eight-year tenure increased the percentage of blacks in city government from 10 percent to 40 percent. Also in 1969, two significant political organizations were created in the black community. Although numerous black political organizations have long existed in the city, only in the last few years have really effective organizations emerged, those whose endorsements carry great weight in the precincts where they operate. This is particularly true of SOUL (Southern Organization for Unified Leadership) in the Ninth Ward and COUP (Community Organization for Urban Politics).[6]

In many respects, the election of Moon Landrieu in 1969 set the stage for Morial's election in 1977. Landrieu's majority consisted of upper-middle and upper-income whites along with widespread support in the black community. In an extensive analysis of the 1969 race, Chubbuck, Renwick, and Walker commented:

> From a racial standpoint, Landrieu received approximately 40 percent of the white vote and slightly over 90 percent of the black vote. The election dramatically illustrates the critical influence the black vote now has on New Orleans politics. Negroes constituted slightly over 30 percent of the regis-

TABLE 10.1   BLACK POOR IN ORLEANS, JEFFERSON, ST. BERNARD, AND
ST. TAMMANY PARISHES, 1970

	Orleans	Jefferson	St. Bernard	St. Tammany
Median income	$4,475	$5,865	$5,119	$4,239
Percent of families poor	68.1	60.1	67.1	76.4
Percent of families below poverty	38.9	31.1	39.0	45.1
Percent of unrelated individuals	56.7	59.3	74.2	60.9
Percent of households in poverty	43.8	35.9	39.8	49.1
Percent of all persons in poverty	43.7	33.3	33.8	53.4

SOURCE: U.S. Census, 1970. Adapted from J. R. Bobo, The New Orleans Economy.

tered voters in the December primary, and the magnitude of the black support for Landrieu gave him a solid base on which to build his majority. Approximately 76 percent of all registered went to the polls. The black-voter participation was slightly higher than that of the whites percent of those registered voting.[7]

In that same election, Morial made an unsuccessful attempt to gain an at-large seat on the city council. Morial was endorsed by Landrieu in the second primary in his race against Joseph V. DiRosa. Both had similar white support. While Morial lost to DiRosa in that race, he later defeated him in the 1977 mayoral contest.

There is no doubt that the coalition of voters that Moon Landrieu put together in 1969 helped pave the way for Morial's victory eight years later: "The socio-economic-racial pattern of Landrieu's support clearly emerges in geographic terms: a combination of upper and middle-SES white areas in uptown New Orleans and Algiers and the predominantly black precincts throughout the city." [8]

Morial lost the 1969 council race to DiRosa by the slim margin of 49 percent to 51 percent. When the two met again in the 1977 mayor's race, the outcome was an almost exact replay in reverse with Morial defeating DiRosa by 51.5 percent to 48.5 percent.

The 1977 Mayoral Contest

Since registered white voters in New Orleans outnumber black voters by 58 percent to 42 percent, Morial clearly had to solidify the black vote and gain one-fourth to one-third of the white vote. Two other obstacles had to be surmounted: (1) a legal hurdle resulting from the fact that Morial held a judgeship while running for a nonjudicial post, a situation prohibited by the Louisiana Constitution, and (2) a scarcity of campaign funds.

Morial's campaign for mayor was accompanied by a lot of legal ma-neuvering. Following his primary victory on October 1, 1977, Morial filed suit in a federal district court against the Louisiana Supreme Court and the State Judiciary Commission whose statutes prohibited a state judge from running for any office except a judgeship. A decision in favor of Morial was made by the federal district court; however, less than two weeks before the general election on November 12, that decision was reversed by the U.S. Court of Appeals for the Fifth Circuit. Morial for-mally resigned from his judgeship on November 4, 1978.

Another important aspect of the 1977 mayoral primary was money. By mid-September the eleven candidates reported already having spent $1.5 million dollars. What follows is a brief description of the four major con-testants and their primary election campaign expenditures.

Nat Kiefer, at age thirty-eight, was an influential white state senator with a large black following. It should be pointed out that the major black organizations supported white candidates in the primary, so their support of Kiefer was hardly unusual. In addition, Kiefer had carefully cultivated support among black voters over the years. By the time of the October primary, Kiefer had spent $435,000. Doubtless large portions of that sum went to SOUL, the black political organization that had supported him in previous elections. However, most of the money was spent for radio and television commercials, which emphasized his legislative accomplishments.

At age thirty-three, State Representative Toni Morrison was the youngest of the serious candidates for mayor. He was the son of former New Orleans Mayor deLesseps Morrison and a former national chairman of the Young Democrats. By the time of the primary he reported $285,000 in expenditures. Morrison's campaign stressed neighborhood preservation and improved streets, a focus much too narrow to inspire the city's diverse voters.

Joseph V. DiRosa was, at age sixty, a senior member of the New Orleans City Council. Moreover, he was councilman-at-large, the traditional route to the mayor's chair. An acknowledged conservative, he campaigned vigorously as the candidate of the "little man," a code for the white working and middle classes. DiRosa spent $300,000 in the primary, most of it on advertisements attacking the municipally owned utility company, New Orleans Public Service, Inc. (NOPSI). Early election returns had shown Senator Kiefer as second to Morial in the nonpartisan primary; however, a recount established that DiRosa was the number-two man.

Ernest N. Morial was an outsider in both the primary and general elections. He was a maverick and laid claim to the office independent of the regular party machinery. Partly this derived from the fact that as a Creole, he was not immediately identified with either blacks or whites in the city. In fact, he was a long-time foe of those blacks who headed the major political organizations in New Orleans (SOUL and COUP, for example), and consequently black groups supported white candidates in the primary. Following his primary victory, the major black organizations gave Morial nominal support in the runoff, but actually he capitalized on the split in their ranks. Prior to the November 12 runoff, Morial worked diligently to cultivate the solid black majority required to win, and at the same time convinced a large segment of middle- and upper-class whites that he could successfully manage the city's economic affairs.

Throughout the campaign, Morial stressed what he called his "executive abilities." He emphasized that he was the best candidate since he possessed the necessary managerial skills "to deal with the urban ills that have created in our cities an underclass whose poverty reaches out to impact the middle and upper economic classes."

Morial spent about $100,000 in the primary campaign. Since he had no specific organizational support, he raised most of his campaign monies from personal resources, mortgages, and various community fund-raising events. Morial's total campaign expenditures were probably not more than $150,000, a sum considerably less than those of his defeated opponents.

Analyzing the Election

To a very large extent, the 1977 mayoral contest between Morial and DiRosa was an exact replica of their 1969 race for the position of councilman-at-large. In that contest, even though DiRosa carried only seven wards and got only 3 percent of the black vote, he beat Morial 84,200 to 78,625. In the 1977 race for mayor, which Morial won with 89,823 votes to DiRosa's 84,352 votes, Morial carried 95 percent of the black vote and expanded his margin of white support by carrying wards he had been unable to secure in the previous councilmanic race. In all, he carried 12 of the city's 17 wards.

As much as Morial tried to downplay the issue of race in the campaign, the fact of the matter is that race was of critical importance to the outcome of the election. Black voters tended to support Morial, and white voters supported DiRosa. Though the population is almost evenly divided between blacks and whites, registered whites outnumber blacks by 58 percent to 42 percent. The crucial differences in the outcome of the election thus derived from the fact that (1) a relatively strong proportion of blacks (76 percent) compared to whites (78 percent) cast ballots, and (2) Morial won a greater percentage of the black vote (95 percent) and siphoned off 19 percent of the white vote (about twice the percentage given to Atlanta's Maynard Jackson in his first election).

That race was a factor in the outcome of the election can also be seen from the fact that Morial carried all seven wards with majority black registration (see Table 10.2). Conversely, every ward carried by DiRosa had white registration majorities. Indeed, DiRosa ran well in the white wards, but not quite well enough. In several of the wards with majority white registration, he gave up just enough votes to ensure his defeat to Morial. This is demonstrated in Table 10.3, which illustrates the extent of support for Morial in white areas.

For example, in the huge Ninth Ward (downtown), even though blacks have slightly less than 50 percent registration, Morial won 55 percent of the vote. In the Sixteenth Ward (uptown), which has only 35 percent black registration, Morial secured a 59 percent majority. Similarly, in the af-

TABLE 10.2   SEVEN WARDS WITH MAJORITY BLACK REGISTRATION CARRIED BY MORIAL IN RUNOFF ELECTION

| | Voter Registration | | Votes Received | |
	White	Black	Morial	DiRosa
First Ward	659	1,270	903	413
Second Ward	507	3,289	2,304	2,448
Seventh Ward	12,764	16,830	13,809	8,900
Ninth Ward	27,405	29,157	23,290	19,316
Tenth Ward	2,091	3,485	2,580	1,308
Eleventh Ward	2,917	6,028	4,999	1,803
Twelfth Ward	4,008	5,645	5,021	2,297

SOURCE: Compiled from data published in the New Orleans Times Picayune and the New Orleans States-Item.

fluent Fourteenth Ward, although it has less than 10 percent black voter registration, 40 percent of its vote went to Morial.

In the final analysis, Morial's strategy was really basic and straightforward. Among his three major opponents—DiRosa, Kiefer, and Morrison—DiRosa was discernibly the most vulnerable, Morial, Kiefer, and Morrison appealed to very much the same voters, black and white. Morial's strategy, therefore, lay in eliminating his moderate opponents (i.e., Kiefer and Morrison) in the primary, thereby earning a place in the runoff against DiRosa. In a recent analysis of the elections Rosenzweig and Wildgen offer the following explanation of Morial's game plan:

> Although Morial developed an in-depth, comprehensive platform during the First Primary, his media strategy was to campaign hard for Black votes. By doing so, he was: (1) appealing to his natural constituency and thereby reaching his most receptive audience; and (2) drawing his support in far greater numbers from Kiefer and Morrison than from DiRosa—who, polls showed, had very little Black following. Thus, by helping himself attract Black votes, Morial was also helping Joe DiRosa's candidacy—by hurting

TABLE 10.3   FIVE WARDS WITH MAJORITY WHITE REGISTRATION CARRIED BY MORIAL IN RUNOFF ELECTION

| | Voter Registration | | Votes Received | |
	White	Black	Morial	DiRosa
Fifth Ward	5,528	3,183	3,190	3,099
Sixth Ward	2,229	1,988	1,773	1,282
Thirteenth Ward	4,800	3,451	3,864	2,567
Sixteenth Ward	3,447	1,830	2,318	1,619
Seventeenth Ward	7,279	6,846	6,506	4,642

SOURCE: Compiled from data published in the New Orleans Times Picayune and the New Orleans States-Item.

the candidacies of Kiefer and Morrison, who were running neck and neck with DiRosa. Indeed, should Morial have received a tiny fraction less of the Black vote than he did, Kiefer rather than DiRosa, would have certainly been in the Second Primary.[9]

Of course, had Kiefer rather than DiRosa been slated against Morial in the runoff, the outcome of the election might have been different, since Kiefer would likely have been a more formidable opponent. As previous mayoral contests in Baltimore and Cleveland have demonstrated, when a black candidate and the leading white candidate appeal to the same white voters, the white candidate may enjoy a moderate advantage, despite the loyalty of the black electorate.[10] This would certainly have been true in the case of Nat Kiefer, whose widespread appeal to a large segment of black voters and middle- and upper-income whites was well established long before his campaign for mayor.

Having survived the primary, Morial recognized the need to concentrate on winning white votes in the runoff. As Rosenzweig and Wildgen point out, "DiRosa's First Primary Black strength suggested very little potential for growth. With Morial's White target areas well identified, the Judge conducted a campaign designed to appeal to the City's better educated, higher income voters—especially those living in the Uptown area."[11]

In short, Morial won because he was able to garner a solid black vote at all income levels while cutting into the white vote in middle- and upper-income areas. Moreover, while Morial was able to capture a significant portion of the white electorate, DiRosa, an acknowledged conservative, was never able to make any inroads into the black vote.

Predicting Mayoral Success

In ascending to the office of mayor of New Orleans, Ernest Morial put together pretty much the same social-racial-economic coalition that had produced Moon Landrieu's victory in 1969. Along the way to city hall he received the backing of New Orleans' major newspapers (the *Times Picayune* and the *States-Item*), a number of influential whites, as well as the Alliance for Good Government, the Independent Women's Organization, and the New Orleans Coalition. In addition he was supported at different times and with varying levels of enthusiasm by several key black groups, for example, SOUL, COUP, the Black Organization for Leadership Development, and the Orleans Parish Progressive Voters League.

On the surface, it appears that the black electorate in New Orleans is cohesive and well disciplined, but such an assertion would be an overstatement. By the same token, it would be inaccurate to characterize black voters in New Orleans as disoriented, leaderless, and totally fragmented. The truth lies somewhere between these two extremes. While there are no fewer than half a dozen black political organizations of any consequence in New Orleans, none exerts a sufficient amount of clout to affect party discipline or citywide unity. In fact, the multinucleated structure of black political organizations hampers party solidarity and contributes to corrupt political practices, especially during campaign seasons when white candidates are flashing thousands of dollars before their eyes.

Probably for these (as well as other reasons), Morial has been at odds in years past with some of the established leaders of black political groups in New Orleans. Some of this enmity is also the result of decades of intraracial rivalries, based in part on mulatto-middle-class-Catholic-Protestant-working-class tensions, already noted. The solid black support that Morial was able to muster (despite the reticence of some black political leaders) suggests that New Orleans' blacks in all income levels can, when called upon, put their jealousies aside and rally behind a viable black candidate. The election of Morial may offer the black electorate an opportunity to repair relationships among its disparate factions and, further, to better define its mission and impose some discipline among its ranks.

Reflections on Mayoral Performance

When Mayor Ernest N. Morial assumed the position of chief executive of New Orleans in May 1978, this writer cited two major priorites: (1) facing squarely the city's revenue problems, particularly since 57 percent of the budget derived from federal and state sources; and (2) selecting a new police superintendent (an undertaking that invariably generates rancor and conflict). These two areas have in fact figured prominently in the mayor's activities.

Like many black mayors across the country, Ernest Morial inherited a city debilitated by decades of neglect. However, unlike many cities its size, New Orleans had been run by a conservative, social elite that had not always been favorable to business. Among Morial's first initiatives was a careful scrutiny of the city's taxes to determine additional sources of revenue.

Almost from the day he assumed office, Mayor Morial began looking for an acceptable means of shoring up New Orleans' sagging fiscal condition. In 1980 Morial succeeded in getting the council to approve two controversial and highly unpopular taxes: a $100 property service charge and a $50 road use tax. From a political standpoint, these taxes generated a substantial amount of criticism, first, because the voters were never asked to approve the taxes in a referendum, and second, due to their highly regressive nature. The imposition of taxes has never been a wise move for those seeking reelection. Since he intended to run for office again in February 1982, Morial was keenly aware of the political difficulties he was creating for himself by advocating these two sources of revenue. Consequently, when it became all too apparent that the citizens of New Orleans would not accept this solution to the city's fiscal problems, he decided to put the issue before the voters.

On November 4, 1980, the voters of New Orleans were asked to approve a one-half cent sales tax. By an extremely close margin of 73,171 to 73,066, the voters approved the tax to be levied beginning January 1, 1981. It replaces the $100 property service tax and the $50 road use tax, which the council later repealed.

Although the mayor may now breathe a sigh of relief, having disposed of the highly unpopular service charge and road use taxes, he surely appreciates the fact that the half-cent sales tax will not eradicate the city's money problems. As one member of the council described the situation,

> It really isn't fair to the public to say we have resolved the problem. . . . We have just postponed the operation. Until the legislature gives us authority [to raise some new form of revenue] or gives us the money to operate city government the way it's supposed to be operated, we're kidding ourselves.[12]

Mayor Morial must also view the passage of the half-cent sales tax as an enhancement of his reelection prospects. In one fell swoop, passage of the sales tax helped deflect potential political flak caused by the earlier service charges that have been removed by the council, and demonstrated that politically, he is still a force to be reckoned with. However, another major problem had to be overcome if Morial was to stem his declining popularity with the black electorate.

Relations between New Orleans' black residents and the police department have never been cozy; and they have become further exacerbated as local economic conditions have worsened. Early on, Mayor Morial realized the importance of selecting a first-rate police superintendent. His selection of James Parsons from Birmingham, Alabama, ultimately proved to be an unwise move.

The immediate events that precipitated the resignation of Superintendent Parsons in November 1980 can be traced to police handling of an investigation into the murder of a white patrolman in the Algiers section of New Orleans. As a local newspaper reporter described it: "Parsons should have known that you don't turn a group of policemen grieved and angry over the murder of one of their own, loose with shotguns on a racially tense community. You don't send them out on a pre-dawn raid to kick down the door on the home of suspects in the murder."[13]

The result of this assault was that four persons allegedly involved in the killing of a policeman were themselves killed. Black leaders were outraged. The killings brought the city perilously close to a race riot and galvanized the city's black residents as never before. The growing disenchantment with Morial was vigorously expressed by black citizens, and it became all too apparent that Superintendent of Police James Parsons had contributed to the mayor's mounting political vulnerability. As more and more young blacks in Algiers-Fischer (a low-income area) were randomly picked up and manhandled by the police, ostensibly in retaliation for the killing of Patrolman Neugarten, the community nudged itself to the brink of an explosion.

Even before the killings in Algiers, however, Parsons' handling of police–community relations had been poor. A police raid on a poverty program operated by COUP, the Seventh Ward black political organization, and coincidentally the mayor's old political nemesis, served to further alienate black citizens. Though several blacks were arrested on allegations of mismanagement of the program, all charges were eventually dropped. Many interpreted this as political persecution by the mayor and his henchman, the police superintendent. It was, therefore, a welcome relief when, in late November 1980, Superintendent Parsons tendered his resignation, and Mayor Morial quickly accepted it.

With his departure, the police superintendent helped defuse a politically volatile situation. Nonetheless, relations between the police department and black citizens will continue to be strained for some time to come. It remains to be seen whether Parsons' graceful exit will enable Morial to restore public confidence in this agency, particularly among the masses of black voters on whom he must depend at reelection time.

Conclusion

Ernest N. Morial, New Orleans' first black mayor, is more than halfway through his first term and will probably run for reelection in February 1982. Granted, it is unfair to filter his every act through the prospects of the 1982 election, but by nearly every indicator, it appears he will stand for reelection. An assessment of his public profile and performance in office to date seems, therefore, appropriate.

Perhaps the central concern of the Morial administration has been economic development. That such an approach is both appropriate and desired is underscored by James Bobo's major study of the New Orleans economy [14] and the mayor's prepared testimony before a congressional subcommittee. [15] To combat the city's economic difficulties, the mayor developed a comprehensive economic recovery plan that proceeds on the following assumptions related to quality of life and perceived business climate:

The basic premise underlying the New Orleans Economic Development Strategy is that the expansion of the private sector employment opportunities for central city residents, particularly for residents of the City's low and moderate income neighborhoods, is a necessary, though perhaps not sufficient prerequisite for reducing both the incidence of the effects of poverty, unemployment, and subemployment.[16]

In the process of attacking the city's sticky economic problems, the mayor discovered that he has another problem—the fact that he is black:

Municipalities managed by black mayors have unique problems, and the treatment of those cities by the county governments, state governments, and even the federal government may be different in many cases than the treatment afforded comparable cities with white administrations. Black mayors have more difficulty doing almost anything, and what we do accomplish, we achieve at the cost of an arm and a leg.[17]

The cost to Mayor Morial has been that he has created an image of being more closely attuned to the wishes of white voters than to black citizens. While Morial clearly has not turned the city's fiscal problems around, his overall approach to economic development has indeed won him high marks with the white business community. Even his political reaction to the shootings of four black Algiers residents was conditioned by the likelihood of a boycott by blacks of the central business district during the holiday shopping season. Only much later, during the protest by black voters, did Mayor Morial begin to play the role of the model black mayor. In the opinion of a keen observer of local politics, one of the mayor's biggest liabilities is that he has never behaved like a black mayor:

He has never seen himself as a "black mayor," but a mayor of all the people. That was not just a political cliché. Morial has never been a spokesman for strictly black interests. And his political philosophy is probably closer to that of the conservative white business leaders he courts than to the political leanings of his black constituency. Morial may be the only conservative black mayor in the United States.[18]

Finally, it should be pointed out that Morial assumed office during an era of strident conservatism and what was perceived as a declining commitment to cities in general and blacks in particular. Needless to say, these twin factors have rendered the life of the mayor doubly difficult and cast a pall of skepticism, cynicism, and recalcitrance over his ambitions and initiatives, however noble and well intended.

We must await the outcome of the 1982 mayoral election to test the accuracy of this observation. Mayor Morial has been an embattled occupant of City Hall since the day he assumed office. Relations with the city council have been less than amicable; he has incurred the wrath of the police department by ordering an independent investigation into the killings of four blacks in Algiers; and his political stock with black voters continues to decline. Through it all, Morial appears sanguine about his chances for reelection. In the remaining months of his current term, he may very well succeed in vanquishing his detractors black and white alike.

As pointed out earlier, in a very real sense political behavior in New Orleans is strongly influenced by life-style values and cultural imperatives that dampen civic responsibility and retard political progress. The requirements of citizenship are at once individual and collective in nature. In order for New Orleans to progress under the leadership of Mayor Morial, basic changes in its political culture will have to occur. At a minimum, success will require increasing active support among both blacks and whites, as well as rich and poor. The mayor's office must not become a hollow prize, irrespective of the race or ethnicity of the incumbent.

Notes

1. See, for instance, H. Paul Friesema, "Black Control of Central Cities: The Hollow Prize," *Journal of the American Institute of Planners,* March 1969, pp. 75–79; Peter Labrie, "Black Control of Cities: Dispersal or Rebuilding," *Review of Black Political Economy,* Autumn 1970, pp. 3–27; Frances Fox Piven and Richard Cloward, "Black Control of Central Cities: Heading It Off by Metropolitan Government," *New Republic,* September 30, 1967, pp. 119–21; and Frances Fox Piven and Richard Cloward, "Black Control of Central Cities: How the Negroes Will Lose," *New Republic,* October 7, 1967, pp. 15–59.
2. James R. Bobo, *The New Orleans Economy: Pro Bono Publico?* (New Orleans: College of Business Administration, University of New Orleans, 1975), pp. 1–2.
3. Ibid., p. 35.
4. Charles Y. W. Chai, "Who Rules New Orleans: A Study of Community Power Structure," *Louisiana Business Survey,* October 1971, p. 10.
5. *Washington Post,* Sunday, April 23, 1978, p. A12.
6. James Chubbuck, Edward Renwick and Joe Walker, "An Analysis of the 1970 New Orleans Mayoral Election," *Louisiana Business Survey,* July 1970, p. 11.
7. Ibid., p. 9.
8. Ibid., p. 11.
9. Allen Rosenzweig and John Wildgen, "A Statistical Analysis of the 1977 Mayor's Race in New Orleans," *Louisiana Business Survey,* April 1978, p. 8.
10. See Thomas F. Pettigrew, "Black Mayoral Campaigns," in *Urban Governance and Minorities,* ed. Herrington J. Bryce (New York: Praeger, 1976), pp. 20–22.

11. Rosenzweig and Wildgen, "A Statistical Analysis of the 1977 Mayor's Race," p. 8.
12. Editorial, *New Orleans Times-Picayune*, November 16, 1980.
13. Iris Kelso, in *New Orleans Times-Picayune*, November 26, 1980.
14. Bobo, *New Orleans Economy*, pp. 3–5.
15. Ernest N. Morial, statement delivered before the Subcommittee on Economic Growth and Stabilization of the Joint Economic Committee of the Congress, March 17, 1978.
16. Mayor's Office of Economic Development, *New Orleans–Economic Development Strategy*, May 1979, p. 2.
17. Mayor Richard Hatcher, quoted in "Black Mayors and the Fiscal Tightrope," *Black Enterprise*, January 1981, p. 31.
18. Iris Kelso, "Morial's Black Strategy," *New Orleans Times-Picayune*, November 30, 1980.

PART FOUR

Reapportionment and Electoral Bias

ELEVEN

Racial Gerrymandering: Its Potential Impact on Black Politics in the 1980s

John O'Loughlin

In Western democracies a common belief holds that if a group or political party gains a certain proportion of votes in an election, that group or party should be rewarded with approximately the same proportion of seats. In most democracies, a matching proportion of seats to votes is guaranteed by the electoral system, a proportional representation system characterized by large multimember districts, multiparty competition, and coalition governments. In this country, the electoral system is "Anglo-Saxon" with two dominant parties, small single-member districts, and majority governments. The Anglo-Saxon electoral system has three intrinsic flaws that become evident when votes are translated into seats. First, single-member districts must constantly be redrawn to match population shifts, thereby inviting abuse by the legislators responsible for reapportionment. Second, regardless of the best and most honorable intentions of the map makers, all redistricting is gerrymandering. (Gerrymandering is both the deliberate manipulation of district boundaries to help or hurt a particular faction or party and the unintentional effects on a group of a particular district map.) A reapportionment plan acceptable to all parties, factions, social groups, and the courts is rare in American political life. Third, since

the vote pattern is on an interval scale but the seats pattern is dichoto-
mous (win or lose), the statewide seats proportion and votes proportion
for a party can diverge substantially.

The single-member system helps majority parties with an even spread
of support. As in the case of the Liberals in Great Britain (seats proportion 7, votes proportion 0.9, in 1970), small parties are hurt disproportionately, especially parties with no concentration of vote strength. Since the
end of large-scale malapportionment in the United States in the 1960s, the
examination of electoral bias (the difference between seats and votes
proportions) has shifted to the role of gerrymandering. After every reapportionment, questions are raised regarding the fairness of the districts to
political parties or racial groups. The focus of this chapter is the impact of
electoral boundaries on the election of blacks. The major legal decisions
are reviewed, and suggestions for challenging suspected gerrymanders are
put forward.

Electoral bias is a persistent feature of American political life. This bias
can be decomposed into three causes: the bias caused by malapportionment (the variation in the population size of districts), the bias caused by
the concentration effect (particularly important for black representation),
and the bias caused by gerrymandering (the correspondence of the election district boundaries and black voters). The components of bias can
easily be calculated for a political party, but the calculation for a racial
group is more complex. Should only black-white contests be examined?
Since this approach would disregard safe seats in both black and white
neighborhoods, it may be better to examine all elections with black candidates. The components of electoral bias, for black voters in Detroit (state
House elections 1972) and New Orleans (city council elections 1977) are
computed in Table 11.1. The elections are for all districts in each city (21
in Detroit, 5 in New Orleans). Noncompetition reflected a realization of
political realities and incumbent strength. Since bloc voting is characteristic, racial lines are more significant than party lines. Consequently, the
votes of whites regardless of party affiliation are compared to those of
blacks, also irrespective of party.

The components of electoral bias are computed from a formula given
by Gudgin and Taylor.[1] Electoral bias is the combination of the three
factors discussed above and will vary from election to election. Since
significant malapportionment no longer exists, the malapportionment factor is composed mostly of the turnout effect. A party or group benefits if
its victories are achieved with a low turnout, which is analogous to a
district smaller than average. The effective vote necessary to win a seat is
small in either case. Since black turnout is usually lower than white (except in racially divided contests), blacks usually benefit from this factor.
We expect blacks in Detroit and New Orleans to be hurt by the overcon-

TABLE 11.1   COMPONENTS OF ELECTORAL BIAS, DETROIT AND NEW ORLEANS

Component	*Detroit* *State House 1972* *(21 districts)*	*New Orleans* *City Council 1977* *(5 districts)*
V	.422	.303
S	.476	.200
B	.054	−.103
$\hat{V}$	.484	.262
M	.062	−.041
D	−.008	.062
$\hat{S}$	.280	.076
D_N	−.204	−.186
D_P	.196	.124

$$B = D_N + D_P + M$$

Detroit:	$.054 = -.204 + .196 + .062$
New Orleans:	$-.103 = -.186 + .124 + (-.041)$

centration of their votes, and the partisan gerrymandering effect will vary based on the spatial pattern of black voter support.

The formulas are very simple and with the exception of $\hat{S}$, the expected seats proportion, are easily calculated.

$$B = S - V \tag{1}$$
$$M = \hat{V} - V \tag{2}$$
$$D = B - M \tag{3}$$
$$D_N = \hat{S} - \hat{V} \tag{4}$$
$$D_P = S - \hat{S} \tag{5}$$

where B is total electoral bias; S is seats proportion for a party or group; V is votes proportion won; M is the malapportionment and turnout component of bias; $\hat{V}$ is the predicted vote proportion and is equal to the mean vote proportion achieved by the party in the districts; D is the distribution or boundary effect and is decomposed into D_N, nonpartisan boundary bias or the concentration effect and D_P, the partisan gerrymander effect; $\hat{S}$ is the predicted total for V, and is usually calculated using the Cube Law

$$\hat{S} = \frac{V^3}{V^3 + (1-V)^3} \tag{6}$$

This Cube Law formulation provides a good fit for the overall seats/votes ratio for blacks in American cities.[2]

The two examples are but two of many that could be selected for analysis of the relationship of votes to seats for blacks or, stated differently, the interaction of the electoral district boundaries and the spatial pattern of the votes. These examples are representative because they point out the often overlooked importance of the concentration effect in black electoral politics. In both Detroit and New Orleans, the concentration effect is negative and large, $-.204$ and $-.186$, respectively. (All figures can be multiplied by 100 to convert them into percentages.) Because the black population is spatially concentrated in American cities, it is practically impossible to avoid this negative impact on black political strength. In many cities the concentration effect is balanced by a favorable relationship between the overall vote proportion and the predicted vote proportion, which is a measure of the gerrymandering effect. This measure is a function of how the seats proportion based on individual districts deviates from the citywide seats proportion. Negative partisan gerrymandering effects are common for a small party that does not have a core of support and is in a minority in all districts. In both Detroit and New Orleans, blacks achieve parity or positive benefits from this factor for small districts (wards, state house, or city council). Frequently, blacks do not form a majority in any city congressional district, either by accident or design, and this D_P factor is negative. The turnout factor is positive for blacks in Detroit (a lower rate is found in black areas) but negative for New Orleans where the presence of Ernest Morial as a mayoral candidate and two black at-large city council candidates helped produce a large increase in black turnout, which surpassed that in white neighborhoods.

Overall, blacks received positive benefits (positive electoral bias) in Detroit in 1972 but negative electoral bias in New Orleans in 1977 from the correspondence of vote patterns to district boundaries. By decomposing this seats-votes difference, we can calculate the contribution made by each element. This method provides a valuable technique for estimating the impact of reapportionment (new district lines) on black representation since it controls for the effects of turnout and concentration. As such, it could become a valuable tool in evaluating the impacts of suspected racial gerrymanders.

The Process of Redistricting

Before proceeding to the legal definitions of gerrymandering, the ways a population can be gerrymandered and the actors involved in the redistricting process are discussed. There are two basic ways to gerrymander a district, and both methods are often used in combination to dilute the vote. Most common is the "wasted vote" gerrymander, and it is achieved by dividing a population into two or more districts so that they constitute an electoral majority in none of the districts. This form of gerrymandering is most visible when the population is small and isolated. Frequently it is found at the outer fringes of a black ghetto and places the blacks in this area in an outer-city or white majority district, preventing the election of a black legislator when racial bloc voting is the norm. The second form of gerrymandering is found in situations in which a group is large enough that they cannot be denied some representation. It is called "excess vote" gerrymandering and concentrates the opposition party or group into as few districts as possible so that their seats are won with huge majorities. It follows the principle that if you are going to lose a district, lose it by as big a margin as possible. By doing so, the possibility exists that some districts with majorities from the gerrymanderer's party can be created. An "excess vote" gerrymander is more difficult to show than the wasted vote version because the retort is often made that at least it guarantees some seats for the gerrymandered group. For an example of an alleged racial gerrymander of the wasted vote variety, refer to Figure 11.1

Redistricting is accomplished by one of three groups of map makers. The most common reapportionment is that done by a legislative committee of the state legislature with the plan voted upon in the general assembly and signed by the governor. The legislature is responsible for the congressional district map for the state as well as those for the state House and state Senate. Greatest potential for political bias exists if the governor and the majority in both houses are of the same party. A second

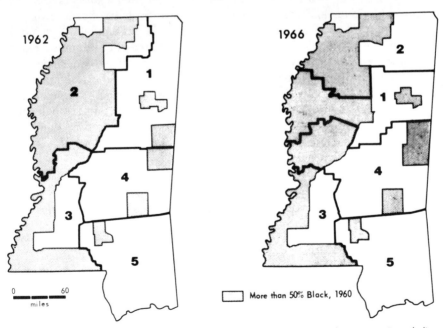

FIGURE 11.1   A presumption of Gerrymandering in Mississippi's congressional districts: 1962 versus 1966.

reapportionment is called "bipartisan gerrymandering." The district map is the result of compromise, political tradeoffs, and intense bargaining. It tries to guarantee the reelection of incumbents of both parties. An increase in the size of election margins and in noncontests in the election immediately after this bipartisan reapportionment would raise suspicions that a gerrymander benefited both parties. Blacks and other minorities have claimed that they are frequently the victims of redistricting agreements since few incumbents are minority and that such agreements virtually prevent elections of new minority legislators.

The third form of redistricting is that done by a nonpolitical body, usually on court orders after the legislators failed to reach an agreement or their plan was not accepted by the courts or Justice Department under the provisions of Section 5 of the Voting Rights Act. (See below for details of this act.) The neutral body is directed to discount political factors, such as the location of the supporters of each party. Instead, use of the commonly accepted guidelines of maximizing district compactness, minimizing population differences, and ensuring contiguity for all districts is mandated. Neutral commissions often use computers to minimize computation difficulties and allow evaluation of many alternative plans. Even though the district map is neutral, its impact is not. Neutral commissioners are neutral only in the sense that the impact of their map on parties and groups is not known until the first election after their plan is accepted.[3] Politicians hate this reapportionment method, probably because of the uncertainty of seats allocation. Computer use is not confined to neutral commissions. To help in the evaluation of hundreds of alternative plans and isolate the most advantageous partisan plan, political parties contract with research firms that provide the computer programs, staff training, and even the computer. While this package is sold as an objective procedure, it also allows the political party to pick a districting arrangement that is difficult to challenge as a gerrymander because the computer program can evaluate hundreds of alternative plans simultaneously. It increases the possibility of scientific gerrymandering.

Population Shifts and Redistricting in Black Neighborhoods

As black urban populations expanded rapidly after the Second World War a growing number of election districts achieved black majorities and later elected black representatives. Since the black residential distribution is not static and district boundaries must be constantly redrawn, the reapportionment of districts for black areas and adjoining white neighborhoods can affect the reelection of black incumbents, black challenges to white incumbents, and the overall seats-votes proportion for both blacks and whites. A review of 1,236 elections involving black candidates in the 18 largest American cities between 1940 and 1975 showed a rapid growth in the election of black representations between 1950 and 1970 and a flattening of the growth curve during the past decade. This present slow growth or stability is attributed to a variety of factors including a reduction in the number of election districts apportioned to cities and, consequently, to black neighborhoods; a lower level of black political activism and turnout; declining populations in inner-city areas, requiring a redistribution of seats from the inner to the outer (often white majority) city; and, most important, the approach of black representation to an upper threshold equal to the number of seats allocated to black majority neighborhoods.[4] Two additional trends were noticed: First, noncontests increased in frequency over time as the method of electing black legislators. Second, the proportion of elections involving both black and white candidates declined. For example, the proportion of state House elections involving black and white candidates dropped from about 90 percent in the 1940–52 period to 38 percent in 1974. In this later year, more black state legislators were elected as a result of noncontests than by defeating white candidates.

These longitudinal trends are partly the result of reapportionment. More incumbents voluntarily retire after reapportionment, when their districts are changed, than are defeated in elections. A redistricting that does not increase the white percentage in a racially changing district is a powerful incentive for a white incumbent to retire. Typically, the winner of the resulting primary is assured a long tenure in office.

Obviously, differences exist from city to city in the success of black candidates, a result of local black political activism, political personalities, issues, role of blacks within the two political parties, and political structure. Wilson has suggested that three factors, in addition to local circumstances, explain black political success at the city level. They are rate of black immigration, the density of the black neighborhood, and the size of the basic political unit.[5] The first reason can be equated to population growth and subsequent neighborhood growth and dominance of more districts. Densely populated neighborhoods allow blacks to form majorities in election districts, and the smaller the size of the political unit, the greater the chance that a citywide black minority can form majorities in some of the districts. Wilson attributed black political success in Chicago to these factors and, conversely, the difficulty of black politicians in New York and Los Angeles is due partly to dispersed ghettoes and large electoral districts.

It has frequently been stated that the proportion of seats won by blacks is consistently lower than the black population proportion.[6] If we look at the seats-votes ratio for black-white contests, however, the bias is favorable for blacks in most American cities.[7] More important, we can examine swing ratio, which measures the responsiveness of the electoral system to changes in voting preferences. For black-white contests in American cities, the swing ratios are small (from 1.357 to .0471) and suggest that the system is slow to respond to changes in vote percentages. It takes a huge shift in votes (although it could be gradual over a long period) in most districts to change the representative, black or white, reflecting in advantages of incumbency and the continuation of racial bloc voting.

The geographic concentration of the black population is critical to understanding the impact of boundaries on black electoral success. Segregation of blacks will result in a number of black representatives since some districts will be black majority. The more concentrated the black population, the more difficult it is to deny them some representation; conversely, the easier it is to prevent them from proportional or greater than proportional representation. The reason for this apparent contradiction can be traced to the fact that black-white contests are rare in American politics and usually occur in fringe ghetto districts. In ghetto districts, elections are contested by two black candidates, and the potential for increased black representation is limited to the number of electoral districts in the black area. These statements are based on an assumption of racial bloc voting, an assumption well documented for elections with both black and white candidates.

Obviously the proportional representation of blacks can be manipulated by gerrymandering. The larger the districts, the easier it is to gerrymander them; and a greater potential exists for negative impacts on minorities from unintentional gerrymandering. Proportionally, the minority will dominate a larger amount of small districts than larger ones. Thus, in Chicago in 1972, blacks formed majorities in 2 of 7 congressional districts, or 28.6 percent, but 17 of 50 wards (city council districts), which was equal to 34 percent. Similarly for New York City, only 2 of 17 congressional districts (or 11.8 percent) were black majority, but 14 of 65 state legislative districts (or 21.5 percent) were black majority.

Claims of Gerrymandering and Legal Guidelines

The basic problem of gerrymandering identification, measurement, construction, and constitutionality is that no objective standard exists against which an alleged gerrymander can be compared. Unlike claims of malapportionment, which can be measured by simple population deviation statistics, the courts cannot easily evaluate claims of vote dilution through deliberate gerrymandering. Ten or fifteen years ago, a common belief existed that if districts had distorted or convoluted shapes, their shapes constituted a reasonable presumption of gerrymandering. Such simplistic thinking ended when it became clear that districting authorities could meet the requirements of compactness, contiguity, and equal population while still creating "excess vote" and "wasted vote" gerrymanders. This progression led to a review of compactness indexes usually based on optimal compactness, a circle. Low compactness indexes supposedly constituted evidence of deliberate manipulation of the boundaries for partisan ends. Thus a comparison of the compactness indexes for sample districts in large American cities for 1958 and 1968 (before and after the major reapportionments of the mid-1960s) showed that the average compactness index for black districts was .40 in 1958 and .45 in 1968, .42 for racially mixed districts in 1958 and .45 in 1968, and .40 for white districts in 1958 and .42 in 1968. The range of the compactness index is 0.0 (least compact) to 1.0 (circle) most compact.[8] Low compactness indexes do not prove gerrymandering, just as high indexes do not prove its absence.

A perfect gerrymander could consist of squarelike districts. Consequently, it was felt that one method of evaluating dilution of the black vote would be to compare the number of black majority districts existing in a city to the number expected from an optimal redistricting of the city using only the nonpolitical, nonracial requirements of compactness, contiguity and equal population. For 8 large cities, the number of black majority districts would rise from 11 to 17 with an optimal districting system. The number of black districts would double in New York and triple in Chicago but remain unchanged in New Orleans and drop from one to zero in Seattle.[9] Since the optimal districts produced for a city are only one set of many such districts that could be drawn, they do not constitute an objective standard against which a legislative plan could be evaluated. It is clear that we need a method for establishing a "reasonable presumption" of discriminatory gerrymandering. Review of the court cases makes this point even more evident.

The vast majority of court cases dealing with legislative districting have concerned the issue of malapportionment, the population differences between districts. Beginning with *Reynolds* v. *Sims* (377 U.S. 533, 1964) the Warren Supreme Court handed down a series of decisions, culminating with *Kirkpatrick* v. *Preisler* (394 U.S. 528, 1969) that declared population deviations from the state average unconstitutional. The 1969 decisions required all deviations from population equality to be justified. This insistence on mathematical equality required districting agencies to violate county, township, and city boundaries in the reapportionment process. The Warren Court rulings on malapportionment had the unintended effect of making gerrymandering easier. Since the legislative commissions could rightly claim that they were not confined to using political subunits as building blocks for the districts (indeed, they could not if they were to meet the *Kirkpatrick* v. *Preisler* guidelines), the number of possible alternative plans jumped dramatically. A New York congressional district plan was struck down in 1969 as unconstitutional since the districts showed a range from plus 6.49 to minus 6.61 percent (*Wells* v. *Rockefeller*, 394 U.S. 542, 1969). Since Republicans controlled both the state House and Senate, as well as the governorship, they drew up a new congressional district plan under which no district deviated more than 0.10 percent. The new plan also produced districts that were more compact and contiguous than the plan struck down by the Warren Court. Yet most knowledgeable observers viewed this new plan as a pro-Republican partisan gerrymander, and the Democrats lost two seats in the resulting election.[10]

The Warren Court rulings had another unintended effect. They prevented "backdoor" challenges to gerrymandering under the guise of a challenge to malapportionment. The Burger Supreme Court has allowed more flexibility in population deviations from mathematical equality (*Mahan* v. *Howell*, 410 U.S. 315, 1973). Since electoral districts represented by blacks lost population during the 1970s, a return to 1969 standards would injure severely the reelection prospects of many black incumbents. The 1973 Court standard allows the possibility of slightly overrepresented black innercity districts. Black areas, like most urban districts, were underrepresented up to 1964. When fair representation was finally achieved, these city districts were already in the stage of large population decline.

A legislative effort in Congress, supported by the civil rights movement, produced the 1965 Voting Rights Act, which attempted to guarantee free and unimpeded access by minorities to ballots. The act initially covered only 7 southern states, but in 1970 it was extended to 3 counties in New York City and 13 counties in the West. It was extended again in 1975, and an additional 45 counties in the West and Texas are covered by the act's provisions. Section 5 of the act requires preclearance by the U.S. Department of Justice for districting plans for state and local government legislative bodies. Numerous invalidations by the Justice Department have occurred, and many of the department's invalidation decisions have been upheld by the courts.[11]

Unlike malapportionment decisions, most court decisions on gerrymandering have concerned abuses on racial rather than partisan grounds. Racial gerrymandering claims rest on interpretation of the Fourteenth and Fifteenth amendments. In 1960 the Supreme Court ruled that a 24-sided new town boundary in Tuskegee, Alabama, which placed almost all black residents of Tuskegee outside the town limits, was unconstitutional (*Gomillion* v. *Lightfoot*, 364 U.S. 399, 1960). This case cannot be used as a precedent for later claims of party legislative gerrymandering because it did not involve voting districts and did not consider party voting issues. In a test of a racial gerrymandering claim, the Supreme Court ruled in a 1964 case from Manhattan that the four congressional districts, based on 1960 population and containing black proportions of 5.1, 27.5, 28.5, and 86.3 percent, did not constitute a racial gerrymander. It was argued by the plaintiffs that these proportions provided evidence of districting based on racial considerations because blacks were placed overwhelmingly in one district; in effect, they alleged an excess vote gerrymander. The Court ruled, 7 to 2, that the plaintiffs "failed to prove that the New York legislature was either motivated by racial considerations or in fact drew the districts on racial lines" (*Wright v. Rockefeller*, 376 U.S. 52, 1964). Speaking for the majority, Justice Black stated that it was the residential concentration of racial and ethnic voters that determined the makeup of the districts. In dissenting, Justices Douglas and Goldberg stated that the boundaries could be explained only in racial terms and that the facts constituted a *prima facie* case of racially segregated districts. The black congressional incumbent from Harlem, Adam Clayton Powell, argued for the status quo claiming that, at least, the existing districting system guaranteed one black representative.

The issue of intent appeared in the New York case and in a subsequent gerrymander case from New Orleans. By selecting the particular congressional district boundaries for the four Manhattan districts, did the New York legislature intend to hinder minority voting strength? The Court said no but Justice Goldberg said that "to require a showing of racial motivation in the legislature would place an impossible burden on complainants" (*Wright* v. *Rockefeller*, 1964, Goldberg, dissenting at 73). It has been suggested that such a requirement of "intent" is analogous to the smoking gun in a murder trial. In the New Orleans case, the city council drew up a plan that was obviously a gerrymander. Despite a city black proportion of 45 percent and black registered proportion of 34.5 percent, the districts contained black voter proportions of 45.2, 41.0, 33.7, 25.4, and 21.5 percent. The Department of Justice refused to preclear this districting arrangement under Section 5 of the Voting Rights Act. A second plan, the Moreau plan, produced districts that had black registration proportions of 52.6, 43.2, 36.8, 23.3, and 22.6 percent and also was turned down by the Justice Department. The appeals court upheld the Justice Department but the Supreme Court in a 6 to 2 decision reversed the appeals court and upheld the Moreau plan. The majority stated that the Moreau plan "did not remotely approach a constitutional violation" (*Beer* v. *United States*, 425 U.S. 130, 1976). The Burger Court's action in the New Orleans case can be understood in the light of a comment by Justice Stevens in a Mobile, Alabama, multimember districting case. In supporting the continuation of an at-large election system, which black plaintiffs claimed precluded the election of blacks in the white majority city, he said that "the proper standard (for proof of gerrymandering) is suggested by three characteristics of the gerrymander condemned in *Gomillion:* (1) the 28-sided configuration was manifestly not the product of a routine or traditional political decision; (2) it had a significant adverse impact on a minority group; and (3) it was unsupported by any neutral justification and thus was either totally irrational or entirely motivated by a desire to curtail the political strength of the minority" (*City of Mobile* v. *Bolden,* 48 U.S.L.W. 4445, 1980).

In another case consequent on Section 5 preclearance, the New York legislature redrew the state House and state Senate districts in Brooklyn so as to create nonwhite majorities of 65 percent in two House and two Senate districts in Williamsburg (the Legislative Committee believed that this was the minimum percentage that would guarantee black representation from these districts). By doing so, the legislature took the tightly knit Hasidic Jewish community of Williamsburg out of a single Assembly district and a single Senate district and divided it into two parts. The Hasidim population of 35,000 did not constitute a population majority in any existing district, but their turnout rate of 85 percent, compared with the black and Hispanic turnout rate of 15 percent, gave them an effective majority. The appeals court rejected the Hasidic Jews' contention that districting along racial lines is per se unconstitutional and further stated that there was no way to preserve "ethnic community unit," as the Hasidic Jews wanted, since there were dozens of identifiable ethnic neighborhoods in Brooklyn, which had only 21.4 seats in the state assembly and 8.6 seats in the state Senate. In upholding the appeals court decision 7 to 1, the Supreme Court stated that a state may sometimes use racial quotas to assure that blacks and other nonwhites have majorities in certain legislative districts and that this was constitutional if the state did it in an effort to comply with the Voting Rights Act (*United Jewish Organizations of Williamsburg, Inc.* v. *Carey,* 430 U.S. 144, 1977). Recently, in two multimember cases from Mobile, Alabama, and Rome, Georgia, the Supreme Court upheld the use of at-large districts in Mobile by stating that the plaintiffs did not prove purposeful discrimination but declared that a switch from a plurality to majority vote and annexations diluted the black vote in Rome under Section 5 of the Voting Rights Act (*City of Rome* v. *United States,* 48 U.S.L.W. 4463, 1980; *City of Mobile* v. *Bolden,* 48 U.S.L.W. 4437, 1980).

From these cases and other related civil rights cases we can see that the Supreme Court decisions establish the principle that proof of discriminatory intent is a necessary element of a Fifteenth Amendment claim. (This amendment acknowledges the right of citizens to vote and prohibits its denial or abridgement on account of race.) By emphasizing this intent principle, the Court has been able to deny the claims of plaintiffs that their vote was abridged because of district gerrymandering. Like the black plaintiffs in Manhattan in 1964 or in New Orleans in 1976, the Hasidic Jews of Williamsburg in 1977 could not prove the existence of gerrymandering. By shifting the burden of proof, a group that feels vicitimized by a districting arrangement can win its case. It is as difficult to prove the nonexistence of a gerrymander as it is to prove its existence. As Justice White said in *Wells* v. *Rockefeller* (394 U.S. 542, 554, 1969), "districting is itself a gerrymandering in the sense that it represents a complex blend of political, economic, regional, and historical considerations." If proof of intent is necessary to support a claim of vote dilution through gerrymandering, what evidence is needed? Justice Marshall, in dissenting from the majority in the Mobile case, stated that he would apply the "common law foreseeability" presumption, which raises a strong inference that the adverse effect was desired. It is easy enough to show discriminatory impact of an electoral system, as was done in the Mobile case. The plaintiffs in the Mobile case showed "that this discriminatory effect could be corrected by implementation of a single-member districting plan. Because the foreseeable disproportionate impact was so severe, the burden of proof should have shifted to the defendants. . . . Reallocation of the burden of proof is especially appropriate in these cases, where the challenged state action infringes the exercise of a fundamental right." (*City of Mobile,* 1980, J. Marshall, dissenting, U.S.L.W. 4458).

If the burden of proof is shifted to the districting authorities (they then must show that they did not intend to discriminate, even though their districting arrangement has a discriminatory impact), it is possible that under Section 5 the Justice Department would not accept the districting proposals. One method of shifting the burden of proof, in addition to that suggested by Justice Marshall, would be to demonstrate through a *prima facie* case that a presumption of gerrymandering is reasonable.[12] As an example of this possibility, consider the maps in Figure 11.1. In 1962 the congressional districts of Mississippi followed traditional regional, cultural, historical, and economic divisions in the state. Few blacks were registered to vote, and so blacks did not constitute an electoral threat, even though they formed a majority in the second district. After the passage of the Voting Rights Act in 1965 and related black political activism, the black registered population rose dramatically. The districts were redrawn to run in an east-west pattern, cutting across the north-south black population concentration so that blacks no longer constituted an electoral threat in any district. Although the state redistricted to correct malapportionment in the aftermath of *Reynolds* v. *Sims,* it devised a system to preclude the election of a black congressman in the bloc-voting situation. A redistricting of such discriminatory impact would constitute a reasonable presumption of gerrymandering and shift the burden to the legislature, which must then justify their choice of district lines, which diverged sharply from those followed for over a hundred years. In addition to this simple method of showing presumption of gerrymandering, a more complicated method based on probability is feasible. It is to this method that we now turn our attention.

The Evaluation of Possible Gerrymanders

It is clear that any particular configuration is only one of hundreds that could be chosen. Even when we introduce stringent requirements of equal population (no district deviates more than 5 percent from the state average), compactness, and contiguity, and use counties, townships, census tracts, and the like as the building blocks, we still have hundreds of possible or feasible solutions. We can view the choice of district lines in a probability framework, just as we view the odds of a number being picked at a Bingo game or roulette table. For each feasible alternative, we can compute some measures of the impact on our group (blacks, Republicans, etc.). We can construct a histogram to examine the overall distribution of these measures. By placing the final plan adopted by the state legislature on the histogram, we obtain an estimate of its odds of being chosen by chance and of its impact on our electoral group, relative to the impacts produced by all other alternatives.[13] An example of a hypothetical histogram is given in Figure 11.2

This histogram is the result of many (usually more than 100) separate redistrictings of a city. The computer algorithm was selected to produce feasible solutions that fall within existing guidelines of equal population, compactness, and contiguity. Suppose there are 4 districts to be formed from 60 census tracts. For each tract, we use only the total population to draw the map. For each alternative plan, we calculate the percentage of the population that is black in each of the four districts. From the histogram, we can see that solutions with high polarization scores (right-tail solution) produce districts with a black majority. The polarization score measures the overall distribution of blacks to whites between and within the districts. If the black population is concentrated in one or two districts, the polarization score will be high, but if it is divided among the four districts (such as in a wasted-vote gerrymander), the score will be low, and the solution will be a left-tail alternative. Depending on the size of the black population in the city, their best solution would be at the far right side (polarization score above 3.5) if they are small and concentrated, or a medium-high score (about 3.5) if they are large and concentrated. An excess-vote gerrymander of the black population would produce a very high score. The optimal solution for blacks in American cities is usually a solution to the right of the modal columns (between 2.0 and 3.0). In this fashion blacks obtain the advantage accruing from their resi-

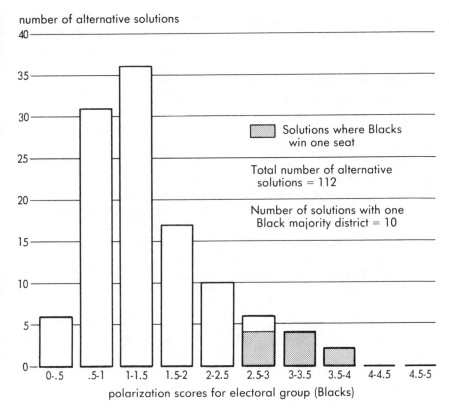

number of alternative solutions

Solutions where Blacks win one seat

Total number of alternative solutions = 112

Number of solutions with one Black majority district = 10

polarization scores for electoral group (Blacks)

FIGURE 11.2   A hypothetical histogram and five alternative redistricting plans in the United States: its impact on black voters.

dential concentration but are not subject to the negative influences of a districting arrangement that overconcentrates them in as few districts as possible. Based on studies in British cities, the histogram generally shows a right-skewed distribution (longer tail to the right), but this form may be a function of the underlying geographic distribution of the Labour and Conservative party votes.[14] The hypothetical histogram portrayed in Figure 11.2 is representative of five alternative redistrictings in the United States.[15]

The histogram can be divided into two regions, titled modal and tail choices. A modal choice (common alternatives) would lie between 0.5 and 2.5 on the histogram in Figure 11.2, while tail choices are between 0.0 and 0.5 (left tail) and between 2.5 and 4.0 (right tail). Since there are many more modal solutions than tail solutions, we expect that a particular districting will show a high probability of falling in the modal region. The polarization scores can be converted in Z scores (standard normal deviates) and a probability associated with each polarization score. If a particular plan had a low probability associated with it, it would raise the suspicion of gerrymandering and could be used to shift the burden of proof. Given the residential distribution of a group, we now have the probability of a certain districting and its impact on their voting strength occurring by chance. Since there are two gerrymander regions on the histogram, we determine *a priori* what the confidence intervals or probability of gerrymandering will be, for example, .10 and .90. If the contested plan's score fell outside these limits, it would constitute a reasonable presumption of gerrymandering. Based on work in Britain and the United States, Gudgin and Taylor show that modal solutions are produced by partisan agencies working for the majority party, by nonpartisan computer redistricting, and by special court-appointed experts working on court orders; tail choices are selected by minority party partisan group, bipartisan gerrymandering, and a neutral commission trying to guarantee minority representation in a plural society.[16]

The use of a probability framework to evaluate a districting arrangement in the context of all feasible alternatives can be illustrated by three alleged gerrymanders. The Supreme Court decisions in two cases, the New Orleans City Council districts in 1976 and the Manhattan congressional districts in 1964, have already been discussed (*Beer* v. *United States*, 425 U.S. 130 and *Wright* v. *Rockefeller*, 376 U.S. 52). The other example also reached the Supreme Court and is portrayed in Figure 11.1. The map shows the reapportionment of Mississippi's congressional districts in 1966. The plan was challenged on the grounds that it diluted the black vote by dividing the black population in the western part of the state into three districts. The federal district court rejected the suit and upon appeal, the Supreme Court affirmed the lower court ruling (*Connor* v. *Johnson*, 386 U.S. 483, 1967).

In the Manhattan case, 4 congressional districts were produced by combining the total populations of the 270 census tracts on the island using a version of the Weaver-Hess algorithm.[17] The program is heuristic and finds an optimal solution (most compact and equal in population) through a trial-and-error process. The compactness of a solution is measured by a moment of inertia index, and the census tracts allocated to each district, the total district population, and an allocation matrix are given for each solution. Since the optimal solution may not be the global, or overall, optimal solution, the algorithm is given different starting points. Intermediate solutions are produced, with associated measures. The algorithm has numerous options such as specifying barriers to district formation, noninteger and integer solutions (census tracts split between districts or not), various distance computation options (straight-line euclidean distance was used in all cases), and holding certain districts fixed while allowing others to vary. Versions of the algorithm have been used in legislative districting studies [18] and are fully described and documented by Goodchild.[19] Only plans whose districts were within 6 percent of the state average and whose districts were contiguous and compact were considered for further analysis. Ninety-two redistrictings of Manhattan were computed using the location and the 1960 population of each census tract. For each district, the total white and black populations were computed and a polarization score (between-district variance divided by the within-district variance, or F-ratio) was calculated for each plan. F-ratio is high when the black population is concentrated in one district and low when blacks are divided into two or more districts. These F-ratios are then converted into Z scores and the probability associated with each computed. The polarization score is also computed for the actual congressional districts challenged as a racial gerrymander in court. The procedure is repeated for the Mississippi and New Orleans samples.

We will examine the Mississippi case first. Sixty-three separate districts, each with 5 congressional districts, were produced using 1960 census data for the 82 counties. The summary statistics were also computed for the old reapportionment and for that performed in 1966. The F-ratios for the black population, the alleged victims of the new reapportionment, were calculated and then converted into Z scores, or standard normal deviates. If the plaintiffs were correct, the Z scores should show a dramatic drop and the post-1966 distribution should fall in the gerrymander region, the left-tail of the distribution. The results of the analysis show a shift in the polarization scores in the expected direction but not enough to merit a presumption of gerrymandering. We start with a gerrymander region of .90 and .10 and a null hypothesis that gerrymandering does not exist. We can reject the null hypothesis only if the computed Z score attains a value less than -1.645. In Mississippi the Z score for the old apportionment was 0.813, which placed it in the modal region at the 21st percentile. The computed odds of picking this arrangement by chance are 21 out of 100; few would claim that these odds are small enough to justify a charge of bias. The post-1966 reapportionment resulted in a Z score of -1.165, which placed it at the 88th percentile, or bordering on the left tail. The odds of this plan being produced by chance are 12 in 100. However, since we established our critical region at .10, we cannot reject the null hypothesis although this plan comes close to the reject region. For comparison, the optimal districting produced a modal solution of $-.099$ which placed it right in the middle of the overall distribution just four percentiles to the left of the mean.

Three caveats are in order. First, the computed Z scores are a function of the sample size. It is practically impossible to compute all feasible alternatives for the Mississippi congressional districts. Second, and as a consequence of the first, since the computed Z score falls so close to the gerrymander region, more alternatives should be computed in order to compute as large a sample as possible of all feasible constitutional solutions. The Z score may change so that it falls below the .10 critical level. Third, because of the huge change in the Z score for the two plans implemented in Mississippi (falling from +0.813 to −1.165 or 67 percentiles) and because the modal solutions for the state clearly indicate one or two black majority districts, this statistical evidence might be enough to persuade the courts to examine the redistricting carefully. Certainly it would appear to be sufficient to persuade the Justice Department to refuse Section 5 clearance for a plan that produced such a dramatic negative shift in black electoral prospects.

In Manhattan the results of the procedure for 92 alternative districtings showed a very low probability of the actual congressional districts occurring by chance. The computed Z score was 4.45, which placed it at the 99.99 percentile. This huge positive value is a result of blacks concentrated into the Eighteenth Congressional District and their relative absence from the other three districts. The modal solution for Manhattan was no black majority congressional district. Adam Clayton Powell, who argued for the status quo, was correct. By concentrating blacks in one district, the legislature guaranteed one black representative. Most of the alternative plans (in our case, 86 of 92) would not have produced a black majority district. Again, the optimal Manhattan solution showed a Z score of +.239, which placed it nine percentiles to the right of the mean within the modal region. We could term the Manhattan districting, which survives in basically the same form today, as a "benign gerrymander," one that clearly favors blacks. Further computation of alternative plans might reduce the absolute value of the Z score, but it would not likely change it sufficiently so that it would fall to +1.645, which would remove this districting from the gerrymandering region on the right-side histogram.

The New Orleans case is very interesting because numerous alternative plans were put forward by local political groups. Each of these plans can be evaluated under the statistical framework proposed here. This districting has also been examined by Engstrom and Wildgen using an alternative statistical arrangement.[20] It is not clear what computer algorithm these authors used to produce their 163 alternative plans using the precincts as the building blocks. They decided a priori that the 45 to 55 percent black registration proportion range constituted the competitive region. Proportions above 55 percent were excess votes, and below 45 percent were wasted votes. They then ranged the percentage black registration along an interval scale from 1 to 3. Forty-five percent or below received 1, and 55 and above received 3. From 45 percent to 55 percent, the scores were allocated according to the formula $[(X-45)/5] +1$ where X

constitutes the proportion black registration. For example, 47.5 percent
black would receive a score of 1.5, 50.0 percent black is 2, etc. The raw
scores are summed for the five districts and then converted into Z scores
and the probability associated with each is computed. For comparative
purposes, the same procedure described above for the New York and
Mississippi cases was applied to the New Orleans data. It should be noted
that the base data differ from the Engstrom/Wildgen study and this one
and that the computer algorithm was probably quite different.

The disputed plan for the city council districts, the Moreau plan, was
reviewed by the Supreme Court. Engstrom and Wildgen compute the raw
score as 6.52, which gives a Z score of $+0.72$ and places it at the 76th
percentile or in the modal region. They conclude that it does not support a
presumption of gerrymandering and would produce one safe black district
(the succeeding election showed this latter point to be accurate). By my
computations, the Moreau plan received a Z score of -1.79, which places
it at the 96th percentile. Within our threshold of rejection or acceptance of
the null hypothesis, we can clearly state that our presumption of gerrymandering has been satisfied. The modal solution for New Orleans is
two black majority districts using our algorithm. Reasons for the huge gap
between Engstrom and Wildgen's result and those reported here must be
sought in the data bases, computer algorithm, choice of polarization
score, and number of iterations. It points to a likely possibility if the
method suggested here for establishing the presumption of gerrymandering were accepted by the courts; the courts would be faced with various
computer programs, academic and statistical experts, and a mountain of
computer output all testifying to the veracity of one system over all
others.

How to Evaluate Redistricting

Gerrymandering is endemic in the American political system. Unlike the
situation in most European countries, redistricting here is controlled by
legislators, who obviously have a vested interest in the outcome of their
deliberations. Only when a deadlock is reached will the courts step in and
appoint a Master (expert). The power to gerrymander can be used effectively, as shown by Sickels.[21] He examined the seats-votes relationship
for states with more than ten districts and divided the parties into two
groups (those in control of the state legislature and possessing the power
to draw the districts and those without this power). Examining parties
with over 50 percent of the total vote, he showed that eight elections
resulted in parties without the power to gerrymander winning a greater
proportion of seats than votes, while thirteen elections resulted in "powerless" parties winning less seats than their votes proportion would

suggest. Conversely, no party with the power to gerrymander (fifty in all) received negative electoral bias. Tufte has suggested that the growing trend toward a bimodal distribution of party votes (more safe seats for Democrats and Republicans with fewer seats won by small margins) can be explained by the increasing tendency to engage in bipartisan gerrymandering. He terms many recent reapportionments as "Incumbent Survival Acts."[22] This trend, regardless of its causes, reduces the voters' power to decide elections. It now takes a huge swing in popular opinion to produce even a modest switch in votes because the party with the loss in popular support can still retain seats in its area of core strength. Unless the group that considers itself to be the victim of reapportionment plans has a set of incumbents who can block a discriminatory plan, its members will probably suffer severely from future redistrictings, thus reducing their future electoral chances.

From a histogram of all alternative solutions to a redistricting problem, we can see that the modal solutions favor the majority party or group. This phenomenon can be explained by the low polarization scores associated with those modal solutions. More solutions with low between-variance measures will be produced because of the geographic concentration of the minority and the greater spread of the majority. The best majority-group solution is where their votes are spread among districts so that they win each with 50 percent of the vote plus 1. This strategy minimizes variance, since when variance is zero, the majority party wins every seat. Such is the case in at-large elections, which prevent minorities from winning seats in a bloc-voting situation. In actuality, there is little difference between the outcome for a minority between most solutions by majority party gerrymandering and those produced by nonpartisan redistricting.

The best strategy for blacks in the reapportionment process is to attempt to gain representation on the elections and reapportionment committees of the legislature. A bargaining position can be defined before the process begins. Black population gains and losses, black voting strength and political allies, tradeoffs on other political issues, and the possibility of a lawsuit can define this position. Alternative plans should be submitted to reapportionment committees, and all plans should outline a compromise position as well as a best solution. (The compromise position might be kept secret pending the outcome of the committee's deliberations.) Avoidance of conflict between black representatives is important if all or most of them are to survive. Since many black districts are losing population, legislatures may be tempted to reduce the total number of black representatives by removing or combining black majority inner-city districts. Such a reduction can be countered by the creation of new black majority districts in the outer city or even in the suburbs of some large cities. Population trends should be analyzed and the tendency for blacks to show a lower turnout than whites kept in mind when alternatives are suggested and proposed plans examined. For example, acceptance of a plan with black minority districts and no immediate prospect of black representation may be preferable to a plan with one black majority district if the demographic trends show the black minority districts becoming black majority in a couple od years.

If political compromise fails, the plan can be challenged in court if its impact is clearly discriminatory against blacks. The costs of such a lawsuit and the fact that the Supreme Court has never turned down a districting plan as a deliberate gerrymander should produce serious consideration of alternatives. In 1973 the Supreme Court clearly set down guidelines for legal challenges to districting. Justice White, speaking for the majority, said "to sustain claims of vote dilution, it is not enough that a racial group allegedly discriminated against has not had legislative seats in proportion to its voting potential. The plaintiffs' burden is to produce evidence to support findings that the political processes leading to nomination and election were not equally open to participation by the group in question— that is, its members had less opportunity than did other residents in the district to participate in the political processes and to elect legislators of their choice" (*White* v. *Regester,* 412 U.S. 755, 1977 at 765–66). In states and areas covered by the Voting Rights Act (the act may expire in 1982) the Justice Department must preclear the plans. If blacks can show that the proposed plan was drawn up at their expense through evidence of discriminatory impact, the Justice Department will probably rule in their favor. Section 5 places a large emphasis on the role of the attorney general and the Justice Department. If the federal authorities adopt a "hands off" policy and do not actively instigate review of districting plans in counties covered by the act, individuals must activate the review. The procedure of preclearance was introduced to avoid the temporal and legal advantages accruing to districting agencies under the process of reapportionment, legal challenges by plaintiffs, court review and decision. However, Section 5 clearly provides a dual standard of justice based on geography. Challenges to reapportionments beyond the jurisdiction of the act are extraordinarily difficult to win.

For areas not covered by the Voting Rights Act, the major effort should be to shift the burden of proof through a presumption of gerrymandering by an assortment of evidence. This package should include information on voting behavior (particularly bloc voting), existing and proposed districts, alternative solutions to the districting question with special emphasis on those plans which would produce proportional representation, the modal solutions, the probability associated with the challenged plan, election results for any election after the contested plan went into effect, evidence of discriminatory impact, and a history of local race relations. The aim, as far as possible, should be to build a sound case around evidence of discriminatory impact and feasible alternatives.[23]

In *Beer* v. *United States* the Supreme Court established the "nonretrogression" principle, which will not allow a diminution of black majority districts during redistricting. The Moreau plan was accepted because two black majority districts were created (one had existed before), and a district in which the black registration exceeded the white registration was carved out. The "nonretrogression" principle can profitably be used in instances where black majority districts are reduced simply as a result of mapmaking and not as a result of population shifts. But is an increase in black majority districts always beneficial? Justice Marshall said in *Beer* v. *United States* that "the Court today finds that an increase in the size of the Negro majority in one district, with a concomitant increased likelihood of electing a delegate, conclusively shows that Plan II (Moreau) is ameliorative. Will this always be so? Is it not as common for minorities to be gerrymandered into the same district as into separate ones? Is an increase in the size of an existing majority ameliorative or retrogressive? When the size of the majority increases in one district, Negro voting strength necessarily declines elsewhere. Is that decline retrogressive?" (*Beer* v. *United States*, J. Marshall, dissenting, at 153–54).

Most voters in the United States would probably agree that it is unfair that a majority party should be allowed to enhance its position simply because it has control of the legislature and thus of the redistricting process. Yet, every decade we witness the exercise of such power and abuse. There seems to be a common feeling that the power to gerrymander is the winner's award. Blacks feel that they are more often the victims than the beneficiaries of redistricting because they do not have enough political strength in the first place to head off its worst effects. Often compromise between two groups of incumbents is achieved at the expense of an increase in the number of black majority districts. Despite many statements and hopes to the contrary, widespread adoption of neutral districting would not produce proportional representation for blacks but it would remove the element of deliberate gerrymandering. Given the constraints of the Anglo-Saxon system of elections, that is the best that can be expected.

Notes

1. Graham Gudgin and Peter J. Taylor, *Seats, Votes and the Spatial Organization of Elections* (London, England: Pion, 1979), pp. 86–91.
2. John O'Loughlin, "Black Representation Growth and the Seats-Vote Relationship," *Social Science Quarterly* 60 (June 1979): 72–86.

3. Stuart S. Nagel, "Simplified Bipartisan Computer Districting," *Stanford Law Review* 17 (1965): 863–77.

4. O'Loughlin, "Black Representation Growth," pp. 74–78.

5. James O. Wilson, *Negro Politics: The Search for Leadership* (New York: Free Press, 1965), p. 25.

6. Lee Sloan, "Good Government and the Politics of Race," *Social Problems* 16 (Fall 1969): 161–75.

7. O'Loughlin, "Black Representation Growth," pp. 80–84.

8. John O'Loughlin, "Malapportionment and Gerrymandering in the Ghetto," in *Urban Policy-Making and Metropolitan Dynamics: A Comparative Geographical Analysis,* ed. John S. Adams (Cambridge, MA: Ballinger, 1976), p. 554.

9. Ibid., pp. 556–62.

10. Gordon E. Baker, "Gerrymandering: Privileged Sanctuary or Next Judicial Target," in *Reapportionment in the 1970s,* ed. Nelson W. Polsby (Berkeley: University of California Press, 1971), pp. 137–38.

11. Stanley A. Halpin, Jr. and Richard L. Engstrom, "Racial Gerrymandering and Southern State Legislative Redistricting: Attorney General Determinations under the Voting Rights Act," *Journal of Public Law* 22, no. 1 (1973): 37–66.

12. Richard L. Engstrom and John K. Wildgen, "Pruning Thorns from the Thicket: An Empirical Test of the Existence of Racial Gerrymandering," *Legislative Studies Quarterly* 2 (November, 1977): 465–79.

13. Allan G. Pulsipher, "Empirical and Normative Theories of Apportionment," *Annals, New York Academy of Science* 219 (1973): 334–41.

14. P. J. Taylor and G. Gudgin, "The Statistical Basis of Decisionmaking in Electoral Districting," *Environment and Planning A* 8 (1976): 43–58.

15. John O'Loughlin, "The Identification and Measurement of Gerrymanders" (paper presented at the 77th Annual meeting of the Association of American Geographers, Los Angeles, April 19–23, 1981).

16. Gudgin and Taylor, *Seats, Votes and the Spatial Organization of Elections,* pp. 146–161.

17. James B. Weaver and S. W. Hess, "A Procedure for Nonpartisan Redistricting," *Yale Law Journal* 73 (December 1963): 288–308.

18. Richard L. Morrill, "Redistricting Revisited," *Annals, Association of American Geographers* 66 (December 1976): 548–56.

19. Michael F. Goodchild, "LAP-Location-Allocation Package," in *Computer Programs for Location-Allocation Problems,* ed. G. Ruston, M. F. Goodchild, and L. M. Ostresh, Jr. (Iowa City: University of Iowa, Department of Geography, Monograph No. 6, 1973), pp. 85–113.

20. Engstrom and Wildgen, "Pruning Thorns from the Thicket," pp. 469–73.

21. Robert J. Sickels, "Dragons, Baconstrips and Dumbbells—Who's Afraid of Reapportionment?" *Yale Law Journal* 75 (July, 1966): 1300–1308.

22. Edward R. Tufte, "The Relationship between Seats and Votes in Two-Party Systems," *American Political Science Review* 67 (June 1973): 540–54.

23. David H. Hunter, *Federal Review of Voting Changes: How to Use Section 5 of the Voting Rights Act* (Washington, DC: Joint Center for Political Studies, 1974).